THE CHAPELS
OF WALES

THE CHAPELS OF WALES

D. Huw Owen

SEREN

Seren is the book imprint of
Poetry Wales Press Ltd
Nolton Street, Bridgend, CF31 3AE

www.serenbooks.com
Facebook: facebook.com / SerenBooks
Twitter: @SerenBooks

Text © D Huw Owen, 2012
Photographs © the photographers, please refer to the acknowledgements

The right of D Huw Owen to be identified
as the author of this work has been asserted
in accordance with the Copyright, Designs
and Patents Act, 1988

ISBN 978-1-85411-554-6

The publisher works with the support of the Welsh Books Council

Printed in Perpetua by Akcent Media Ltd

CONTENTS

ACKNOWLEDGEMENTS

I wish to acknowledge the information provided by the ministers, officers and members of the chapels selected for consideration. They responded readily to my requests for relevant details, and ensured that I had full access to the buildings during my visits to the chapels. Some are mentioned in the text, but the assistance of all those persons who helped me in various ways is greatly appreciated.

I am also indebted to the following for their guidance on specific issues: Richard Price Baskwill (Delta, U.S.A); Edward Bevan (Trebanos); Peter James Cousins (Bangor); John Crowter-Jones (Devon); Brian Davies (Pontypridd); D. Leslie Davies (Aberdare); Eirlys Davies (Radyr); Twynog Davies (Lampeter); Gwynfor Ellis (Mynytho); D.J. Goronwy Evans (Lampeter); Muriel Bowen Evans (Tre-lech); Martin Evans-Jones (Ruthin); Susan Fielding (Aberystwyth); Luned Gonzales (Gaiman, Patagonia); John Green (Carmarthen); Philip R. Hobson (Cardiff); Evan Hughes (Melbourne, Australia); Richard Huws (Bontgoch); Penny Icke (Aberystwyth); Alun Jones Caernarfon; Alwyn Harding Jones (Taffs Well); Anthony Jones (Chicago, U S.A); David Jones (Llanelli); Eric Jones (Pontarddulais); Ieuan Gwynedd Jones (Aberystwyth); Islwyn D. Jones (Blaenclydach); J. Gwynfor Jones (Cardiff); J. Towyn Jones (Carmarthen); Michael Jones (Merthyr Tydfil); Phylip Jones (Resolven); Neil G. Kirkham (Llandudno), Andrew Lambert (Machynlleth); Don Llewelyn (Pentyrch); Lionel Madden (Aberystwyth); Andrew Mathieson (Welshpool); Susan Morgan (London); Judith Morris (Penrhyn-coch); Llinos Morris (London); Lisbeth McLean (Merthyr Tydfil); Rob Nicholls (Cardiff); Dafydd H. Owen (Cardiff); Goronwy Prys Owen (Bala); Gruff Owen (Tremadog); John Owen (Ruthin); David Peate, (Newtown); D. Ben Rees (Liverpool); Marian Rees (Tal-y-llyn); Nia Rhosier (Pontrobert); Eluned Richards (Tregaron); the late Stuart Rivers (Llandudno); Robert Rudge (Aberystwyth); Joel Sainsbury (Cardiff); Robert Scourfield (Cresswell Quay); Meriel V. Simpson (Toronto, Canada); Hywel Thomas (London); Peter Thomas (Aberystwyth); Richard Thomas (Rhyl); William Troughton (Aberystwyth); Huw Walters (Aberystwyth); Hywel Wigley (Pentyrch); Carol Wilkinson (Pontypool); Gareth Vaughan Williams (Wrexham); Marc John Williams (Cardiff); Megan Williams (Dolgellau) and Laurie Wright (Aberystwyth). Information on St. John's, Colwyn Bay, was kindly provided by L. Colin Williams, who delivered a talk at the Capel meeting, held at St. John's in 2008; on G.E. Dickens-Lewis by Dr. W.T.R. Pryce; information on Solva and Caerfarchell by the Rev. Wiliam T.E. Owen.

I greatly benefitted from my discussions with them and their positive comments, but I am aware that I alone am responsible for any errors or omissions in the volume.

I also wish to acknowledge the efficiency and co-operation of the staff of various institutions, including The National Library of Wales; Royal Commission on the Ancient and Historical Monuments of Wales; St Fagans: National History Museum; Cadw; Ceredigion Library (Aberystwyth); Carmarthenshire Libraries (Carmarthen, Cross Hands, Llanelli); Cardiff Central Library; Cardiff Fairwater Library.

The following have very kindly allowed me to publish their photographs: Marian Delyth [2, 7, 13, 21, 65, 72, 73 (exterior), 76, 77, 85, 90]; Mick Felton [56, 57, 58, 59, 100, 102, 103 (exterior), 110, 111 (exterior), 112, 113]; Andrew Lambert of MOMA Machynlleth (Introduction, p.20); David Puleston Williams [1]; Richard Hayward [22, 23, 24]; John Evans [25]; Edgar Lewis [35]; Robert Scourfield [38, 47, 67, 71]; Islwyn D. Jones [48, 73 (interior), 79 (interior), 81]; Eleanor Jenkins [89]; iz Mckean [108]; the late H. Wyn Jones [114]; Trevor Jennett [116]; Nick Bucknall [117]; Sion Gough Hughes Photography [118]; Richard Price Baskwill [119]; Laurie Wright [120]; Muriel Simpson [121]; Pablo Pappolla [122].

The other photographs were taken during my visits to the individual chapels.

I received every assistance by the staff of Seren, and I wish to especially thank Mick Felton for his full co-operation, his agreement to the proposal to commission a number of photographs by Marian Delyth, and his immense patience in view of the unavoidable delay in submitting the text for the volume which was scheduled to be published in 2008.

That delay was caused by a long family illness and subsequent bereavement, and my greatest debt is to my family for their constant encouragement and unfailing support over an extended period of time. Valuable assistance was provided by my late son Tomos, despite his cruel illness; my wife Mary; and son Hywel. It is with the greatest pleasure that I dedicate this volume to Mary and Hywel as a small expression of my appreciation for their constructive comments on the text and numerous practical contributions whilst the volume was being prepared.

LIST OF ABBREVIATIONS

A: Apostolics; Bw: Baptists, [Welsh language]; Be: Baptists, [English language/ bilingual]; C: Congregational; E: Evangelical; I: Welsh Independents; Mw: Methodists, [Welsh language]: Me: Methodists [English language]; Pw: Presbyterian, Welsh language; Pe: Presbyterian,English language; R: United Reformed Church; Sa: Salvation Army; So: Society of Friends / Quakers; U: Unitarians; Un: United congregation.

INTRODUCTION

In recent years there has developed an enhanced awareness of the significance of Nonconformist chapel buildings in the landscapes and townscapes of Wales. Welsh architects, contractors, builders and craftsmen, using local materials, were responsible for building and furnishing the vast majority of the chapels of Wales. Anthony Jones, who has been in the vanguard of efforts to promote an appreciation of the value of chapel buildings, referred in his *Welsh Chapels* (1992) to Welsh streets, "littered with the decomposing hulks of chapels, hundreds of abandoned Bethels and Bethesdas", and described chapels as being "once the architectural celebrities of every street and country lane", and also being "without question the national architecture of Wales". Anthony Jones's views have been endorsed by Simon Jenkins, who commented in his *Wales: Churches, Houses, Castles* (2008) that chapels "make every Welsh settlement instantly recognizable as such, in a religious pluralism replicated in no other community in Europe". A comparison of the earliest and latest volumes published in the *The Buildings of Wales* series, established by Sir Nikolaus Pevsner (1902-83), those on Powys in 1979 and Gwynedd in 2009, reveals the considerable increase in the emphasis placed on chapels. However, Richard Haslam, in the earliest volume, that on Powys, described chapels as "the most characteristic of all Welsh building types, visually the focal point of so many rural communities, and of so many landscapes and townscapes". Also, John Newman, in his volume on Glamorgan (1982), referred to chapels as "the building type people most readily associate with Glamorgan".

It is a paradox that these positive comments on the significance of Welsh chapels are in marked contrast to views expressed in an earlier period, when adherence to Nonconformist causes was far more widespread. Prominent literary figures, writing in both Welsh and English, were critical both of the physical nature of chapel buildings and also their powerful influence. T. Rowland Hughes, the Welsh novelist and poet, referred to chapels as "addoldai llwm...yn flychau sgwar, afrosgo, trwm" [poor places of worship ... square, clumsy, heavy boxes], and several Anglo-Welsh authors, including Caradoc Evans, T. Harri Jones, Gwyn Thomas and Dylan Thomas emphasised the harmful claustrophobic consequences of a dominant Nonconformist culture. Gwyn Thomas, who was one of the most severe critics of an all-pervading Nonconformist influence, referred to "marathon stints of piety that are the cultural paving stones of a Rhondda boyhood". Yet he also stated, in *A Welsh Eye* (1964), that "The chapel has been a characteristic part of our idiom.... not a single artist in Wales today who, in his earliest years, was not made aware and communicative by the cult of self-expression developed in the teeming vestries of our valleys".

The increasing emphasis on chapel architecture has coincided with the dramatic decrease in membership of the mainline Nonconformist churches and growing secularization of Welsh society, with pluralism and diversity replacing the traditional concept of the chapel forming the bedrock of settled and cohesive communities. The dominance of Nonconformist chapels was reflected in the actual buildings which often literally towered over the surrounding buildings in the towns and villages of Wales. Some of the more impressive buildings attracted differing responses even when Nonconformity was at its most influential.

Tabernacl chapel, Morriston [90] (known as the 'Cathedral Church of Welsh Nonconformity'), was described in a contemporary local-based newspaper as "the one great redeeming feature in the whole of that huge manufacturing district – it is an oasis in the desert". Iorwerth C. Peate, the founder of the Welsh Folk Museum, now the St. Fagans National History Museum, was very critical of the decline in architectural standards and cited Tabernacl as a glaring example of this trend, with the ornate place of worship in stark contrast to a simple, unadorned but dignified 'Bethel' which had previously been the meeting place for a small congregation. He was answered by the Rev. Trebor Lloyd Evans, minister of the Tabernacl and author of the volume presenting the history of the chapel, significantly entitled *Y Cathedral Anghydffurfiol Cymreig* ['The Welsh Nonconformist Cathedral'], who asserted that the pulpit and communion table were in a central position, wrapped around by every seat in the chapel.

The central location of the pulpit where the preacher would deliver the sermon reflected the fundamental theological basis of the Nonconformist churches which emphasised the preaching of the Word (*y Gair*). A feature of the early meeting houses, which were usually built for groups which had previously held services in private homes, barns or outhouses, was that the pulpit was placed either in the centre of the long wall façade, or in the centre of the short wall. Windows would normally be arranged on either side of the pulpit, and often with tall windows also placed above the pulpit, thereby providing the preacher with sufficient light to read and consult the Bible. The entrance was by means of a door, or doors placed either alongside the pulpit or on the rear wall facing the pulpit. Early examples of religious meeting houses discussed in this volume include Maesyronnen [49], built *c.* 1696, the earliest chapel which continues to be used by a congregation for worship, and the Pales, Llandegley [46], probably built in 1717, the oldest Quaker meeting house in Wales. Capel Newydd, Nanhoron [12], built *c.* 1770 in the Llŷn peninsula, and Pen-rhiw chapel [99], built in 1777 in the Teifi Valley but now located at the St Fagans National History Museum, are examples of early chapels which have survived largely unaltered, and were possibly once a barn, or possibly a cowshed which had been converted into a chapel. Capel Newydd, Nanhoron continues to have its earthen floor and pews along the long wall. Hen Gapel John Hughes, Pontrobert [37] was built in 1800, with the minister's house attached to it, and similarly the chapel and house at Soar-y-mynydd [55] were built in 1822 under the same roof,

Nanhoron [12], an early rural chapel

with the stable nearby, and the second chapel at Caerfarchell, Solva [67], replacing the original 1763 structure, was built in 1827. These chapels again have survived with relatively very few changes made to them, but a number of other early chapels were renovated, including Capel Cildwrn, Llangefni [3], in 1846-49; and Capel Gwynfil, Llangeitho [56], in 1861-63; and a new chapel was built at Rhydwilym [72] in 1875.

The growing strength of Nonconformity in Wales, and a dramatic increase in the population, especially in the industrial areas led to a realisation of the need for a larger chapel. One consequence for chapel architecture was the trend to move the pulpit to the rear gable wall, as a rule facing members of the congregation who would enter the chapel on the front gable. The entrance at the gable end formed part of the main façade, and this then became a distinctive feature of the Welsh chapel. Other integral elements were the *sêt fawr* [great pew], placed immediately in front of the pulpit, and occupied by the elders or deacons elected by the members; and the unadorned Communion Table. Galleries or balconies, normally on three sides, provided accommodation for the members and also the *gwrandawyr* [listeners] who often represented a significant element in the congregation. The intense theatrical atmosphere in a confined auditorium presented opportunities which could be utilised by an eloquent preacher.

Many of the larger chapels of the nineteenth century were designed in a Classical style, with an emphasis on columns, pediments, pilasters and balustrated parapets. An early and exceptionally influential example of a Classical chapel was Peniel Tremadog [17], which was probably based upon Inigo Jones's design of St. Paul's church, Covent Garden, London. Developments of this style were the chapels of

Crane Street, Pontypool (1846) [111]; Seion, Llanelli (1857) [81]; Bethesda, Mold (1863) [34]; Tabernacl, Cardiff (1865) [103]; Tabernacl, Morriston (1873) [90] and Tabernacle, Haverfordwest (1874) [70].

Gothic features constituted the other main architectural style adopted by chapels. An early example was Ebeneser, Caernarfon (1826) [10], but on the whole this was the style favoured by English-language chapels, such as Castle Square, Caernarfon (1883) [9]; the English Presbyterian Church at Menai Bridge (1888) [5]; St. John's Uniting Church, Colwyn Bay (1888) [25]; and Gloddaeth United Church, Llandudno (1891) [22], with their naves, aisles, towers and spires resembling those of Anglican churches.

The more elegant chapels were associated with professional architects, and an effort has been made in this volume to provide information on the architect who designed a chapel, and also on the firm responsible for supplying the organ: these details are frequently absent from many chapel histories. Several of the chapels discussed in this volume represent examples of the work of Welsh architects such as

The interior at Tabernacle, Pontypridd [105]

Hyfrydle, Holyhead [1]; Moreia, Llangefni [4]; Capel y Drindod, Pwllheli [14]; and Capel Als, Llanelli [79] (Owen Morris Roberts); Jerusalem, Bethesda [6]; and Pendref, Denbigh [31] (Richard Davies); Zion Baptist Church, Newtown [42]; the English Baptist Church, Carmarthen [75]; and Greenfield, Llanelli, [80], schoolroom and renovation (George Morgan); Tabernacl, Morriston [90] (John Humphrey); Bethania, Maesteg [94] (W. Beddoe Rees); and Mynydd Seion, Abergele [27]; Castle Square, Caernarfon [9]; Bathafarn, Ruthun [32]; Crescent Christian Centre, Newtown [41]; China Street, Llanidloes [43]; and Seion Aberystwyth [53] (Richard Owens). The latter was based in Liverpool, and other examples in this volume of chapels designed by English-based architects include Capel Tegid, Bala [21] by William Henry Spaull, Oswestry, and Bethesda, Mold [34], by W.W. Gwyther, London, whilst the City United Reformed Church, Cardiff [100] was designed by Frederick Thomas Pilkington, Edinburgh.

A number of chapels were designed by ministers, such as the Rev. Edward Roberts, who designed Tabernacle chapel, Pontypridd [105] (*opposite*), currently the Pontypridd Museum. The Rev. William Jones, a prominent preacher and minister of Jerusalem, Tonpentre, who had been apprenticed as a carpenter, is said to have designed over 200 chapels in south Wales. His father, William Jones was the builder of Capel y Garn, Bow Street [50], and his brother Thomas was the builder when the chapel was later renovated. The Rev. Robert Ambrose Jones (Emrys ap Iwan) was closely associated with planning Tabernacl, Ruthin [33]. One of the most prolific architect-ministers was the Rev. Thomas Thomas, minister of Seilo, Landore, Swansea. Known as 'Thomas Glandŵr', he made extensive use of the 'great arch', probably based upon the one in the San Andrea church, Mantua, Italy, as the main feature of the gable and the design of the Dre-fach, Capel Seion [78]; Gellimanwydd/Christian Temple, Ammanford [84]; and Tabernacl, Efail Isaf chapels [95] have been attributed to him. The illustrated study of him, 'Thomas Thomas, 1817-88: the first national architect of Wales' by Stephen Hughes was originally published in *Archaeologia Cambrensis*, 152 (2003), and then reprinted as a monograph.

The biography by David Farmer, *The Remarkable Life of John Humphrey, God's Own Architect* (1997) focused attention on the architect of Tabernacl, Morriston [90] with its eight massive Corinthian towers, and clock tower with steeple. John Humphrey and Thomas Thomas appear on a list, compiled by Vernon Hughes and Malcolm Seaborne, of Welsh chapel architects mentioned in the periodical *The Builder* between 1843 and 1890. This list was published in the *Capel Newsletter*, 21 (1993-94), and the same publication also contains information on a number of architects, including William Henry Spaull, 8 (1989); Sir William Beddoe Rees, prepared by Brian James, 9 (1989); George Morgan by Thomas Lloyd, 11 (1990); Richard Owens, by Malcolm Seaborne, 19 (1993); and Eryl Wyn Rowlands, 38 (2001): the latter also provided biographical details on Owen Morris Roberts and R.G. Thomas, 39 (2002); and Richard Davies, 39 (2002) and 41 (2003).

Sir Clough Williams-Ellis, the renowned creator of the 'Italianate' coastal village of Portmeirion, designed Moreia, Llanystumdwy [16], a notable example of a chapel built in the twentieth century. The dramatic decrease in the congregations of Nonconformist denominations in Wales in the late-twentieth century, emphasised by D. Densil Morgan, *The Span of the Cross, Christian Religion and Society in Wales, 1914-2000* (1999, 2nd ed. 2011), and Paul Chambers, *Religion, Secularization and Social Change in Wales* (2005), was accompanied by the closure of many chapels. John Davies, in his *A History of Wales* (1993), commentated that "religious decline is one of the most striking aspects of the history of Wales in the period after the Second World War", and that "the empty chapels were a cause of sadness and regret even to those who never darkened their doors"; and Martin Johns, in the concluding chapter of his *Wales since 1939* (2012), referred to the "passing of the chapels' grip on communities".

Some chapels have been replaced by new buildings, such as Seilo, Caernarfon (1976) [11]; Capel y Groes, Wrexham (1982) [35], and Berea Newydd, Bangor (2003) [7] which offer far better facilities for their congregations. Another positive development resulted from the establishment of Berea Newydd. One of the five churches which had united to form Berea Newydd had previously been known as Tŵr-gwyn, the interior of whose chapel has been significantly adapted for use by the church now known as Penrallt Baptist Church [8] but with also extensive provision for the local community. The nature of the work undertaken at Penrallt Baptist Church was outlined at the Capel Lecture delivered at the Ebbw Vale National Eisteddfod in 2010 by Alwyn Harding Jones, a contemporary architect renowned for his expertise in the sensitive adaptation and conversion of chapels. He was also responsible for designing an extension at Salem Canton [102], the conversion of Horeb, Pen-tyrch [97] into the Acapela concert hall and recording studio, the conservation project at the Pontypridd Museum [105], and the work undertaken at Gwaelod-y-Garth [96] and Tabernacl, Efail Isaf [95]. Another example of the sensitive conversion of a redundant chapel to a different use is that of the former Tabernacl, Machynlleth into a centre for the performing arts, alongside the Museum of Modern Art, Wales [45]. In Aberystwyth, following the opening of the new St Paul's Centre [54] in 1992 by the English and Welsh Wesleyan Methodists of the town, the former St. Paul's Methodist chapel has been converted into the public house known as the 'Academy'. Several redundant chapels have been converted into private residences, and an on-going example of a sensitive conversion is that of the former Welsh Independent Gwilym Hiraethog Memorial Chapel in Llansannan.

The need to provide a positive response to the rapidly-increasing rate of chapel closures was the establishment in 1986 of Capel, the Chapels Heritage Society, whose objectives include the encouragement of the study and preservation of the Nonconformist heritage of Wales; the provision of information and advice to congregations on ways to maintain their buildings and preserve their records; and support efforts to ensure the sympathetic conversion of chapels no longer required

The interior of Llwynrhydowen [61], acquired by the Welsh Religious Buildings Trust

for their original purpose. A newsletter is produced twice a year and a regular feature is a list of chapel closures and planning applications, which have been considered by specialist architects aware of Capel's priorities. Accounts are also presented of the two visits arranged each year by Capel, and information leaflets describing the chapels in these areas visited by the society are also published. I have personally benefitted from these visits and publications, and a number of the chapels featured in this volume were first visited during meetings organised by Capel.

Concern with regard to the threat to chapels was expressed by the parliamentary Welsh Affairs Committee in a report in 1993 which emphasised the need to safeguard historic buildings and ancient monuments. The government responded to this report by accepting the need for arrangements to be made with Nonconformist denominations in relation to their redundant religious buildings. Following a seminar to consider the future of redundant buildings organised in 1994 by Cadw, the historic environment division of the Welsh Government, a working party was established which produced in 1996 a comprehensive report, *Redundant Historic Chapels in Wales*. A direct result of the report was the establishment of the Welsh Religious Buildings Trust, Addoldai Cymru, which, partly funded by Cadw, is required to take into its care a representative collection of non-Anglican redundant religious buildings which are of particular historic or architectural interest. To date, six chapels have been acquired, of which four are discussed in this volume: Bethania, Maesteg [94]; Yr Hen Dŷ Cwrdd, Trecynon [106]; Llwynrhydowen [61]; and Peniel

Tremadog [17]. The Trust's annual *Newsletter* contains information on these chapels, and other valuable publications for two of these chapels are David Barnes's *People of Seion* (1995) [Llwynrhydowen] and D. Leslie Davies's *'They Love to be Dissenters': the Historical Background of Hen Dŷ Cwrdd, Aberdare, 1650-1862* (2012). The Trust, and also Capel, were fully involved in the Ceredigion Faith Trail discussions, organised by Ceredigion County Council, which resulted in the installation of information panels outside religious buildings, including chapels, and the publication of the information leaflets, *The Cilgwyn Trail* and *The Unitarian Trail.*

In addition to these bodies, national institutions, local authorities and the media have paid attention to the importance of the Nonconformist heritage. Reference has already been made to Cadw, which has prepared detailed descriptions of a large number of the more important chapels as part of the listing process, and the Grade 1 and Grade 2* designations awarded by Cadw have substantially influenced the selection of chapels included in this volume. In 1999 Cadw published the illustrated booklet *Chapels in Wales, Conservation and Conversion,* the opening sentence of which declared that "The thousands of chapels built in Wales over the last two centuries are a quintesssential part of the country's architectural heritage". Striking colour illustrations were presented of external views of three chapels considered in this volume: Tabernacl, Morriston [90]; Maesyronnen [49]; and the City United Reformed Church, Cardiff [100]; and also of the external view and interior of the Museum of Modern Art, Wales, Machynlleth [45], formerly the Tabernacle Chapel, which represents a fine example of a chapel converted to another use.

The text was prepared by John Hilling, whose other publications in this field include *Cardiff and the Valleys* (1973), *The Historic Architecture of Wales* (1979), the

The Museum of Modern Art, Wales, Machynlleth [45], formerly the Tabernacl Chapel

chapter 'Architecture in Glamorgan' in the *Glamorgan County History*, vol. VI, *Glamorgan Society, 1780-1980*, ed. Prys Morgan (1988); and *Cardiff's Temples of Faith* (2000). He described the latter as "an architectural and historical romp to as many places of worship as possible", with the text accompanied by Mary Traynor's drawings of the various buildings. His article 'The Architecture of the Welsh Chapel' in the *Transactions of the Honourable Society of the Cymmrodorion* (1983) significantly contained the statements that chapels "rarely seem to have been taken seriously as architecture or as works of art", "Books on the subject of Welsh chapel architecture are almost non-existent" and "chapels have been for too long treated with scorn or ignored with undeserving contempt". His own publications since 1983, and the numerous references in this text to books on the subject reflect considerable advances in this field.

Capel contributed to the extensive project organised by the Royal Commission on the Ancient and Historical Monuments of Wales to record all the Nonconformist chapels of Wales. As a result images of every surviving chapel in Wales are available in the National Monuments Record for Wales at the Commission in Aberystwyth, and the entries for more than 6,400 chapels may be consulted on the Commission's website: www.coflein.co.uk. The Commission has extended the scope of this project and it is envisaged that a major study based on the chapels project, *Welsh Chapel Architecture*, will be published in 2014 by the Royal Commission. Publications by members of the Commission staff include David Percival's 'Inventory of Nonconformist Chapels and Sunday Schools in Cardiganshire', which contains details of the architect, builder, carpenter and designer and costs involved, in the *Cardiganshire County History*, vol. 3, 'Cardiganshire in Modern Times' (1998); and Stephen Hughes's *Copperopolis, Landscapes of the Early Industrial Period in Swansea* (2000), which provides valuable information on chapels and chapel architects and builders in the Swansea area. Reference has already been made to his published work on one of, if not the most significant of these local architects, the Rev. Thomas Thomas, minister of Seilo Landore. Also, Susan Fielding presented a survey of the subject and of recent activities in Tim Rushton's *Capeli/Chapels* (2012), which contains a collection of colour photographs of 120 chapels, predominantly located in north-west Wales.

Pen-rhiw chapel [99], one of the most important historical chapels of Wales, has been preserved at the St Fagans: National History Museum. In 1984 the National Museum of Wales published Anthony Jones's booklet, *Chapels of Wales*, to accompany the influential exhibition organized by the Museum. Two extremely popular television programmes, *On the Chapel Trail*, presented by him and shown on HTV, again emphasised the significance of the history and deteriorating condition of many Welsh chapels. These programmes, together with a range of visual material, were shown in the exhibition *Temples of Devotion*, organized at the National Library of Wales in 1996. The collections of the Library include many pictures and drawings of chapels by artists including John Piper, John Petts, John Elwyn, Kenneth Rowntree, A.F. Mortimer and Cefyn Burgess; and photographers including John Thomas, Geoff Charles, Graham Rosser and Islwyn D. Jones. The Library published in 1994 *Nonconformist Registers of Wales*, edited by Dafydd Ifans, a list of the registers of the Nonconformist chapels of Wales which have been deposited in public libraries and record offices in England and Wales.

Local authorities have also been increasingly aware of the importance of chapel buildings, and planning officers regularly submit details of building applications to Capel. An extremely important initiative was the MSC-funded scheme organised by the Planning Department of the former Mid Glamorgan County Council, under the direction of Mr. Alwyn J. Williams, whereby young people were recruited to undertake a survey of 636 pre-1918 chapels. Measured drawings were prepared of these chapels, and information assembled on approximately two-thirds of them. This valuable archive, relating to many chapels which have by now closed, been demolished or converted to another use, is preserved at the Glamorgan Archives. Another MSC scheme organised in Clwyd in the 1986-89 period resulted in the deposit in the county's record offices of photographs, information sheets and schedules of records. Chapel photographs are regularly displayed in libraries and museums, and the photographs by Islwyn Jones of a number of local chapels were exhibited in various libraries in the area administered by the Rhondda Cynon Taff Council.

The detailed descriptions of Cadw have been consulted when the entries in this volume have been prepared, especially those in the Grade 1 or Grade 2* category, as also have the relevant sections of the volumes in the series *The Buildings of Wales*, established by Sir Nikolaus Pevsner. To date, seven volumes have been published: *Powys*, ed. Richard Haslam (1979), *Clwyd*, ed. Edward Hubbard (1986, 2001), the two volumes edited by John Newman, *Glamorgan*, (1995) and *Gwent / Monmouthshire* (2000); the two volumes edited by Thomas Lloyd, Julian Orbach and Robert Scourfield, *Pembrokeshire* (2004), and *Carmarthenshire and Ceredigion* (2006); and *Gwynedd : Anglesey, Caernarvonshire and Merioneth*, eds. Richard Haslam, Julian Orbach and Adam Voelcker, with contributions by Judith Alfrey (2009); and another volume on Powys is currently being prepared by Robert Scourfield.

Considerable attention has been paid in recent years to chapel architecture and the significance of Nonconformity in the visual culture of Wales. Significant publications in this field include Anthony J. Parkinson's chapter 'Chapel Architecture' in *Methodism in Wales, A Short History of the Wesley Tradition*, ed. Lionel Madden (2003); John Harvey, *The Art of Piety: The Visual Culture of Welsh Nonconformity* (1995); and his *Image of the Invisible: The Visualization of Religion in the Welsh Nonconformist Tradition* (1999); Peter Lord, *Imaging the Nation: The Visual Culture of Wales* (2000); and *Biblical Art from Wales*, eds. Martin O'Kane and John Morgan-Kane (2010). High-quality illustrations, accompanied by detailed descriptions, appear in T.J. Hughes, *Wales's Best One Hundred Churches* (2006) which includes fourteen important chapels.

Descriptive entries on selected chapels, as well as churches, are presented in Jonathan Wooding, *Churches and Chapels of Wales* (2011). Also, D. Huw Owen emphasised the contribution of the Calvinistic Methodist/Presbyterian Church of Wales to the visual cultural heritage of Wales in his chapter in *The Bible in Church, Academy and Culture*, ed. Alan P.F. Sell (2011).

Valuable local-based publications include the collection of chapel illustrations in *Marching to Zion: Radnorshire Chapels*, eds. J.B. Sinclair and R.W.D. Fenn (1990), which succeeded in its objective of placing the 'Nonconformist chapel architecture of Radnorshire into its historical and social perspective.' A comprehensive narrative and visual survey of 180 Nonconformist places of worship in one area was presented in Alan Vernon Jones's *Chapels of the Cynon Valley: Capeli Cwm Cynon* (2004). Information was provided on the main architects and builders, and detailed descriptions of architectural features, accompanied by a range of illustrative material, including a large number of measured drawings, plans and elevations, and colour and black-and-white photographs of the exterior and interior of chapels in the area extending from Ynysybwl in the south to Penderyn in the north. Anglesey chapels were described in Geraint I.L. Jones's *Capeli Môn* (2007), and Huw Edwards's comprehensive survey of Llanelli chapels, *Capeli Llanelli: Our Rich Heritage* (2009), enhanced an understanding of the importance of the Nonconformist heritage: he is now preparing a similar volume on Welsh chapels in London.

Publications comprising various local photographs also constitute important sources of information on Nonconformist buildings. Recent volumes relating to the Rhondda Valley and Pontypridd include Aldo Bacchetta and Glyn Rudd, *Porth and Rhondda Fach* (1996, new. ed. 2003) which contains photographs of the old (1778) and new (1870) buildings of Capel y Cymer, Porth; the opening of Ebenezer Chapel, Maerdy in 1912, and the demolition of Penuel, Ynyshir in 1991. A second collection by the same compilers (1998, reprinted 2002) contained photographs of the conversion of two Calvinistic Methodist chapels in Ynyshir: Tabernacl which is now a British Legion Club and Moriah a Boys' Club. A collection of chapel photographs presented in Dean Powell, *Pontypridd, A Market Town* (2005), includes the exterior of Penuel demolished in 1967 before the opening of the Fraternal Parade shops; the interior and exterior of Carmel chapel, Graigwen, demolished in 1969 with the Plas Carmel flats afterwards built on the site; and also three chapels converted to other uses: Capel Eglwys-bach, Berw Road, the Wesleyan chapel built in 1899 in memory of the Revd. John Evans, Eglwys-bach and now a medical surgery; the Wesleyan Chapel, Gelliwastad Road, the site of the Muni Arts Centre; and Tabernacl Chapel, Bridge Street, the present-day location of the Pontypridd Museum. Simon Eckley's compilation in *Pontypridd* (1994 contains two fascinating photographs taken in 1907 of the interior of Capel Rhondda, Hopkinstown, one before, and the other one after the installation of the organ in the Baptist chapel. A photograph of Ebenezer, Glyntaff, taken soon after it was built in 1896, represents a valuable record as this chapel was demolished in the 1970s at the time of the widening of the A470 road.

Studies of the history of denominations include T.M. Bassett, *The Welsh Baptists* (1977); R. Tudur Jones, *Congregationalism in Wales* (2004); A.H. Williams, *Welsh Wesleyan Methodism 1800-1858* (1935); *Methodism in Wales*, ed. Lionel Madden (2003) and Eric Jones, *The Good Ground* (2009), an outline of the history of Unitarian churches in Wales. Three Welsh-language volumes tracing the history of the Welsh Calvinistic Methodists/Presbyterian Church of Wales have been published, in 1973, 1978 and 2011; and an English-language version of the latest publication, concentrating on the period *c*.1814-1914, together with a final volume covering the period extending from 1914 to the present day are at present being prepared for publication.

Several valuable articles have also been published in denominational historical journals. Huw Walters's detailed list of books and pamphlets on the history of Independent churches in Wales, which represents an extremely important contribution to the historiography of Nonconformity in Wales, appeared in *Y Cofiadur*, the historical journal of the Welsh Independents. The history of the Baptist church in Hengoed was examined by Avril Padfield in 1990 and E. Keri Edwards in 1996, in *Trafodion Cymdeithas Hanes y Bedyddwyr* [Proceedings of the Historical Society of the Baptists], with information provided on the construction of a new chapel in 1829 at a cost of £420 to replace the early meeting house built in 1710; and also the building of a number of chapels in the Rhymney Valley, including Tonyfelin, Caerphilly in 1865 at a cost of £1,000; Calfaria, Nelson in 1878 at a cost of £386; and Bryn Seion, Ystrad Mynach in 1905-06 at a cost of £700. J. Gwynfor Jones's study in this journal of the contribution of local Baptists to the growth of Welsh civic consciousness in Cardiff in the period 1890-1914 emphasised the importance of the central location of Tabernacl Chapel, with the first chapel constructed in 1821 and the present building in 1865. B. Tudor Lloyd's article on 'William Griffiths (1788-1861), Apostle of Gower', which contained valuable information on the Gower chapels of Bethesda, Burry Green [89] and Trinity, Cheriton, built through the patronage of Lady Barham, and Ebenezer, Old Walls, dependent on the financial support of her son, Lord Barham, was originally published in the *Journal of the Historical Society of the Presbyterian Church of Wales*, and subsequently in the volume *Pleasant Places: A Tribute to the Gower Ministry of Rev. B Tudor Lloyd*, ed. Eifion Evans (2006).

Other standard denominational histories and many contributions to the historical journals are in the Welsh language, as also are the histories of individual Welsh-speaking churches: details of relevant volumes and journals which may provide further information are listed at the end of each entry. Reference has also been made in the relevant entries to information provided by the Religious Census of 1851, and published in *The Religious Census of 1851, A Calendar of the Returns relating to Wales, vol. i, South Wales*, eds. Ieuan Gwynedd Jones & David Williams (1976); *vol ii, North Wales*, ed. Ieuan Gwynedd Jones, (1981). I have benefitted from my discussions with Professor Jones whilst selecting chapels for inclusion in this volume.

In the two volumes published by Y Lolfa: Penry Jones, *Capeli Cymru* (1980), and D. Huw Owen, *Capeli Cymru* (2005), an attempt was made to provide a brief history of the chapel and the church in which it met, a description of the chapel and references to significant events and individuals associated with the church. Penry Jones commented on the undoubted deterioration which had occurred by 1979-80 when he was writing his volume but yet he added that there was still a considerable amount of life left in them. This was also my impression with regard to most of the churches visited during the preparations for my volume, despite the further deterioration which could be observed by 2004-05. There was also no doubt concerning the enthusiasm, energy and determination of the ministers and officers who assisted me at that time, and again while preparing this volume, to overcome all the problems and difficulties experienced, and respond positively to my requests for information.

The failure to elicit a response from a very small number of persons explains the omission of some chapels which I had intended to include. Whilst my main criterion in selecting a chapel was on the basis of the architectural importance of the building, I also hoped that some indication would also be provided on the significance of the Nonconformist heritage of Wales, and its unique contribution to the distinctive life and culture of Wales. This is relevant in view of both the English and Welsh-language chapels selected for inclusion. With regard to the latter, there has been an awareness of the value of providing those readers with a limited or non-existent knowledge of

Change of faith: the former Welsh Presbyterian chapel, Crwys Road, Cardiff [101]

the Welsh language with some indication of their distinctive contribution to the heritage of Wales, especially as in some instances the available sources are understandably exclusively in the Welsh language.

As has been previously stated, one of the key factors influencing the selection of chapels to be included in this volume was the grading of the chapel by Cadw. An attempt has also been made to provide a balanced selection, reflecting the various denominations and localities of Wales, the different architectural styles of the buildings, and a broad chronological span extending from the late seventeenth century, when Maesyronnen [49], the earliest chapel which continues to be used by a congregation for worship was built (c. 1696), to the first eleven years of the twenty-first century, when developments have included the opening of Berea Newydd, Bangor [7]; renovation of Penrallt Baptist Church, Bangor [8] and Tabernacl Efail Isaf [95]; the extension to Salem, Canton [102]; and adaptation of Horeb, Pen-tyrch [97]; Soar, Merthyr Tydfil [108], and Seion, Llanelli [81]. Whilst the emphasis has understandably been on Nonconformist churches, there have also been references to the activities of other religious groups, such as the Anglican Church in the Welsh Church, Aber-carn [110]; the Greek Orthodox Church in the vestry of Soar, Lampeter [59]; and the Shah Jalal Mosque, the Islamic Cultural Centre in the former Welsh Presbyterian chapel in Crwys Road, Cardiff [101] (*see previous page*).

1.HOLYHEAD, Hyfrydle Unedig [United] (Pw)

OS: SH 244 825

The Calvinistic Methodists at first held their meetings on the outskirts of the town of Holyhead to avoid persecution, as they faced fierce opposition from Thomas Ellis, the vicar of Holyhead. The town was visited by many of the early Methodist leaders, and William Williams, Pantycelyn, is believed to have composed the hymn '*Mae'r iachawdwriaeth fel y môr, yn chwyddo byth i'r lan*' ['Salvation is like the ocean, swelling constantly to the shore'] after he had seen the tide wash ashore at nearby Porth Dafarch. Services were regularly held in private homes by 1749, and early meetings in the town were held in the home of Richard Jones, a prominent local Methodist who encouraged the purchase of an empty house, Ty'n y Llidiart which was adapted as a meeting house. The first chapel, built in 1808 was very small and measured just 12 yards x 9 yards. Named 'Hyfrydle' it was also known as Capel yr Allt or Capel Mawr, and was enlarged in 1815.

In the early nineteenth century members of Hyfrydle were accused of taking advantage of goods washed ashore during the numerous shipwrecks which occurred off the coast of Anglesey. The Rev. John Elias was requested by the Anglesey Presbytery to investigate the charge, and at a church meeting held at Hyfrydle he apparently discovered that the members had been involved in handling tobacco and cotton from a wrecked ship. He excommunicated all the members who then departed, leaving John Elias alone in the chapel. Following their public confession of guilt and repentance, they were readmitted to membership about a month later.

The growth in the local population in a period which witnessed the completion of Telford's road in 1826 and the railway in 1848 was accompanied by an increase in the number of local Calvinistic Methodists. The chapel was demolished in 1847 and a new chapel erected, which was then enlarged in 1856. The Religious Census of 1851 recorded that on 30 March 577 were present in the morning service and 1,038 in the evening. The need for a new building was again recognised, even after an enlargement in 1856, and the purchase of the freehold of the chapel, together with four houses in Thomas Street and Mill Street, enabled the building of a new chapel facing the main street. This new chapel, designed by O. Morris Roberts, Porthmadog, with a stucco facade, arched upper windows, galleried interior with ornate ceiling, and with forecourt railings made at a local foundry, was opened in 1888. The cost of £3,511 included a payment for the land, and, seating 1,000, this is Anglesey's largest chapel. By 1901 the debt had been paid, and another £1,517 was spent on the building in the period 1906-1911.

The first full-time minister, the Rev. W.R. Jones (Goleufardd) was inducted in 1880, and served until 1894. Two years later the church bought a stock of hymn books for the use of the congregation, and it is possible that up to that time the tradition continued of a hymn being read out in parts before those sections were sung.

Two mission causes had been established by Hyfrydle in Holyhead. The one in Bont Ddu moved in 1881 to a new schoolroom built in London Road, at a cost of £445, and an increase in the adherents and scholars led to a desire for improved facilities, and eventually to the establishment of Disgwylfa church in London Road. A new schoolroom was built for the mission cause which had been commenced in 1859 at Ponc y Felin, and here again a successful operation resulted in the extension and re-building of the schoolroom in 1900 at a cost of £750. In addition to supervising these mission endeavours, Hyfrydle also supported the English cause whose first services were held in the Town Hall in 1885, leading to the formation of the church the following year. A pipe organ, made by the prestigious Willis firm, was installed at Hyfrydle in 1949 at a cost of over £5,000, and the composer W. Bradwen Jones was the organist from 1952 until 1970.

For many years there was a close association between Hyfrydle and the Welsh church in Talbot Street, Dublin, which opened in 1838, and John Roberts, an elder at Hyfrydle, had travelled to Dublin to arrange the purchase of the land on which the chapel was located. Calvinistic Methodist ministers from the town regularly visited Dublin until the inter-war period to conduct services.

The closure of several Welsh Presbyterian churches in Holyhead which had developed from branches established by Hyfrydle, resulted in them uniting with Hyfredle.

Present position: The church has been without a minister for some years; 55 members; Sunday service, 10 a.m; an active society meets during the winter months.
Further reading: I.C.M. Dodd, *Eglwys Hyfrydle Caergybi* (n.d.); John Pritchard, *Methodistiaeth Môn o'r Dechreuad hyd y flwyddyn 1887* (1888); David Puleston Williams, 'Hyfrydle: Calvinistic Methodist (Presbyterian)', *Capel Local Information Sheet 36, Holyhead* (2010).

2. RHOSMEIRCH, Ebeneser (I)

OS: SH 462 777

This is the oldest Nonconformist chapel of Anglesey, and has been described as '*crud Ymneilltuaeth Môn*' ['the cradle of Anglesey's Nonconformity']. The cause was established in 1744 by William Pritchard, Clwchdernog, who had been evicted from the farms of Glasfryn Fawr, Llangybi, Caernarfonshire and Plas Penmynydd, Anglesey on account of his religious beliefs. Caeau Môn, the home of John Owen, was registered as a place of worship in 1744 and, when it became too small for the congregation, the first Ebeneser was built in 1749. This was a thatched roof, one-floor building which stood on a site now part of the present-day graveyard. The Rev. William Pritchard (1741-73) was buried under the floor of the original chapel, and there is in the graveyard a memorial to him and to Abraham Tibbott, one of his co-ministers who has been described as being prepared to use his fists to defend his beliefs. The building was also used by Baptists and Calvinistic Methodists before they opened their own chapels, and John Wesley and George Whitefield are reputed to have visited the chapel. The 1851 Census recorded that there were 40 free seats, 170 others and room for 60 to stand. On 30 March 110 were present in the morning service, 96 in the afternoon and 150 in the evening, and 80 scholars and 16 teachers attended the afternoon Sunday school.

The present chapel was built in 1869 to a classical design, with a stuccoed façade and an arch cutting across the lower line of the pediment. It is an elegant building with the entrance facing the congregation. There are behind the pulpit memorial tablets to the Rev. William Pritchard and a number of other early ministers of the church, including the Rev. Abraham Tibbott, and also the Rev. Benjamin Jones, who was involved in the conversion of the hymnist Ann Griffiths when he preached at Llanfyllin in 1796. In 1998, at the celebration of the 250th anniversary of the opening of the first chapel, a memorial to John Owen was unveiled. A notable twentieth century minister was the Rev. Ll.C. Lloyd, minister from 1923 until 1954 and, a gifted musician, the founder of the Anglesey Orchestra. A chapel house is located behind the chapel and a small vestry beyond the house.

Present position: No minister; 84 members, three children; Sunday service, normally at 10.00 a.m., Sunday school p.m.; Prayer meeting every month
Further reading: E.B. Jones, *Plannu'r winwydden ym Môn* (1923); *CAPEL Local Information Sheet, 21, Llangefni* (2002).

Ebeneser, Rhosmeirch (*top*) and Cildwrn, Llangefni (*above*)

3. LLANGEFNI, Cildwrn (E)

OS: SH 452 760

The original chapel, Ebenezer, was built in 1781 on the site on the outskirts of Llangefni and this was the first Baptist chapel in north Wales. The second minister, from 1791 until 1826, was the Rev. Christmas Evans (1766-1838), the famous preacher described as *Esgob y Bedyddwyr* [the 'Baptist Bishop'] who preached, evangelised and established churches throughout Wales. The chapel was rebuilt in 1814-15, using local rubble and a gallery was installed. Christmas Evans resided in the neighbouring chapel house, and he is commemorated in the slate plaque placed on it by the county council. His wife Catherine, who died in 1823, is commemorated by a memorial tablet in the yard in front of the chapel. The chapel was remodelled in *c.* 1846-49 when the roof of the chapel was raised, the beams covered and the pews re-arranged, with local craftsmen presumably responsible for organizing and undertaking the work. Other distinctive features dating from this period include a gallery with raking pews and panelled front, and a high pulpit raised by six steps and with a panelled front. On 30 March 1851, 157 were present in the morning, 129 pupils in the afternoon and 259 in the evening service, and there were in the chapel 28 free seats and 260 others.

Following protracted discussions, it was decided to build a new chapel in the town centre and in 1897 this was opened as 'Capel Coffa Christmas Evans' [Christmas Evans Memorial Chapel]. This action was responsible for the survival of Capel Cildwrn as an unspoilt chapel dating back to the first half of the nineteenth century. The chapel remained empty for many years but was renovated and reopened for services in the 1980s. The building was essentially intact, and the plan is nearly square, with entrances on each side of the pulpit, and with six stairs leading to it. The chapel was listed Grade 2* by CADW as an unusually well-preserved eighteenth-century chapel and chapel house, whose original character had been remarkably-well preserved, despite some nineteenth century modifications, and which is of historic interest on account of its association with Christmas Evans.

The chapel now houses Capel Cildwrn, and also the office of Tearfund Wales, of which the minister of the church is the Director.

Present position: Minister: Rev. Hywel Maredudd; 20 members, 6 children; Sunday services, 10.a.m, 6 p.m., with translation facilities, weekly prayer meeting and coffee bar.

Further reading: Capel Local Information Sheet, 21, Llangefni (2002).

4. LLANGEFNI, Moreia (Pw)

OS: SH 459 756

This is the third chapel built by the Calvinistic Methodists in Llangefni, and represents a fine example of a town chapel designed by professional architects.

Howel Harris and Daniel Rowland, the Methodist leaders had visited the locality in the mid-eighteenth century, and a small chapel, Capel Dinas, had been built on the outskirts of Llangefni in 1806-07. A larger chapel had been built in 1836, and, measuring 61 x 46 feet, was described as the finest chapel on Anglesey. In 1851 it contained 74 free seats, 510 others and space for 120 to stand. On 30 March 162 pupils were present in the morning Sunday School, 391 persons in the afternoon service and 420 in the evening service. John Elias, '*y Pab o Fôn*' ['the Pope of Anglesey'] was associated with this chapel. This is where his funeral service was held in 1841, and the tablet on the wall of Moreia had been moved here from Capel Dinas in 1898.

As a result of difficulties experienced with renewing the lease on the land on which Capel Dinas stood, and also a wish to move to the centre of a town which was developing rapidly, a plot of land was purchased on Glanhwfa Road for the purpose of building a chapel. Money was raised largely through the endeavours of James Donne, a businessman who had served as minister of Capel Dinas for many years, and the new chapel was named in memory of John Elias as 'Capel Coffadwriaethol John Elias' [John Elias Memorial Chapel]. The contributors included two wealthy brothers reared in Capel Dinas: Richard Davies, Treborth, Member of Parliament for Anglesey from 1868-1888, and Robert Davies, Bodlondeb, High Sheriff of Anglesey in 1862. Plans were prepared by R.G. Thomas, Menai Bridge, the architect of the Baron Hill estate, and his grandiose plan included a large classical portico standing on four Corinthian columns with four steps leading to three doors. Unfortunately there were not available sufficient funds to pay for this ambitious design, and another architect, O. Morris Roberts, Porthmadog was called in to prepare a cheaper and simpler version. This led to a bitter dispute between the two architects and the chapel's building committee. Eventually, the portico was omitted, two doors replaced the three envisaged, and they were moved to each side, and three round-headed windows were added.

The chapel was built by R. & J. Williams Ltd. Bangor, and despite an effort to complete the work in advance of the completion of the Baptist Capel Coffa Christmas Evans, Moreia was opened in 1898. The cost was £5,500 and the entire debt had nearly been cleared by 1903. An organ chamber had been included in the original design, but the installation in 1928 of an organ, built by the Ernest Wadsworth company, Manchester represented a major change to the chapel. The organ was officially inaugurated by John Williams, the organist of Tabernacl, Bangor and was restored on several occasions later in the century. More restoration work was undertaken on the chapel in the 1980s when dry rot was discovered in the façade.

The chapel has been listed Grade 2* by CADW on the basis of its importance as an urban chapel, its ambitious Neo-Classical style, and its elegant entrance and interior. Reference was also made to the chapel as an integral part of the civic and religious structures built at the turn of the twentieth century at the time of Llangefni's development as the main town of Anglesey.

Present position: No minister since departure of Rev. Christopher Prew to Porthmadog in November 2010, discussions in progress with regard to establishment of area ministry; 130 members, 15-20 children; Sunday service with Sunday school, 10.00 a.m., weekly youth club, devotional services, literary society meets six times.

Further reading: Eryl Wyn Rowlands, *Mirain Moreia* (1997); CAPEL *Newsletter*, 40 (2002); *Capel Local Information Sheet, 21, Llangefni* (2002).

5. MENAI BRIDGE, English Presbyterian Church (Pe)

OS: SH 558 718

This chapel represents the only example on Anglesey of a fully-ecclestiastical, Gothic-syle Nonconformist building.

The English-language cause at Menai Bridge was established largely through the influence of the Rev. Joseph Jones, who had been inducted in 1868 as minister of Capel Mawr, the Welsh church in the village. He had preached at the very first English service held at Menai Bridge on 16 June, 1867, and was the minister of the two churches from 1867 to 1878, when his pastorate became solely concentrated on the English church. For several years English services were held in the New Hall, loaned to the new church by Richard Davies, Treborth Hall, M.P. for Anglesey. A Band of Hope had been held in the hall for some time, and in 1882 the Sunday school moved here from the British School where it had been held since 1873, and which was an important venue for various activities and religious meetings, such as the United Saturday Evening Prayer Meeting, commenced in May 1872; the Mission to Fisherman, first held in 1878; and the temperance meetings held for many years on the last Sunday of the month. It was later used as a cinema; 'pictiwrs bach y Borth' in the words of the popular Welsh song; and then as a paint shop.

Several unsuccessful attempts were made to secure a plot of land for a chapel, but eventually land was acquired in Telford Road on which the elegant chapel was built. The chapel was designed by R.G. Thomas (1847-1909), who had been born in Menai Bridge, and who was responsible for preparing the plans of many chapels, including Gorslwyd, Rhosybol and the recently-demolished Graig, Penrhosgarnedd and the Howel Harris Memorial Chapel in Trefeca; and also the restoration of St. Peblig church, Llanbeblig, Caernarfon. In 1872 he had been responsible for designing an extension to Treborth Hall, and in 1880 he was appointed architect of the Baron hill estate. He also designed the Town Hall in Llangefni, the fire station in Beaumaris, several houses in Menai Bridge and also possibly the Victoria Hotel, next door to the Presbyterian chapel. The chapel has an octagonal spirelet, and the interior is also of an ecclesiastical nature with a wide central nave, and a stone pulpit at the side of the chancel.

Richard Davies, his wife Anne (the daughter of the Rev. Henry Rees, the prominent Calvinistic Methodist minister) and his brother Robert, Bodlondeb, were fervent supporters of the new church from the outset, and the family are reputed to have had a private entrance to the chapel. The two brothers had prospered as a result of their wood-exporting and shipping businesses, and they were generous patrons of many religious institutions and educational and charitable activities. Several unsuccessful attempts were made to secure a plot of land for a chapel, but eventually land was acquired in Telford Road on which the elegant chapel was built. The cost of £6,000 was paid by Robert Davies, and when the chapel was opened on 14 June

1888 Richard and Anne Davies were also thanked for their contribution to the building costs and towards the purchase of furnishings, and the acquisition of the organ. The generous support of this family was acknowledged by the stained glass chancel window commemorating Robert Davies and depicting four scriptural scenes, accompanied with eight inscriptions, four in Welsh and four in English; and the marble tablets to the Treborth family and the architect. A baptismal font was presented in 1930 to celebrate the half century since Robert Davies had been an elder in the church, and an oak lectern with a carved eagle head was donated in memory of Miss A.M. Davies, daughter of Richard and Anne Davies.

Present position: No minister since retirement of the Rev. Edward G. Kielty in 2009; 36 members; Sunday service, 10.30 a.m, weekly devotional meeting.
Further reading: *Hanes M.C. Môn 1880-1935*, ed Hugh Owen (1935).

6. BETHESDA, Jerusalem Unedig (Un)

OS: SH 624 667

Prior to the formation of a united church in 1996 when an Independent minister was invited to become the pastor, Jerusalem had been a Calvinistic Methodist /Presbyterian church.

The first chapel, designed by T. Evans, Bangor, had been built in 1842 and was described as one of the largest, finest and most valuable chapels in Wales. The Calvinistic Methodists had already built chapels in the area: Capel yr Achub in 1794 and Capel Carneddi in 1816. Following a substantial increase in the local population as a result of the development of local quarries, it was decided to build a chapel in the centre of the village. A site was secured on a lease granted by E.G.D. Pennant, Penrhyn Castle, and after 195 members had left Carneddi, the members were required to endeavour to drain the land which was described as a wet and infertile marsh. In 1851 there were 162 free seats and 905 others, and on 30 March 437 scholars were present in the Sunday school held in the morning, 402 persons and 365 scholars in the afternoon and 388 with 330 scholars in the evening. The secretary also noted that a temperance meeting was held in the chapel every third Sunday throughout the year between the afternoon and evening service.

Substantial changes were made to the chapel in 1872-75, which, designed by Richard Davies, Bangor, and with Owen Williams, also of Bangor, as the builder, included the addition of stucco detail and a large porch with a monumental round arch. The remodelled interior had a semi-circular plan which involved the creation of an amphitheatre effect. The U-plan gallery was supported by 11 plain iron columns, the free standing pulpit was in polished mahogany and the pews were painted in an oak colour. A central rose was a prominent feature of the large saucer-shaped ceiling. The windows were fitted with obscured glass, with stained glass in the rear ground floor window, next to the porch, and these were made by Forrest & Co., Liverpool. When the chapel was re-opened in May 1875 there was room for a congregation of 950. A new lecture hall, schoolroom and classrooms were built from c.1896 and an organ loft in 1903-05, with the organ, built by Peter Connacher, and purchased from Huddersfield Town Hall in 1903, installed in this period.

The memorial erected in the chapel's grounds in 2001 commemorates those who, in the words of the inscription, 'withstood Lord Penrhyn' during the Penrhyn Lockout from November 1900 until November 1903. In December 1903 the elders of Jerusalem expressed their concern that in their religious work "there are signs that we are failing from exhaustion". Large congregations attended services at the chapel in November 1904 at which the Rev. Hugh Hughes, the local Wesleyan evangelist, preached, and 500 women met daily at afternoon prayer meetings in the village. However, the bitterness caused by the strike may well have been responsible for the relatively-limited success of the Revival in Bethesda, in marked contrast to

other slate-quarrying communities in north Wales, such as Blaenau Ffestiniog and the Nantlle valley.

The chapel has been listed Grade 1 by Cadw as a chapel of remarkable scale and dignity which was unusual for the 1840s with a richly detailed interior of the 1870s.

Present position: Minister: Rev. Geraint S.R. Hughes; 127 members, 25 children; Sunday services, 10.00 (with Sunday school) and 5.00, weekly devotional, literary, women and youth group meetings.

Further reading: *Jerusalem Bethesda, Dathlu canrif a Hanner 1842-1992* (1992); R. Merfyn Jones, *The North Wales Quarrymen, 1874-1922* (1981).

7. BANGOR, Berea Newydd (Pw)

OS: SH 569 701

This is one of Wales's newest chapels with the Berea Newydd church having been formed in January 2003 following the union of five Presbyterian chapels in Bangor and the surrounding area, namely Berea, Twr-gwyn, and Y Graig in the city, together with Caerhun and Pentir in the surrounding villages.

The decision to unite was made partly because of a consciousness of the advantages of ensuring modern facilities and avoid spending large sums of money on maintaining five ageing buildings, and compliance with the requirements of disability, and health and safety legislation. There was also an awareness of the decrease in the membership of the various churches, especially those in the villages. Moreover, another inducement was the financial offer by developers anxious to buy and demolish Berea chapel on Caernarfon Road, as part of a proposed development on the site of the former St. David's Hospital.

In 2001-02, local members agreed on the need to rationalise the Presbyterian ministry in the locality. The membership of Twr-gwyn was transferred to the new united church, and Twr-gwyn was then sold to the English Baptist church which had resolved to relocate, and this chapel, now renamed Penrallt Church, which is a Grade 2 building, continues to be a place of worship (see [8] Bangor, Penrallt). The Ap Thomas Partnership architecture practice designed the new chapel, and the minister, the Rev. Eric Jones and the elders discussed the plans in detail with the

architects and the developers.

Photographs of the five chapels were displayed at the service which established the new church. Also, having observed the logo largely designed by the children, illustrating five rays of the sun and the dawn breaking in the light of the Cross, tribute was paid to the history and heritage of the five churches, with reference also to the former churches of Tabernacl, Hirael and Lôn Bobty. The distinctive features which adorn the chapel include the coloured windows created by Meri Jones, Llangollen and designed by Gwawr Roberts, one of the members. The glory of the creation is conveyed, and the centrepiece of the middle window is the Celtic stone cross, representing the resurrection of Christ. The force of the sun is represented by the yellow glass of the windows; the earth by the green colour; and the local river Adda and also all the rivers and seas of the universe by the blue colour. The electronic organ was produced by the Makin Company, Oldham.

Present position: Minister: Rev. Eric Jones; 350 members; Sunday services, 10.00 with Sunday School (70 children) and Sunday School for 10 adults afterwards, 5.30 p.m, bi-monthly and in August evening united services with Penuel, Baptist and Pen-dref Independent chapels, weekly devotional, literary and women's meetings.
Further reading: 'Pump yn dod yn un', *Y Goleuad*, 14 March 2003; *Capel Newsletter 59* (Spring 2012).

8. BANGOR, Penrallt Baptist Church (Be)

OS: SH 589 038

The history of the first chapel on this site, Tŵr-gwyn, may be traced to a Sunday school held in a carpenter's workshop, c.1850 and to the efforts of the Tabernacl Calvinistic Methodist church to establish a church in upper Bangor. This chapel was designed by Thomas Evans, with John Parry as the builder, and was opened in 1854. Soon afterwards a chapel house and schoolroom were also built, again by John Parry. A marked increase in the congregation led to the chapel being extended and a gallery built in 1865, and the changes which resulted in an elegant two-storey façade and interior, containing a panelled gallery and ribbed ceiling, were designed by Kennedy and Rogers. This represents the only known Nonconformist building for which they were responsible: other places of worship in north-west Wales were all Anglican churches and included the nearby St. James's church at Bangor (now the Roman Catholic Church of Our Lady and St. James), and the churches at Cerrig Ceinwen, Llandyfrydog, Llanfwrog, in Anglesey; Gyffin and Llanystumdwy in Caernarfonshire.

The fore-runner of Penrallt Baptist Church was established by Penuel Welsh Baptist Church 140 years ago in response to a demand from English-speaking railway workers for services in their own language. For many years the church was supported by the Welsh Baptists who paid the final instalment of the costs of the chapel built in Penrallt isaf, near to the university. A close connection between the

two churches has continued to the present day, and in January 2011, the respective ministers exchanged pulpits for the first time.

In recent years Penrallt has grown and changed. The congregation increased to such an extent that there was no spare space in the chapel. In 1999 a second service had to be held on a Sunday morning, but the congregation continued to out-grow the chapel, and the morning service had to be held in Ysgol Tryfan. In 2004 Twr-gwyn chapel in Upper Bangor was purchased from the Presbyterian Church of Wales, and this followed the transfer of the membership of Twr-gwyn to the newly-built Berea Newydd church (see 7, Bangor, Berea Newydd).

A sum of over half a million pounds was spent on the adaptation of the building, and the existing pulpit, organ, great pew and wooden pews were taken out and replaced by comfortable chairs, a projector, theatre lighting and a modern sound system. The congregation on a Sunday has grown and many have accepted the Christian faith by means of an Alpha Course. A full-time youth worker was recently appointed for the first time. The morning service has facilities for children and young people with crèche, classes, and a worship style for all ages. Following the service, a 'bring and share' lunch is arranged on the first Sunday of the month, with tea and coffee provided on the other Sundays. The evening service, which often incorporates times of symbolic and informal prayer, is more meditative in style. During university term time, a 'Faith Café' is held after the evening service, with an opportunity provided for students and other young adults to meet together, with food and a light magazine-style programme of interviews and music.

The minister emphasised that Penrallt has been converted into a bilingual church which united local residents and newcomers to north Wales to serve God. In an area where approximately 70% of the population are Welsh-speaking, the use of the Welsh language has been integrated into the life of the church. The hymns are simul-taneously projected onto the screen in English and Welsh, with the congregation able to choose their preferred language. Approximately thirty per cent of the congrega-tion, of whom most are learners, speak Welsh, and this has enabled the old Welsh hymns to be presented to the church, together with a simultaneous translation on the screen, for the benefit of the non-Welsh speakers who include students and visitors. One of the ten house groups conducts its meetings in Welsh, and the use of Welsh has also been developed in praising God, by training musicians from other local churches and teaching them new songs.

At the outset it was decided that the rear part of the building should be made available for use by the local community, and this led to the establishment of Canolfan Penrallt Centre which is regularly and extensively used by various commu-nity groups. The Centre's aim is to promote, encourage and develop a sense of community in Upper Bangor and the surrounding area by the provision of facilities for meetings and activities that promote community life. Following the complete refurbishment of the building, the facilities available include a large hall, modern kitchen, small meeting rooms with projection facilities, and crèche and play area for children. The results have been extremely positive with the building in use every day of the week by community groups, frequently three or four in one day, and on one occasion, seven different groups in one day! Those using the facilities include six different dance groups; two choirs; various bands, student societies; Welsh-language learners, social services, the Duke of Edinburgh Scheme and music classes. Private parties are also held here.

Present position: Minister: Peter James Cousins; 110 members, Sunday services, 10.30 a.m. and 6.00 p.m. (7.00 p.m. in June, July, August). Weekly 'house groups' for Bible- study and prayer meetings (120 persons) and 'Faith Café' after Sunday evening service (between 40 and 60 students and young persons). Activities organised for young people and children, parent and toddlers, as well as the over 60 age group, and Alpha Course offered for those interested in finding out more about the Christian faith.

Further reading: W. Ambrose Bebb, *Canrif o Hanes y Tŵr-gwyn (1854-1954)* (1954); *Capel Local Information Leaflet*, 40 (October 2011).

9. CAERNARFON, Castle Square (Pe)

OS: SH 480 526

In 1873, six years after the formation of the first English-language Presbyterian church in north Wales, at Menai Bridge, a meeting held at the Welsh church of Moriah, Caernarfon led to the holding of English services at Turf Square chapel, recently built for mission work by Moriah, with a Welsh Sunday school on the ground floor and the upper floor allocated to the English congregation. The English church was formally established the following year when the four elders elected included Hugh Pugh, Llys Meirion, one of the group of Moriah members who had become members of the new church. A banker, he was mayor of Caernarfon in 1876 and married to the daughter of Sir Hugh Owen, the educationist, who occasionally attended services at Turf Square when visiting Llys Meirion. The first minister at Turf Square was inducted in 1875, and the succession of ministers at Castle Square has included the Revs. David Hughes (1892-1934) and D. Elwyn Edwards (1951-85).

The growth of members led to discussions relating to the possible building of a new chapel with the local architectural firm of Thomas and Ingleton, but eventually the plans of another architect, Richard Owens, Liverpool were accepted. The new Gothic-style chapel, built of yellow, rock faced Cefn sandstone with grey limestone, was opened in Castle Square in July 1883, with a 100 foot tower and spire in the west front of the chapel, facing the town square, and with three stained-glass lancet windows. The interior, seating 400, measures some 70 feet in length, with five pairs of lancet windows, each set within an arch, along each side. An arch above the organ on the east side is supported on each side by a pair of gilded columns, and contains a stained-glass window. The total cost amounted to nearly £4,400, with £1,550 paid for the purchase of houses in Castle Square, £2,422 to R.R. Williams, the contractor, £100 to Richard Owens; £161 for gas fittings and heating apparatus, and £125 for furnishing. Strenuous efforts were made by the congregation to raise funds with over £1,700 collected by members, a concert and bazaar held in the Caernarfon Pavilion, and a substantial donation was received from Richard Davies, the Anglesey Member of Parliament. By 1885 a debt of £1,250 remained to be cleared, and in the following years several sales of work, concerts and organ recitals were organised to raise funds.

A major development in 1887 had been the installation by Rushworth & Co. of an organ which had been offered for sale in Liverpool and purchased for a sum of £215. Closely involved in this decision was J.H. Roberts, the church organist from 1879-97 and composer of a number of popular hymn tunes, including Mawlgan (to the words 'Bendigedig fyddo'r Iesu') The organ had been built in the early 1880s, probably for a private residence, by Edward Franklin Lloyd, who, born in Holywell, and having been apprenticed with 'Father' Henry Willis, the renowned English organ builder, had his own organ-building business in Liverpool. The organ case had been

made by Robert Garnett and Sons, a firm of Warrington cabinet makers which had undertaken work in many stately homes in the north of England. The opening recital on 21 March 1887 was given by W.T. Best, organist of St George's Hall, Liverpool who had opened many organs including the one at the Albert Hall, London in 1871. The organ was renovated in 1907 and the alterations, involving the replacement of four of the twenty stops, aroused the ire of John De Gruchi Gaudin, Roberts's successor as organist who became headmaster of Caernarfon County School in 1901. Organ recitals were often held over the years, and concerts held included the performance of Stainer's *Crucifixion for Easter* by the chapel choir in February 1920.

An increase in activities and in the numbers attending the Sunday school resulted in the building of a new schoolroom, formally opened in October 1897 and designed by Richard Lloyd Jones, Caernarfon. He also was responsible for the design of the memorial tablet, produced by Italian sculptors from white Sicilian marble, commemorating three members killed during the 1914-18 war, and unveiled on 3 July 1921. In 1909 there were 184 members and a total congregation of 353. Those attending the various chapels of Caernarfon were counted on 12th January 1913, and in Castle Square there were present 117 in the morning service, 140 in the evening, and with 104 in the Sunday school. An invitation to join the church was made at the time of the closure of the Castle Square English Methodist Church in 1926 and resulted in the addition of a number of active families. The membership increased from 179 in 1936 to 226 in 1943, but then declined to 173 in 1970 and 133 in 1982.

The chapel and organ have been regularly renovated over the years. Repair work was undertaken to the spire in 1934 and to the three stained-glass windows in the west front following storm damage in 1936. In 1955, and again in 1974, after the chapel roof had been damaged by a storm, extensive renovation work on the organ was carried out by Rushworth and Dreaper, and the re-roofing of the chapel and schoolrooms in 1976 cost nearly £8,000.

Present position: No minister; 20 members; Sunday service, 10.30 a.m., occasional other services, including Carols at Candlelight, at Christmas, rambling club, monthly coffee morning on Saturdays, visitors welcomed to church on Wednesdays in summer.

Further reading: Alun Jones, *A History of Castle Square Presbyterian Church Caernarfon* (1983).

10. CAERNARFON, Ebeneser (Mw)

OS: SH 480 626

This was one of the first chapels in Wales built in the Gothic style and is the largest Wesleyan chapel in Wales. It was erected in 1826, near to the site of the first Wesleyan chapel in Caernarfon, built *c.* 1805 as a result of the missionary efforts of Owen Hughes and John Hughes who preached in the town in 1800. W. Evan Roberts, a carpenter from Denbigh, designed a schoolroom built in 1805 and this was extended in 1815. An engraving of the 1826 chapel, designed by John Lloyd, is displayed today in the schoolroom. The foundation stone was laid on 1 March 1825 and the two trustees were W. Davies, the minister, and Richard Preece, who had been born in Cowbridge and who, having moved to Caernarfon, and sworn in as a burgess of the borough in 1823, established a school in the town. Eloquent in English and Welsh, Preece preached throughout the county and raised funds for the new chapel. His son,

Sir William Preece, F.R.S. became the chief electrical engineer of the General Post Office, London, and is commemorated in a tablet on the wall of the Caernarfon Post Office as the first honorary freeman of the borough. The chapel has a broad ashlar front and a basement underneath, and is approached by a ramp and steps.

The 1851 Census recorded that the chapel contained 82 free seats and 1,116 others. 289 were present in the morning service on 30 March 1851, and 509 in the evening service, but George Gregory, 'Local minister', commented that the congregation on that morning was less numerous than usual because of illnesses and deaths in families belonging to the church. The need to modify the building was soon appreciated, but no action was taken for some time because of the heavy debt incurred in building the chapel. The chapel was renovated in 1875-76 at a cost of £2,300 with seats for 900-1,000 persons. The plans were prepared by Richard Davies, regarded as the Connexion's architect, and the builder was Hugh Rowlands, Caernarfon. An attempt was made to keep to the Gothic style, but apart from maintaining the walls, substantial changes were made to the interior with the floor levels amended, the floor of the chapel raised and the gallery lowered. A handsome new Gothic porch was added, with Anglesey marble columns, three coloured-glass windows behind the entrance, and a pulpit and communion area. It is also probable that new seating was placed on the ground floor and in the gallery, and the previous one re-used in the extensive schoolroom under the chapel, and in the 'Rhestrau' [Lists] rooms leading from the schoolroom. These rooms were intended for meetings held by elders, who were responsible for a specific section of the membership, the List, but were later used for Sunday school classes. Sir William Preece recalled his experience of attending a school underneath Ebeneser chapel, in a "small, dark, dreary, dirty school-room", studying "underneath that upright Christian, John Jackson, I commenced to master the three Rs."

Ornamental features were added to the porch in 1893 and in 1905 it was recorded that there were 780 seats in the chapel and 680 seats in the schoolroom. A mission room was built beside the chapel in 1912 with an effort made to evangelise among the poorer townspeople, and thereby complement the similar campaign by Seilo by means of Seilo Bach located across the road from the chapel. The room is now used as a workshop.

A later development was the extension of the gallery across the four sides of the chapel with space reserved on the front side for the organ chamber. An electronic Viscount organ has been placed in front of the *sêt fawr*.

Present position: Minister: Rev. Gwynfor Williams; 120 members (arranged in 8 lists) 9 children in the Sunday School, 31 children associated with church; Sunday service, 10.00 a.m. with Sunday School.

Further reading: E.C. Baker: *Sir William Preece, F.R.S. Victorian Engineer Extraordinary*.

11. CAERNARFON, Seilo (Pw)

OS: SH 480 629

This is one of the most modern chapels in Wales, and was constructed due to the need to demolish the former chapel when a new road through the town was being built. A substantial sum was received from the Welsh Office, the forerunner of the Welsh Assembly, and the cost of the new building was £300,000. The chapel was opened in October 1976 by the late Rev. William Morris, the chaired bard and archdruid, and former minister of Seilo.

The new chapel was designed by Gerald Latter, of the Colwyn Foulkes practice. It is an octagonal building, with a cross on one of the outer walls, and a high wooden ceiling in the interior. The pulpit was placed in the centre of the front of the chapel, with an organ, made by George Sixsmith, behind it, and with the pipes on a brick wall. An aisle extends through the middle of the floor of the chapel. Associated with the chapel is a theatre used by the church for the children's Sunday School and its various societies, and also by various local cultural societies. Large audiences are attracted to the pageants and dramatic and musical productions performed by Cymdeithas y Gronyn Gwenith, which includes members from local Presbyterian churches. One notable production was that of *Etholedig Arglwyddes* by the Rev. Harri Parri, minister of Seilo from 1976 until 2000 (see 12, Nanhoron, Capel Newydd for the background to the events portrayed).

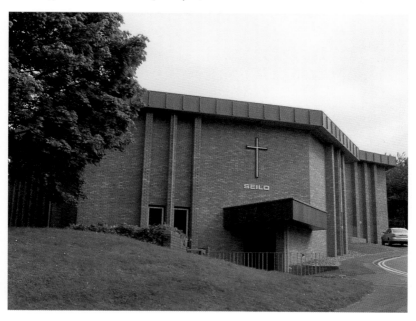

Present position: Minister: Rev. Gwenda Richards; 573 members, 140 children; Sunday services: 10.00 a.m. and 5.30 p.m., Sunday school on Sunday morning at the same time as the morning service; week-night meetings during the winter: society (*seiat*) and prayer meeting, every week; literary society, women's society, and walking club, every month; Cwmni Theatr Seilo [Seilo Theatre Company]: theatrical presentation performed every spring.

Further reading: W. Gwyn Lewis, *Calon i Weithio: Hanes Eglwys Seilo Caernarfon* (1986).

The rural chapel at Nanhoron

12. NANHORON, Capel Newydd (I)

OS: SH 286 309

This is the oldest Nonconformist chapel in north Wales, and only a very limited number of changes have been made to it since it was built *c.* 1770. Meetings were held in the local homes of Independent adherents before the chapel was built on land belonging to the Nanhoron estate. The simple building, constructed of rubble stone and with earthen floors is a typical early Nonconformist chapel, and it is probable that it represented an adaptation of a barn or cowshed. The characteristic entrance is by means of two plank doors located on the long wall on either side of the lateral pulpit, and box pews were placed on each side of the central aisle running through the middle of the chapel. The low plastered walls have been whitewashed, and candlesticks hang from the tall ceiling.

One of the pews had been extended and reserved for the use of Catherine Edwards, the widow of Captain Timothy Edwards, and one of the enthusiastic supporters of the church. After she had travelled to Portsmouth to meet her husband who was due to arrive there, she learned that he had died during the voyage. It is possible that she was treated with great kindness there by an Independent minister, and then, after she had returned home, she joined the church at Nanhoron. She donated a set of communion cups for the use of the members, and her devotional book is kept under the pulpit. The Rev. Harri Parri has portrayed her association with Nanhoron in the historical novel, *Etholedig Arglwyddes* (1993), and in the drama based on the novel which was performed at Theatr Seilo, Caernarfon in 2005.

On 30 March 1851, 73 were present in the morning service, 60 in the afternoon and 15 in the evening. There was one free seat, 26 others and room for 312 to stand. The average attendance over a six-month period was 298, and 120 pupils. Following an increase in the population of the nearby village of Mynytho, Horeb chapel was built there by the Independents in 1872. Services continued to be held for a period in Capel Newydd but the chapel began to deteriorate. The building was safeguarded through the efforts of the Caernarfonshire County Council, the county's Historical Society and several other bodies. The chapel was officially opened on 26 July, 1958, and a trust was established to care for it. One of the most prominent individuals involved in the restoration of the chapel was Gwilym T. Jones, Clerk of the County Council, and a commemorative tablet, placed on the wall of the chapel, contains a couplet by the chaired bard Cynan which states that after his death, this chapel stands as a memorial to his zeal. The considerable amount of restoration work undertaken in recent years includes repointing the stonework.

The chapel has been listed Grade 1 by Cadw as an exceptionally early nonconformist building with one of the few surviving early chapel interiors.

Further reading: Trefor M. Owen, 'Capel Newydd Nanhoron', *Capel Newsletter 20* (Autumn, 1993).

13. BARDSEY, Capel Enlli

OS: SH 121 222

The 1851 Census referred to a Calvinistic Methodist schoolroom which had been erected in 1825 and which was not used exclusively as a place of worship. On 30 March 17 were present at both the morning and evening services, and 24 scholars attended the morning Sunday school and 29 the evening Sunday school.

This chapel and adjoining chapel house were built through the patronage of Lord Newborough in 1875, and this is recorded on a plaque placed above the doorway. The local Calvinistic Methodist presbytery expressed their appreciation in an illuminated address which was sent to the lord who had "built at your own expense the handsome chapel and the comfortable house attached... for the islanders, irrespective of all denominational differences". The chapel was officially opened on 30 August 1876, and one tradition records that the local inhabitants selected a chapel when they were given a choice between a chapel and a mill. At the time new houses and farms were being built on the island, and the chapel was of a similar solid construction.

The chapel is sited near to the abbey which, dating from the eighth century, had been the destination of pilgrims over the centuries. It was built of rubble, with sandstone quoins and yellow brick dressings, and a slate roof. It has been suggested that stones from the walls of the ruined thirteenth-century Augustinian abbey were used for building the chapel.

The chapel is of a Gothic architectural style and the impression of a church atmosphere is strengthened by the bell, made by Mears and Steinbank Founders, Whitechapel Road, London, and housed in a tall brick bellcote above the entrance porch. Seats were provided for approximately 70 persons, and this was the number of the residents of the island recorded in the 1881 census. In front of the central wooden pulpit, made of dark oak, a brass surround has been engraved with various symbols illustrating various aspects of the crucifixion.

The chapel used to belong to the Calvinistic Methodists, but by now it is not attached to any denomination and is used by Protestants and Catholics. It is owned and managed by the Bardsey Island Trust.

Further reading: H.D. Williams, *Across the Bardsey Sound* (1982); R. Gerallt Jones and Christopher J. Arnold, eds. *Enlli* (1996).
Website: www.bardsey.org

14. PWLLHELI, Capel y Drindod (Pw)

OS: SH 377 352

Following efforts to meet in various localities in Pwllheli, a house, Pen-y-mount, was purchased in 1780 and adapted as a place of worship. Within twenty years the chapel was too small, and after its demolition a new chapel was built on the site in 1802-03. The Rev. Michael Roberts, who opened a school in Penmount in 1803, ministered to the church and recorded 120 members in 1803. In 1833 about 400 adults and children attended the Sunday school, and in 1840 there were 340 members, 98 men and 242 women. For several years an attempt had been made to secure land for a new chapel, and in 1841, a new chapel was built. This was designed by William Thomas, architect and county road surveyor, who had also designed St. Peter's Church which had opened in 1834. The new chapel measured 72' x 54' and cost £2,348. As with the 1801 chapel, the pulpit stood between the two doors, with a gallery above it where the precentor and his assistants were seated, and rows of seats were placed behind them, as far as the wall. An oval-shaped gallery surrounded the other walls, and as with the ground floor was filled with benches. The pulpit was high enough for a tall man to walk beneath it, and between it and the ground floor benches was the *sêt fawr*. A sum of over £330 was collected to pay for the new chapel, with the contributions ranging from a few pence to £20, and in the following years strenuous efforts were made to clear the debt of slightly over £2,141 recorded at the opening of the chapel. There were according to the 1851 Census 170 free seats, 1,000 others and standing room for 1,050 persons, and on 30 March 450 were present in the morning service, 361 scholars in the afternoon service, and 750 in the evening service. A note was added by Owen Edwards, draper and elder, that the average attendance was much higher, and the corresponding figures were 650, 461 and 1,100.

Despite the continuing debt gas lighting was provided in the chapel at a cost of £25 18s 6d, and in 1859 more seats were provided to replace benches at a cost of £126.10s 8d. There was a marked increase in the membership after the Revival of 1859-60 and, with many listeners (*gwrandawyr*) attending the services, the chapel with room for 2,000 was often full to the rafters. A fierce debate centred on the financial implications of the installation of a new ordained minister led to a number of members deciding to leave the church in 1862. As a result, a new chapel, Salem, was opened in 1864 on land provided by Lord Newborough, but yet there continued to be 402 members in Penmount at the end of 1863.

The defects of the chapel resulted in extensive renovation in 1881, with the pulpit, seating and galleries removed, leaving only the walls and roof. The work was designed by O. Morris Roberts and the builder was William Jones both of Porthmadog, and the cost was slightly in excess of £2,500. New galleries and seating were provided in the renovated building, which was stuccoed with a hipped roof, 3-

bay recessed entrance with round-headed doorways, divided by Ionic columns. The work undertaken on the interior was characterised by fine craftsmanship, especially the gallery front and sweeping pulpit staircases, and the ceiling had a coved cornice and a large ornate rose. Also built in the same year was the large vestry, again designed by the same architect but the builder was John Jones, Pwllheli, who had also built the small vestry in 1861. This cost slightly over £600, and with a total expenditure of over £3,140 the collection of a sum of £977 following the distribution of collecting cards resulted in a substantial debt being again incurred. Following the revival of 1904-05 the membership increased from 446 at the end of 1904 to 537 at the end of 1906. Further building work was undertaken in 1911-12, at a cost of £2,820 when an extension was added behind the pulpit to house the new organ built by Messrs. Blacket and Howden to replace the harmonium previously in use. Also introduced at this time were central heating, ventilation and electric light, produced with the assistance of an oil-fired machine. A full electricity system was installed in 1927. Dry rot presented a considerable problem, and over £7,000 was spent since 1967 on measures to counter-act its damaging effects. Further costs, amounting to £15,000, were incurred in 1977 because of the need to paint the chapel, improve the heating system and restore the organ.

Penmount, Salem and South Beach churches were united in 1997 to form Capel y Drindod church. Subsequently, South Beach chapel has been sold, Salem is at present for sale, and a considerable amount of work has been undertaken on the building of Penmount, with the renovation of the roof, electricity and heating system, adaptation of the vestries, and re-painting of the chapel.

Present position: Minister: Rev. W. Bryn Williams; 207 members, 40 children; Sunday servioces, 10 a.m. and 5 p.m; weekly devotional and women's meetings, childen and youth club, drama group, and cultural society.

Further reading: D.G. Lloyd Hughes, *Hanes Eglwys Penmount Pwllheli* (1981).

15. CRICIETH, Berea (Bw)

OS: SH 500 338

Berea is an exception among Welsh chapels in that it has belonged to three separate denominations. As a result of the efforts of Baptists from south Wales to evangelise in north Wales, services were held in houses in Cricieth *c.* 1780. Pen-y-maes chapel was built in 1791 and licensed as a place of worship in 1794. Christmas Evans is reputed to have preached his first sermon in north Wales here. In 1798 the congregation adopted the principles of the Scotch Baptists, which represented the most extreme form of Protestantism, and the area was undoubtedly influenced by the teachings of J.R. Jones, Ramoth, who argued in favour of a split with the 'Babilonian Baptists' [*Bedyddwyr Babilonaidd*]. Pen-y-maes remained faithful to Scottish Baptist principles until 1841 when, swayed by the teachings of Alexander Campbell, it registered as a Church of the Disciples of Christ: another name given to the congregation was that of 'Campbellite Baptists'. There was no paid minister, and over a period of many years Dafydd Llwyd, and then his son Richard Lloyd, served as ministers with the sect at Pen-y-maes. The chapel is now a private house and a

memorial garden was created in the graveyard in 1980.

There was a close connection between Pen-y-maes and Berea which was built on a site in the town of Cricieth known as Capel Bach, where the town's chandler traded, and opened in 1886, when the membership amounted to 63. The money to build the chapel, which probably amounted to £500, was borrowed from Dafydd Jones, Siop Pen-y-bont, Llanystumdwy, who was not a Baptist. One of the first duties of David Lloyd George, the politician and statesman, as a solicitor was to complete the transaction which provided the trustees of Berea with the title to the land on which the chapel stood. In 1909 a special meeting was held at Berea to celebrate Richard Lloyd's ministry for 50 years. Richard Lloyd's nephew, David Lloyd George, was a member of this church throughout his life. His nephew, W.R.P. George, the chaired poet and archdruid, described in his autobiography, *88 Not Out*, his mother, who had served as organist of Hermon, Fishguard, moving to Cricieth following her marriage to his father, Dr. Wiliam George in 1910 and persuading the deacons of Berea to install a harmonium for the first time. Berea joined the mainstream Baptists in 1939 and the first paid minister, the Rev. T.R. Lewis was appointed in 1942.

There is currently some uncertainty as to the future of the chapel. The facilities are used at present in August for activities organised by Clwb Gwyliau Cricieth Holiday Club organised by the Scripture Union, the successor to the Children's Special Service Mission, which held in 1904 the first beach mission at Cricieth: these activities have been held on Cricieth beach every year since that time apart from during wartime.

Present position: No minister; three members; Sunday service, 10.30 a.m.
Further reading; W.R.P. George, *The Making of Lloyd George* (1976); *88 Not Out* (2001); 'Lloyd George and Nonconformity', *Capel Newsletter*, *23* (Winter, 1994), *Capel Local Information Sheet*, *8* (1994).

16. LLANYSTUMDWY, Moreia (Pw)

OS: SH 475 387

This chapel was opened in 1936 and replaced a chapel which had been accidentally burnt down. A large house now stands on the site of the original chapel which had been built in 1866 near the village bridge and was an exceptional building with a vestry and chapel house underneath the chapel. Land for the new chapel was provided by J.E. Greaves, Broneifion, Cricieth on condition that the chapel be designed by his nephew, Sir Clough Williams-Ellis. The chapel has been listed Grade 2* by Cadw, and has been described as an important example of the work of the renowned architect. The Italianate aspects of some of the features may be compared to similar ones in the village designed by him at Portmeirion.

The chapel stands in the middle of the village, opposite the Lloyd George Museum, which displays items illustrating the life of the famous statesman. The exterior seems to resemble a school rather than a chapel, with the longer side facing the street and the entrance in one of the semi-circular apses on a gable end. Within the chapel a proscenium arch replaces the traditional pulpit and the window arrangement provides a balance of light. The chapel was built of local rubble with a slated roof. A distinctive feature is the bellcote with swept pyramidal copper roof. The central three windows are round-headed and grouped together under a pediment which contains an oval date plaque while the outer windows are square-headed.

The front walls and gates enclosing the forecourt to the chapel were built in 1936, at the same time as the chapel and, again designed by Clough Williams Ellis, are also listed by Cadw. The low rubble stone walls with integral pointed copings are symmetrical and curve inwards.

A recent development was the provision of facilities for the disabled, including a ramp and toilet.

Present position: No minister; 37 members; Sunday service, 2.00 p.m.
Further reading: 'Lloyd George and Nonconformity', *Capel Newsletter*, *23* ((Winter, 1994); *Capel Local Information Sheet*, *8* (1994).

17. TREMADOG, Peniel (Pw)

OS: SH 563 399

The crucial factor in the background to the building of this chapel was the construction by William Alexander Madocks, Member of Parliament for Boston, of the embankment – the Cob – (1808-12) which succeeded in reclaiming land from the sea in Cardigan Bay. This resulted in the draining of Y Traeth Mawr and the establishment of the towns of Tremadog, and then Porthmadog. Services were held in local houses by Calvinistic Methodists who had been attracted to Tremadog, and, encouraged by Thomas Charles, Bala, a Sunday school was established in 1805. The increase in the local population led to a realisation of the need for a chapel, and a petition signed by Methodist leaders requesting land for the construction of a chapel was submitted to Madocks. His grant of a plot of land on a 99-year lease and peppercorn rent was bitterly criticised by the Bishop of Bangor, but he responded by stating that he had built a church with its foundation on a rock whereas the land provided for the chapel on the other side of the road was on the sand. However, both church and chapel were envisaged as integral features of the public buildings for Madocks's new planned town of Tremadog.

The work of building the chapel commenced in 1808. At the opening of the chapel in 1810, the persons seated prominently in the front included Madocks and several members of his family; the Methodist leaders, Thomas Charles and John Elias; and the poet and dramatist Thomas Edwards (Twm o'r Nant), who worked as a mason in the construction of the embankment. The chapel was registered as 'Peniel' on 14 March 1810. The total cost of £858 10s 6d included payments of £264 for wood, £150 to the masons and £121 to the carpenters.

Following an increase in the membership a gallery was built on one side in 1840, and in 1849 an open portico in Classical style, supported on circular Tuscan columns, was added. The work was supervised by John Williams, steward of the Tremadog estate, and he contributed £10 towards the costs as the inclusion of the columns had been part of the original plan. The original chapel had seats along the two sides and benches in the middle of the floor. Additional seating was provided in 1860, and in 1905 there were 600 seats in the chapel and 100 in the schoolroom, built in the late nineteenth century. The gallery had been extended to the three sides of the chapel in 1880, a new pulpit and elegant great pew were installed in 1898, and in 1908 the present ceiling was built. Gas lighting had been provided in 1857, and electricity was introduced in 1953.

Peniel is one of the small number of places of worship in Wales accorded a Grade 1 status by Cadw, and has been described by John Hilling as "an iconic gem". The unusual qualities of this Classical building, possibly influenced by Inigo Jones's St. Paul's Church, Covent Garden, London (1638), included a generous scale and gable-ended front, in contrast to the contemporary trend of small chapels with long wall

facades and the pulpit located between the two entrance doors. Gradually, this style was generally adopted in Wales, and Peniel is regarded as having been of critical importance in the process with congregations appreciating the advantages of an auditorium experience. The chapel was formally transferred to the Welsh Religious Buildings Trust / Addoldai Cymru in March 2010, and members of the church now worship at the Memorial Hall sited on the square in Tremadog.

Present position: Rev. Christopher J. Prew, 60 members; Sunday service (at Memorial Hall), 9.45 a.m.
Further reading: R.G. Jones, *Hanes Cychwyn yr Achos yn Nhremadog, Peniel M.C.* (1960); Beazley, Elisabeth, *Madocks & the Wonder of Wales* (1967, 2nd ed. 1985); D. Huw Owen, 'Peniel Tremadog transferred to the Trust', *Welsh Religious Buildings Trust Newsletter* (Spring 2011).

18. CEFNCYMERAU, Salem (Bw)

OS: SH 597 273

The painting of the scene inside Salem chapel by Sydney Curnow Vosper, the Devon-born artist is one of the most familiar images of Wales. Art historian Peter Lord has drawn attention to the date of the picture, painted in 1908, immediately after the Revival, and regarded by the Welsh people as "a national icon". He described it as "redolent of the virtues of Nonconformism – pious, unpretentious and built around the centrality of the Word". Vosper was a popular artist and the painting was bought for 100 guineas by the first Lord Leverhulme when it was exhibited at the Royal Academy in 1909. Large numbers of prints of the picture are found today in many Welsh homes, having come into the possession of numerous Welsh people as a result of a vigorous marketing campaign by the Leverhulme company, which offered prints of the painting when a specific quantity of Sunlight soap was purchased. The original painting may be viewed in the Lady Leverhulme Gallery, Port Sunlight.

The Baptist cause in this area may be dated to *c.* 1820. Services were held in homes before a plot of land for the building of a chapel and graveyard was leased for 999 years at an annual cost of 'one shilling'. The chapel was opened in 1850. Lighting was provided by oil lamps and there was no form of heating until a wood and coal stove was installed when the chapel was extended in 1860. A gallery was added and this is its present form, with the pulpit now facing the entrance rather than being placed between the doors, as had been the arrangement in 1850. Electric lighting

and heating were introduced in 1950 when the centenary of the chapel was celebrated. There is no baptistry, and baptisms are held near the chapel in the Artro river: this is a continuation of a tradition extending back to the time before the building of the chapel, and the words '*Bedydd Lyn*' [Baptism Lake] appear on the large stone above the lake.

The Rev. William Evans, known as 'William Evans y Clocsiwr' as he was also a clogmaker, was the minister from 1847, before the chapel was built, until 1889, when the largest number of members: 70: was recorded, with 64 pupils in the Sunday School and nine teachers.

Present position: No minister; five members; afternoon Sunday service every fortnight.
Further reading: Tal Williams, *Salem, Y Llun a'r Llan, Painting and chapel* (1998).

The imposing front of Salem, Dolgellau [19]

19. DOLGELLAU, Salem (Pw)

OS: SH726 177

Several Methodist leaders, including Howel Harris, *c.*1760, encountered persecution in Dolgellau. Services were held in private houses, and on one occasion a service led by the Rev. Peter Williams, Carmarthen was disrupted with the furniture broken and the worshippers forced to flee. One tradition refers to the attempts by local people to disturb David Jones, Llangan when preaching in the town *c.* 1787 by shaking chains and shouting, and that David Jones responded by stating that a chapel would be built, come what may. Soon afterwards land was bought in the area of the town known as Penucha'r Dre from Dr. Henry Owen, a local Quaker. The chapel subsequently built here was extended by the addition of a gallery, and later sold, together with attached houses, for £500 to the Independents after the purchase for £235 of land nearby at Penbryn, on which the new chapel, Salem, was built. The two denominations held services together in the old chapel until Salem was opened in May 1809. Described as the largest chapel in Gwynedd, the new building cost £1,500 and the debt was eventually cleared by 1833. A crucial factor was the need to locate the chapel as near as possible to the homes of most of the members and therefore near to the town centre. However the limitations presented by the sloping site at the rear, the road below and the close-knit housing development on each side resulted in an unusual town church building which has been set well back from the road.

113 members were recorded in 1815. The graveyard behind the chapel dates from 1831 and in 1840 the chapel was registered for marriage services. The first minister, the Rev. Edward Morgan, Dyffryn, served from 1847 until 1849. In 1851 there were, according to the Census taken that year, 180 free seats, 423 others and room for about 400 to stand. On 30 March there were present 340 in the morning service and 500 in the evening service, and this number included the scholars in the Sunday school usually held in the morning. The early nineteenth century long wall chapel was considerably modified in 1893-94 by the pedimented stucco and pebbledash centrepiece designed by Richard Davies with arched windows and the outer bays showing the original porches. Steps lead up to a small forecourt on either side of which are small pavilions, each of which contains an entrance to the chapel. The interior was also extensively changed at the same time, and has a deep-coved plaster ceiling, panelled gallery and carved pulpit in front of an organ by Wadsworth. A graveyard is located to the rear of the chapel. Whilst the chapel has been renovated over the years, much of the rear could possibly date from 1809. The vestry attached to the chapel dates from 1904.

Two offshoots of Salem were established in 1877: Bethel, in Smithfield Street, designed by Richard Owens and built by John Thomas, Dolgellau; and the English chapel in Glyndŵr Street, designed by Humphrey Jones, Tanybryn, Dolgellau. Both were built at a cost of £2,000 and were reputed to hold congregations of 2,000. They have closed by now and Bethel is now the Spar shop and the English chapel is a theatre.

Recent building work has included the provision of a committee room and new kitchen, and the schoolroom underneath the chapel, has been renovated.

Present position: No minister since retirement of the Rev. Megan Williams in June 2011; 150 members, 16 children; Sunday services. 10.00 a.m. and 5.30 p.m., Sunday school during the morning service, weekly devotional service, and a cultural society meeting during the winter months.

Further reading: Robert Owen, *Hanes Methodistiaeth Gorllewin Meirionnydd*, vol. 1 (1889); *Capel Local Information Sheet, 3* (1991).

20. TAL-Y-LLYN, Ystradgwyn

OS: SH 729 113

Preaching services were held in the late eighteenth century in the locality near to Tal-y-llyn at the foot of Cader Idris known as Mawnog Ystradllyn, the word 'mawnog' referring to the practice of harvesting peat. The Rev. John Roberts, Llangwm encountered considerable hostility when he attempted to preach here. A daily and Sunday school were established following a visit by the Rev. Thomas Charles in the early years of the nineteenth century, and the Rev. John Elias, Anglesey is reputed to have preached here in the open air. The chapel appears to have been built *c.* 1828-29, and 30-35 members from the village of Corris, about three miles to the south, joined the church but continued to return to their mother church for the communion service. It is probable that the church membership never exceeded the number at its foundation, with the local area able to support only a low population base, and also suffering from the effects of depopulation.

The 1851 Census recorded 64 free seats, 50 others and standing room for another 20. On 30 March there were present 38 in the morning service, 41 scholars in the afternoon Sunday school, and 47 in the evening service. John Owen, the steward who provided these statistics, added the note that they were lower than the average, that is, corresponding numbers of 70, 50 and 90 because "it was a rainy afternoon".

The empty chapel has been bought by Marian Rees who lives nearby and has established at the chapel a Welsh Heritage Centre whose purpose is to welcome visitors and to give a taste of the history and culture of Wales through a varied programme of live interpretation and entertainment, and a series of walks and lectures have been organised in the summer months.

Further reading: Robert Owen, *Hanes Methodistiaeth Gorllewin Meirionnydd*, cyf 1 (1889).
Website: tal-y-llynheritagecentre.co.uk

21. BALA, Capel Tegid (Pw)

OS: SH 927 359

This was one of the main centres of the Calvinistic Methodists in north Wales. Howel Harris visited the town eight times during the period 1740-1751, and despite persecution, a *seiat* [society] was established here in 1745. The first chapel was built in 1757 at Tegid Place near to the location of the present chapel. Early members included the preacher John Evans, whose portrait by Hugh Hughes has been described as one of the 'classics of our visual art', and also Simon Lloyd and his wife Sarah, who were members of the Trefeca Family: their son was the Rev. Simon Lloyd who had arranged for Thomas Charles, his friend and fellow-student at Oxford, to come to Bala. He became a curate at Llanymawddwy, and after marrying Sally Jones, a Bala resident, he settled in the town, published here a number of theological works and established a network of Sunday schools, and then the Bible Society in 1805. He had established in 1785 a Sunday school at the chapel, which had been enlarged in 1782, and again in 1792, and a new chapel, called 'Bethel' was built in 1809. This chapel, which held a congregation of 1,000, was a large, square building with the pulpit placed between the two doors. Lighting was provided by candles and three chandeliers, and heating by a large stove. It was the venue for the historic Association of 1811 when Thomas Charles was responsible for arranging the service whereby eight ministers were ordained: an event parallelled by a similar one held in August at Llandeilo for south Wales resulting in the Calvinistic Methodists henceforth becoming a separate denomination. Prospective ministers were trained at the college established beside the chapel, and students are reputed to have been able to listen to sermons by opening internal windows separating the two buildings. One of the lecturers was Lewis Edwards who had married Thomas Charles's grand-daughter, and was principal of the Bala Theological College. In 1845 he established, with Roger Edwards, the journal *Y Traethodydd*, and also served as minister of the chapel. He recorded in the 1851 Census that there were 500 free seats in the chapel, 627 others and space for another 250 to stand. There were present that year on 30 March 472 in the morning service, 361 scholars in the afternoon Sunday school and 588 in the evening service. The average attendance was 500 in the morning, 380 in the afternoon and 650 in the evening.

There was a further increase in the membership after the Revival of 1859 and after the acquisition of land in 'Cae Capel' a new chapel was opened in 1867. The architect was W.H. Spaull, Oswestry who designed many chapels for the Wesleyan Methodists and had been a consultant for a period to the diocese of St. Asaph. Following the construction of the chapel he presented a stained glass window which was placed in the eastern end of the chapel, above the pulpit. W. Thomas Ltd., Menai Bridge were the contractors and the clerk of the works was Evan Jones, father of the Rev. John Puleston Jones, the Calvinistic Methodist minister, writer and theologian.

Granite from the Fron Quarry was used for building the chapel and for the Bala Theological College, also opened in 1867, and built on a site overlooking the town. The chapel, a Gothic-style building with a stone tower and spire, held a congregation of 1,000, with 594 on the ground floor and 406 in the gallery, and had been built at a cost of £4,000. A feature of the interior are the galleries with painted panels on iron columns, beneath another layer of columns with timber arcades.

The membership continued to grow, especially as a result of revivals, such as the Richard Owen Revival of 1884 and the Revival of 1904-05. A new vestry was built in 1894 and a pipe organ, built by Conacher of Huddersfield, was installed in 1897. Following an influx of English labourers to the area c. 1880 to build the railway line to Blaenau Ffestiniog, Capel Tegid was responsible for building a chapel, known as Y Capel Bach [The Small Chapel] in Plase Street for the local community, and it has been suggested that the Great Western Railway may have contributed to the building costs. A Welsh service was held in the morning, a Sunday School in the afternoon and an English service in the evening, and many who attended regularly would never attend Capel Tegid. Stories of the chapel, its Sunday school and its football teams continue to be recounted in Bala. The lease of the land reverted to the County Council in 1980, and the building, known as Canolfan y Plase, became the home of the Bala and Penllyn Heritage Society. Capel Tegid has also been responsible since 1907 for the old Anglican chapel of ease which, as a branch of Capel Tegid, has been used for English services.

The condition of the spire of Capel Tegid caused concern over the years, until it was demolished in the year 2000. The upper section of the tower was restored in 2004, and the spire replaced by one in metal in 2006. The substantial costs of nearly £250,000 were paid by Cadw, the Snowdonia National Park and the Presbyterian Church of Wales. Also renovated at this time was the statue of Thomas Charles, by William Davies, Maenorydd, which had been erected outside the chapel in 1872.

Present position: Voluntary minister: Rev. Eric Green; 220 members, 10 adults, 28 children in Sunday school; Sunday services, 10.00 a.m., with Sunday school for children; Sunday school for adults 11.00 a.m., 5.30 p.m.; informal service at 6.00 p.m on 3rd Sunday, weekly devotional meeting, fortnightly cultural society and two women's meetings.

Further reading: D. Francis Roberts and Rhiannon Francis Roberts, *Capel Tegid y Bala, daucanmlwydiant 1757-1957* (1957); Goronwy Prys Owen, 'Capel Tegid y Bala', *CAPEL Newsletter*, 42 (Autumn 2003); *Capel Local Information Sheet* 23 (2003); D. Densil Morgan, *Lewis Edwards* (2009).

22. LLANDUDNO, Gloddaeth United (Pe)

OS: SH 780 825

An Anglican minister who had retired to Llandudno because of ill-health and had joined Seilo, the Welsh Presbyterian chapel, was actively involved in the efforts to provide English services for visitors attracted to the growing tourist resort. At first, meetings were held at the Masonic Hall in Mostyn Hall. Then a corrugated iron building, the original church building on the present site, was constructed in May 1880 with financial help provided by Seilo, located across the road. The growth in numbers led to an awareness of the need for a new chapel, and the present school-room was built alongside the existing one and used for worship while the iron hut was demolished and the present church built.

Two of the church elders had been so impressed by a church in Italy which they had seen whilst on holiday that they paid for an architect to visit it and copy the design. The new church, designed by T.G. Williams, Liverpool, was opened in 1891 at a cost of £5,819 including furnishings. The architect's plans are kept at the church and are available for viewing. Sandstone from Wyddfydd quarry was used for the building, together with dressings of Cefn stone. The space beneath the extensive

conical-shaped roof, measuring 58' by 55' and spanned by interior beams in cartwheel formation is not interrupted by supporting pillars. An unusual aspect of the interior is that whilst it appears to be a standard nave and transepts design, the plan is of a large, undivided oval space with a strongly raked floor and circular curved pews. Other features include an organ by Charles Whitely & Co., and a very large pulpit, behind which three carved panels bear the inscription 'Carved by Emma Ridge, January 1891'. A fine gas candelabra, a Scott-Thorp corona light, was converted to electricity c. 1960, and removed approximately ten years later. The schoolroom, which also has a raked floor, contains wooden roller shutters which when opened connect with the church to provide additional 'overflow' space.

A derelict garage nearby has been purchased. This had a large petrol tank under the floor which had to be filled in. It had previously been a carpet warehouse and many years ago the storage for horse-drawn fire engines. Following renovation, it is now extensively used for activities by the church and other organisations. Recent developments include the provision of new lighting, repairing the windows, painting the exterior of the chapel, and provision of wheelchair access and space, disabled toilet and hearing loop in the main auditorium.

Present position: Minister: Rev. Neil G. Kirkham, 107 members, two Sunday services, 9.45 a.m, traditional service followed by Sunday school which runs in parallel with modern service, 11.15 a.m., numerous activities during the week include devotional meetings in church, garage and homes, ladies guild, luncheon club and parents and toddlers groups.

Further reading: *Capel Local Information Sheet*, 13 [1998].
Website: www.gloddaeth.com

23. LLANDUDNO, Seilo (Pw)

OS: SH 780 825

The present building is the fourth built by the Calvinistic Methodists in the town and the second on this site. The first chapel, opened in 1855, was a very simple building but the best-quality materials were used in its construction. A gallery was added in 1874, and a chapel house and schoolroom were built in 1884.

Younger members requested the provision of an organ, and despite the opposition of a third of the members, the request was approved and a new chapel, including an organ, was built in 1901-05. The cost was £8,779, and approximately £900 was paid for an organ by Peter Conagher of Huddersfield. The architect was G.A. Humphries, steward of the Mostyn estate, who was responsible for many of the town's buildings, including the Tabernacl chapel (see 24). Seilo, a notable building which has been listed Grade 2 by Cadw, has two large sandstone cupolas. It is of grey and purple ashlar, with two storeys, the ground floor of purple Cheshire sandstone and the upper floor of grey limestone with extensive purple dressings. The impression is of a baroque cathedral church. The interior is of a traditional plan with a large open space, and three-sided, curved-ended gallery supported on iron columns with curved seating. 920 persons may be seated in the chapel, which is the largest chapel in the town. It is often used for meetings and concerts, with the large *sêt fawr* being removed to enable choirs to hold concerts in the summer months.

The four Nonconformist denominations in Llandudno have worshipped together since 1 January 2000, and a number of improvements have been made following the decision to locate at Seilo the united church for Llandudno. The entrance porch has been enlarged to accommodate two toilets, the chapel ceiling has been painted, and the original benches in the schoolroom have been removed to be replaced by chairs and small tables. New furniture has been placed in the elders' room, which also serves as a computing suite. An additional facility for members and visitors is the car-park outside the chapel. The chapel has a seating capacity of over 1,000 and is a popular venue for concerts in the summer months.

One of the eminent former ministers of Seilo was the Rev. E.O. Davies (1910-25), who made a significant contribution to secure a parliamentary measure to improve the constitutional status of the Presbyterian Church of Wales and extend its legal rights.

Present position: The minister, the Rev. Dafydd Rees Roberts has recently retired on health ground; 203 members in the united church, 77 in Seilo; 30 children in the Sunday school; weekly devotional meeting, fortnightly cultural meeting.
Further reading: 'Chapel Tour', *Capel Newsletter*, 30 (Autumn, 1997); *Capel Local Information Sheet*, *13* (1998).

24. LLANDUDNO, Tabernacl (Bw)

OS: SH 780 826

Meetings were held by Baptists in the area as early as 1776 but the Baptist cause at Llandudno may be dated to 1813 when the first Welsh Nonconformist chapel was opened here. Following an increase in the membership, another chapel, designed by Roger Jones, Baron Hill, was built on the site in 1835. The present chapel, designed by Richard Owens, was built, again on the same site, in 1875, and has been described as "Italianate stucco with an open-pedimented centrepiece and Gothic detail". This chapel was renovated and extended in 1902 by G.A. Humphries (see [23] Llandudno, Seilo) with the building of a schoolroom and a new entrance, featuring the classical addition of an Ionic colonnade-style porch. The chapel now occupies a prominent position at the junction of Mostyn Street and Llywelyn Parade, with the Great Orme in the background. The interior is unusual with the gallery extending into the two transepts, and the baptistry located on a higher level than the *sêt fawr*. Also in 1902 an organ was bought from the Anglican Christ Church and occupied the space originally intended for the organ.

An extensive amount of work was undertaken in 1998-99 to repair and renovate the chapel at a cost of £200,000 and a substantial contribution, amounting to 75% of the total expenditure, was received from the Heritage Lottery Fund with the remainder contributed by Conwy County Council, Cadw and the funds of the church. The original intention was to use this chapel for the services of the newly-formed Llandudno united church, but a decision was later made in favour of Seilo.

The church has played an important role in improving and maintaining social and moral standards in the town. The Rev. Lewis Valentine was the minister from 1921 until 1946, and he is commemorated in the plaque located outside the chapel. Whilst minister of Tabernacl, he composed the hymn 'Dros Gymru'n Gwlad' which has been described as the "hymn of the Welsh people".

Following the decision of the four Nonconformist denominations to hold their services at Seilo, Tabernacl chapel has housed the Llandudno Heritage Centre, and at present art classes in watercolour, acrylic and textile techniques, and temporary art exhibitions are held in the chapel schoolroom.

Present position: see entry 23, Llandudno, Seilo; 26 members in Tabernacl.
Further reading: J. Roberts, *Hanes Bedyddwyr Cylch Llandudno* (1925); *Capel Local Information Sheet*, 13 (1998); Gwilym Williams, 'The Restoration of Tabernacl, Llandudno', *Capel Newsletter*, 38 (Autumn 2001).

25. COLWYN BAY, St John's Uniting Church (Un)

OS: SH 846 791

The establishment of St. John's Methodist Church, regarded as the cathedral of English Methodism on the north Wales coast, may be traced to the vision and determination of the Rev. Dr. William Morley Punshon to build chapels in the new coastal resorts which were developing in the second half of the nineteenth century. St. John was one of the beneficiaries of the fund, known as 'The Watering Places Fund', which he had established for this purpose, and following his death the Rev. Frederick Payne, appointed in 1879 by the Wesleyan Conference as minister at Rhyl and 'North Wales Coast Missionary', embarked on the construction of a church, schoolroom and manse. A brass plate on the nave wall commemorates his significant role in the history of the church. He was also closely involved in the establishment of Penrhos college for girls and Rydal School which opened with 15 scholars in 1885 and which has had close links with St. John's since its foundation. Stained glass windows in the church commemorate Miss Rosa Hovey, headmistress of Penrhos for 34 years, and T.G. Osborne, the founder of Rydal School. The church is used at present by the Rydal Penrhos school on a daily basis for assemblies and other school services, and ancillary church premises are also used by the school.

Plans were approved in 1881 for the building of a church in the Gothic style to hold a congregation of 625, designed by the architect Robert Curwen, Liverpool and London, and the builder appointed was T. Foulkes, the father of the architect S. Colwyn Foulkes, who designed alterations and extensions to Rydal School, and also many public buildings, cinemas and houses in Colwyn Bay and in north Wales, and Tabernacl Welsh Baptist chapel, Colwyn Bay (see entry 26).

The first stage was the construction of the boundary walls, lych-gate and manse, and preparation of the foundations when the funds ran out. The manse was completed in 1882 and named 'Tranby' after the Punshon home in London. The schoolroom was completed in 1883 and used for services until 1888 when the church was completed. The intention and subsequent delay in building such a large and imposing church aroused amazement and the site was described as 'Wesley's Folly' by local residents. A sum of £5,700 had already been spent, and another £4,750 was required to complete the project. The structure was a combination of granite, limestone and sandstone with a Welsh slate roof. In many respects it resembles an Anglican church with its aisles, transepts and spire. An early collecting book issued by the Rev. Payne referred to the church as an 'English Wesleyan Chapel, *Puncheon Memorial*'. An extension to the church was added in 1908, involving the addition of a link corridor, 'Ladies Parlour' and a kitchen. This area has in recent years been upgraded to provide an enhanced meeting room and toilets.

Over the years St. John has played a prominent role in the life of Colwyn Bay, and also in the Colwyn Bay and Llandudno Methodist Circuit. At present the church

is a united church comprising Methodist, Baptist and United Reformed congregations.

Present position: Minister, Rev. Malcolm Chester; 71 members, four to five children in the Sunday school; Sunday service, 10.30 a.m., weekly prayer meeting, fortnightly Fellowship Circle.

Further reading: Norman Tucker and Ivor Wynne Jones, *Colwyn Bay, its history across the years* (2001); *Capel Local Information Sheet, Colwyn Bay*, 32 (2008).

26. COLWYN BAY, Tabernacl (Bw)

OS: SH 852 787

Tabernacl chapel was built in 1888 on Abergele Road for the English-language Baptists of Colwyn Bay, and was also used for two years by the Welsh-language Baptists who had previously held prayer meetings in a house in Station Road. The cost of building the chapel, schoolroom and associated rooms, designed by S. Colwyn Foulkes, Colwyn Bay, was £1,800. In 1900 £126 was spent on building a chapel house. In the same year another chapel was built for the English Baptists, and since that time the Welsh-speaking congregation has had sole use of the Tabernacl. Two tablets on the chapel walls, one in Welsh and the other in English, refer to two men who died in 1889 and who made significant contributions in the early days of the chapel: John Showell, architect and surveyor who was largely responsible for building the chapel, and William Hughes, a member who bequeathed a sum of £1,000 to clear the debt which had been incurred.

A new pulpit was installed in 1928 and an elegant vestry was added in 1932. The chapel was re-modelled in 1936-37 for the installation of an organ by Rushworth and Dreaper, built to a design by Dr. Alfred Hollins and originally placed in 1924 in the music room of Bryn Eisteddfod, Glan Conwy, the mansion of Edward Blackburn, formerly a cotton manufacturer in Manchester. Following his death in 1936 the organ was moved to Tabernacl, and on 9 June, 1937 an organ recital was presented by Leslie D. Paul, the organist of Bangor Cathedral Church.

The first minister at Tabernacl was the Rev. William Hughes, who had been brought up at Capel y Beirdd, Caernarfonshire. He had been a missionary in the Congo from 1882 until 1885, and after he had been inducted as minister of the church established in Colwyn Bay for the local English and Welsh-language Baptists, he decided to concentrate on the English church established in 1890. Whilst minister of Tabernacl, he established a training college for negroes, and by 1894 there were 15 negro youths in the Colwyn Bay Institute. It has been estimated that 87 students were educated here, some later became political leaders in Africa. Despite this, financial difficulties were experienced and after a harmful court case the Institute was closed in 1912.

Another minister of Y Tabernacl was the Rev. J.S. Jones (1919-49) who closed his sermon by singing part of a hymn. David Lloyd George, the Prime Minister, was present at Tabernacl in October 1920 and before the close of the service paid tribute to the force of the Welsh pulpit in moving his heart – 'yn cyffwrdd â'm calon'.

Present position: Minister: Rev. Gwilym Hughes; 13 members; Sunday service, 2.30 p.m.

Further reading: *Bedyddwyr Cantref y Rhos*, ed. Rev. T. Frimston (1924); Ivor Wynne Jones, 'Hughes the Congo; the rise and fall of the Congo institute', in A *Tolerant*

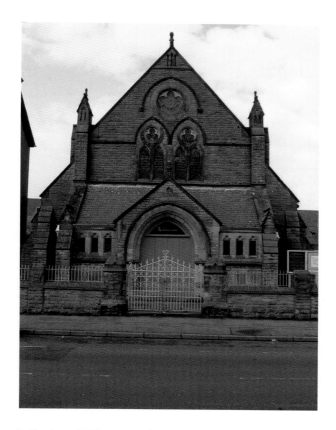

Nation, eds.Charlotte Williams, Neil Evans and Paul O'Leary (2003); Marc J Williams, *Bedyddwyr Bae Colwyn* (n.d.); *Capel Local Information Sheet, Colwyn Bay*, 32 (2008).

27. ABERGELE, Mynydd Seion (Pw)

OS: SH 944 774

The nearest chapel to Methodists in the Abergele area was Tan-y-fron, and one of the farms where Edward Parry preached was Y Nant, in the parish of Abergele. A *seiat* was established in Bryngwyn sometime before 1778, and prayer services were held in the town in Chapel Street. A chapel had been built on the site by 1791 and registered as a place of worship in 1797. It was extended in 1808 and in 1851 363 reserved seats and 96 free seats were provided: and also standing room for 104 persons. On 30 March 201 were present in the morning service, 371 in the afternoon and 329 in the evening service. The accompanying note, submitted by John Jones, deacon and 'Druggist, Market Street' refers to the occasional practice of having an afternoon sermon as the Sunday school was usually held in the afternoon. The average attendance over a 12 month period was 200 in the morning, 235 scholars in the afternoon, and 340 in the evening.

The need for additional space was soon appreciated, and a new chapel was opened in 1869 on an adjacent site. The architect of the new chapel was Richard Owens, Liverpool. The chapel has a Gothic plan, and it was built of dark grey, polygonal Penmaenmawr granite with a narthex, transepts and an apse with a gallery to the rear. The cost was nearly £4,000, and a considerable amount of voluntary work was undertaken with 28 farmers providing transport for moving building-material from the quarry and railway at Pensarn. Richard Owens was also probably responsible for the small schoolroom built in 1887 in a new modern style. In 1901 an organ built by Conacher was installed. Following its restoration a recital by Huw Tregelles Williams in a concert held on 5 June, 2005 celebrated the re-opening of the organ. The work of renovating and cleaning the chapel and introducing electricity in 1927 cost £1100. Additional improvements were made in 1963, and the costs were nearly £6,200. The old chapel continues to be used as a multi-purpose hall. It has been a refectory for the primary school for years, and improvements were made in 1960 with the gallery taken down, a new kitchen installed and also a porch inside the door. Recent developments include the further adaptation of the old chapel and vestry, with the provision of a new kitchen and the numerous users of the premises include the Action for Children charity, Llandrillo College, Merched y Wawr and a local choir and drama group.

There was a close and long-standing connection between Mynydd Seion and the family of Bryngwenallt, which was also designed by Richard Owens. The leading figure involved in the building of the new chapel in 1869 was David Roberts, the founder of the substantial commercial company in Liverpool and one of the founders of Bangor Normal College. His son John was the Member of Parliament for the Flintshire Borough (1878-92), and his grandson, John Herbert Roberts, the first Lord Clwyd, had been the Member of Parliament for West Clwyd (1892-1918)

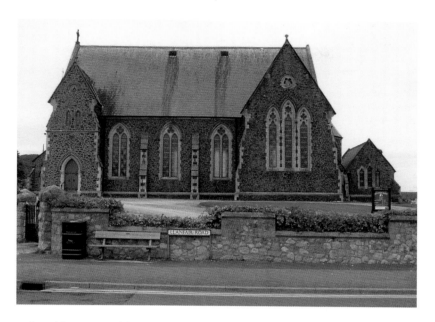

and an elder in Mynydd Seion for a total of 68 years (1887-1955). John Roberts was an enthusiastic supporter of the 'English causes' of the Calvinistic Methodists and one of his leading opponents was the Rev. Robert Emrys Jones (Emrys ap Iwan), who started preaching in this church and who taught the children of Mynydd Seion from 1876 until 1883.

Present position: Minister, Rev. Ifor ap Gwilym; 190 members, Sunday services 10.00 a.m. with Sunday School (25 children and 10 adults) and 5.00 p.m., monthly prayer meeting and fortnightly men and women's meetings.

Further reading: Ellis Wynne Williams, *Hanes Eglwys Mynydd Seion, Abergele* (1968); *Capel Local Information Sheet*, 17 (2000).

28. RHYL, Clwyd Street (Pw)

OS: SJ 010 814

The Calvinistic Methodists extended their activities to Rhyl from Rhuddlan, with members of the Rhuddlan society holding meetings in local homes. The congregation and Sunday School grew, and a lease was signed on 28 September 1824 for the erection of "a good and substantial edifice chapel or meeting house of stone or brick... to be used for the worship of Almighty God ... by the Society or Congregation of Protestant Dissenters commonly called the Calvinistic Methodists...". Bethel chapel was opened in 1826, but by 1840 this chapel was too small, and the new chapel opened in 1843 later evolved into the Wellspring Christian Centre in Vale Road. Following the coming of the railway in 1847 Rhyl developed as a holiday resort. On 30 March 1851, 159 were present in the morning service, 153 scholars in the afternoon and 252 in the evening service. The chapel had 100 free seats and 300 others.

Clwyd Street chapel was opened in 1855 and it is probable that this was the only chapel designed by W. Owen, Llanrwst. This was in the simple Gothic style, in a hard brick with stone dressings. Bethel was retained for the Sunday school, prayer meetings and occasional preaching services, and was reopened in 1867 as many in the area felt uncomfortable in the more fashionable part of the town. This was a problem which also affected the Wesleyans and Anglicans, with the vicar declaring that "the church was being built here to minister to the wants of the poorer parts of Rhyl." The membership of the Clwyd Street church continued to grow, and in 1873 an extension, designed by Richard Davies, and including schoolrooms, was built in the same style. These buildings, gate piers, gates and railings have been listed Grade 2 by Cadw, which described the chapel as a notable example of chapel architecture, with a complete, richly detailed interior. Richard Davies also designed the same denomination's English-language chapel which, built in red brick with stone dressings and an octagonal corner turret with spirelet, opened in Princes Street in 1885 with 52 members. An organ built by Wadsworth was installed in Clwyd Street in 1897, and was completely restored in 1966.

Present position: Minister: Brian Huw Jones; 92 members; Sunday services: 10.00 and 5.30; weekly devotional meeting.

Further reading: R.H. Evans (ed.), *Hanes Henaduriaeth Dyffryn Clwyd* (1986); D. Elwern Jones, *Dathlu Cant a Hanner, 1855-2005*, *Eglwys Bresbyteraidd Cymru, Clwyd St. Y Rhyl* (2005), *Capel Local Information Sheet*, 25 (2004).

29. DENBIGH, Capel Mawr (Pw)

OS: SJ 053 662

Meetings were held on this site in a barn c.1790 and a small chapel, measuring 10 square yards, was built on the corner of Lôn Swan and Beacons Hill. It was extended in 1805, and again in 1813, and this was the chapel ministered by Thomas Jones, the author, hymnist and main leader of the campaign in north Wales to establish the Calvinistic Methodists as a separate denomination. A new chapel was built in 1828, measuring 20 by 24 yards. It was described in the 1851 Census as 'Middle Chapel', with Thomas Gee as the minister, and with seats for 600 and space for 1,000 to stand. On 30 March there were 502 present in the morning service, 515 in the afternoon Sunday school and 785 in the evening.

The chapel was closed in 1880 for extensive adaptations which cost £2,000 and which included the addition of a porch with arched windows on the old side-wall façade replacing the front of the chapel and the seats, and installing an U-shaped gallery supported on cast iron colonnettes with foliated capitals. This is the current form of the chapel which has been listed Grade 2* by Cadw as an impressive late nineteenth-century galleried chapel, built of limestone in a restrained Italianate style, with a symmetrical façade and slate roof. The fine interior also includes a central semi-octagonal pulpit with panelled front, and flanking stairs, sêt fawr with curved enclosing rails, and ceiling with fifteen panels, five of which have floral centrepieces. The large organ behind the pulpit was built by Alexander Young.

A schoolroom, with an asymmetrical limestone ashlar façade and slate roof was erected at the northern end of the chapel in 1892, and consists of a large hall with a stage. This is where the Twm o'r Nant Welsh school was held before moving to new premises. Thomas Gee, founder of the Gwasg Gee publishing firm and the publisher of the Welsh encycleopaedia, Y Gwyddoniadur Cymreig, the journal Y Traethodydd and magazine Baner ac Amserau Cymru, served as minister in the nineteenth century. Several prominent residents of the town were faithful members, including the novelist Dr. Kate Roberts, and the poet Gwilym R. Jones, both of whom taught in the Sunday School.

Recent building developments, costing £60,000 and funded by Cadw and the church, include the provision of a new roof, kitchen and porch. An office is provided at the chapel for a presbytery worker, and the vestry is regularly used by Coleg Llandrillo Cymru, Colwyn Bay. Former ministers include the Revs. W.I. Cynwil Williams and W.H. Pritchard.

Present position: Minister: Rev. S. Wayne Roberts; 147 members; 52 children; Sunday services, 10.00 a.m. and 5.30 p.m.; monthly prayer and Yr Aelwyd cultural meetings, lunch for district churches.

Further reading: W.H. Pritchard, *Dysg i'm Edrych* (1993).

30. DENBIGH, Lôn Swan (I)

OS: SJ 053 662

The Lôn Swan Independent church was established in 1662, the year of the eviction of two thousand clergymen. Services were conducted furtively for several years but the early members included some wealthy individuals: in 1715 one individual was valued at between £4,000 and £5,000, and three at over £500. The first meeting house on this site in Lôn Swan was built in 1742. The chapel was renovated and extended in 1813, and then, following a further substantial increase in the congregation, a larger chapel again was built at a cost of £1,200 in 1839, when the Rev. William Rees (Gwilym Hiraethog) was the minister. On 30 March 1851 277 were present in the morning service, 257 in the afternoon Sunday school, and 480 in the evening service, and it was recorded that there were 352 free seats, 424 others and space for 200 to stand. It was also pointed out that these statistics were lower than

usual, and the average attendance was stated to be 600 in the morning, 500 in the afternoon and 550 in the evening service.

A U-shaped gallery supported on cast iron colonnades, central semi-octagonal pulpit and new seating were installed in 1875, and the debt for this work had been cleared by the 1880s. In 1891, during a period when the church was without a minister (1887-93) a single-storey porch was installed, and also a new organ, by Bellamy of Denbigh, at a cost of £1,500. By this times most of the construction work had been completed, and the present chapel has been listed Grade 2* by Cadw as an especially fine mid-Victorian chapel with "bold well-detailed façade and retaining good galleried interior". The chapel has been built in an Italian Renaissance style, of rubble construction with a red/brown brick façade with limestone ashlar dressings, arched windows and pitched slate roof. Other features in the impressive interior include a *sêt fawr* with curved enclosing rails, and a ceiling with three large ceiling roses and foliate plasterwork.

The ministers of Lôn Swan have included the Rev. Robert Everett (1815-23) who later emigrated to the United States where he made a significant contribution to Welsh American society as a powerful preacher, prominent anti-slavery campaigner and editor for thirty years of the missionary magazine, *Y Cenhadwr Americannaidd*; and the minister, editor, and hymnist William Rees (1837-43); and the members have included Edward Williams, the influential divine who became principal of the Rotherham Academy; William Williams (Caledfryn); Robert John Pryse (Gweirydd ap Rhys); and L.W. Lewis (Llew Llwyfo).

Present position: Minister: Rev. G. Graham Floyd; 60 members; Sunday services; 10.00 a.m. and 6.00 p.m.; Sunday school at 2.00 p.m.

Further reading: *Gwylio Gorymdaith*, ed. Dafydd Owen (1992); Jerry Hunter, 'What can the Welsh do, Robert Everett and the creation of a Welsh-American Abolition Movement, *c*.1840-4'in *Wales and the Wider World*, eds. T.M. Charles-Edwards & R.J.W. Evans (2010).

31. DENBIGH, Pendref (Mw)

OS: SJ 052 662

Pendref chapel was built in 1802 as a result of the efforts of a number of Wesleyan Methodists, including Evan Roberts and Edward Jones, who had been motivated by Oldham Street church, Manchester. Evan Roberts was a carpenter and he was largely responsible for building the original chapel, at a cost of £700, after the purchase in 1800 of a plot of land measuring 21 yards by 20 yards on the road near to the Factory. Several seats were placed on the gallery and floor, with benches provided in the middle of the floor for poorer persons. The chapel was lit by candles with a bronze star holding a number of candles hanging above the floor. Hugh Jones claimed in his history of the Wesleyan Methodists, *Hanes Wesleyaeth Cymru*, that this was the first Welsh Wesleyan chapel to be built.

In 1851 there were 80 free seats and 300 others, and on 30 March there were present 151 in the morning service, 37 in the afternoon and 259 in the evening service. In his *Ancient and Modern Denbigh* (1856), John Williams referred to the Welsh Wesleyan chapel, which contained an upper room where English services were held. The chapel was extended in 1861 at a cost of £365. In 1883 a large schoolroom was built, and two smaller ones where the Sunday school and weekly meetings were held, and heating equipment was also installed. The architect was Richard Davies and the cost was £1,297. In 1900 a chapel house was built next to the chapel. More renovation work was undertaken in 1908, under the supervision of James Hughes, the town mayor and local architect. A chamber was installed to house the new organ built by Charles H. Whiteley, Chester. This work cost approximately £900 and the chapel was reopened in 1909.

One of the prominent ministers of Pendref was the Rev. E. Tegla Davies who, in his autobiography *Gyda'r Blynyddoedd*, described the town as unbearably English, and his church, Pendref, especially so. This comment was cited by Frank Price Jones in his volume *Crwydro Gorllewin Dinbych*, but accompanied by the comment that the minister had expressed the view, on a later visit to the town, that the condition of the Welsh language had improved by that time, especially as a result of the ministry of a successor, the Rev. T.G. Ellis after the Second World War.

Recent work undertaken includes renovating the roof and organ, with the latter work costing £12,000, pointing the walls of the chapel, schoolroom and chapel house, and painting the buildings in distinctive heritage paint.

Present position: Minister: Rev. Tudur Rowlands; 24 members; Sunday service, 10 a.m., occasional interdenominational services.

Further reading: Medwyn Jones, *Dathlu Daucanmlwyddiant Capel Pendref 1802-2002* (2002).

32. RUTHIN, Capel Coffa Edward Jones, Bathafarn (Mw)

SJ 125 584

The name of the chapel refers to the earliest period of the history of Wesleyan Methodism in Wales with Edward Jones, brought up on Bathafarn farm near Ruthin, one of the early leaders of the Wesleyan Methodists in Wales. Whilst working in Manchester in a cotton mill he was influenced by Methodists and when he returned to Ruthin in 1799, he sought to evangelise in the town. In 1800 he hired a room at the Prince of Wales Inn and services were held here for two years. In time this building was demolished and later the site became part of the Castle Hotel. Also in 1800 Edward Jones is believed to have led a group of youths from Ruthin to the summit of Moel Famau early in the morning to welcome the Rev. John Bryan who was travelling from Chester to preach at Ruthin at 9 a.m. A plot of land was acquired in Mill Street and Capel-y-Felin was opened on 16 November 1802 when Edward Jones, who had previously become an elder, and then been ordained as minister, conducted a communion service attended by a congregation of 300. He then supervised activities in various areas, including Caernarfon, Machynlleth and Haverfordwest. He moved to Leek, Staffordshire in 1837 but before taking up his appointment as supervisor he died after suffering a serious accident. He was buried at the Mount Pleasant Chapel, Leek but when this church closed, his memorial stone was moved in 1982 by the Historical Society of the Methodist Church and placed outside the chapel in Ruthin.

The membership of the church in Ruthin had grown and 92 scholars were present in the Sunday school held on the morning of 30 March, 1851, 162 scholars in the afternoon and a congregation of 202 in the evening service. There were in the chapel 122 free seats, 177 others and space for 90 to stand. The need for a larger chapel was responsible for the decision in 1865 to build a memorial chapel to Edward Jones, which was opened in September 1869, with the cost of the land and buildings £1,500. Red bricks were used for the building of the chapel which has a Classical style, designed by Richard Owens. The organ was built by Crewe and Sons, Wrexham and Liverpool.

A memorial tablet to Edward Jones was placed behind the pulpit, and the wording in Welsh refers to him as an instrument to bring Wesleyan Methodism in the language of the common people to Wales, and as a holy man, a pure evangelist and a successful minister, and it was through him that many were brought to the Lord. In 1872 a schoolroom was built, behind the chapel, and contains a stone which had stood above the door in Capel-y-felin, and also the communion cups used there, with a reference to the date 1802. In 1887 a house for the minister was built beside the chapel and the cost of this work was £687.

Recent building developments include repairing the roof after the movement of coping stones and pointing the walls. A contribution was received from Cadw but

most of the sum of £60,000 was raised by the church.

Present position: Hon. Minister: Rev. Martin Evans-Jones, 50 members including 20 young persons recently received as members; Sunday service, 10 a.m., weekly youth club and monthly society.

Further reading: *A Dictionary of Methodism in Britain and Ireland*, ed. John A. Vickers (2000); Glyn Tegai Hughes, 'Welsh-speaking Methodism' in *Methodism in Wales*, ed. Lionel Madden (2003); *Capel Local Information Sheet*, *28, Ruthin* (2005).

33. RUTHIN, Tabernacl (Pw)

OS: SJ 126 583

A small number of Calvinistic Methodists travelled to worship at Bontuchel before holding a Sunday school in an old barn in Rhos Street, Ruthin, c. 1788. A plot of land in this street was bought in 1789 for £20 and a chapel, Capel y Rhos was built upon it. Thomas Jones ministered to the congregation during the period 1804-09, and it is believed that he composed some of his hymns at this time. He was later succeeded by the Rev. John Jones, father of the hymnist Edward Jones, Maes-y-plwm who also held a school at the chapel. The first permanent minister was the Rev. John Mills (1841-46). In 1851 there were in the chapel 600 free seats and 400 others. On 30 March 170 were present in the morning service, 167 scholars in the afternoon and 373 in the evening service.

The present chapel was built between 1889 and 1891 at a total cost of £3,500 for the land and construction-work, with a number of houses demolished to make way for the new building. The builder was Thomas Williams, and the minister, the Rev. Robert Ambrose Williams (Emrys ap Iwan), the minister, literary critic and writer on political and religious topics, was closely involved in planning the chapel, which is believed to have been strongly influenced by his experience whilst visiting France. The chapel was opened on 5 April 1891 and the new chapel made a considerable impression with its spire described as a directing sign to heaven (*mynegfys i'r nefoedd*). The exterior front is convex and the interior is dominated by the array of organ pipes with the pews are arranged in a semicircle. The roof comprises broad hammer beams and the chapel is lit by traceried windows. Two houses were built next to the chapel in 1892, one for the minister and the other for the caretaker. The minister tendered his resignation the following year, but expressed his affection for Tabernacl in his homilies, declaring that she was his first love and the wife of his youth (*fy nghariad cyntaf a phriod fy ieuenctid*). A sum of £600 was paid in 1894 for an organ built by Wadsworth of Manchester, and a special concert was held to celebrate the occasion with E.T. Davies as the guest organist. The chapel was renovated when the organ was installed, and other improvements made since that time have included the restoration of the organ and the painting of the chapel in 1966.

Former ministers include the Rev. R. Bryn Williams (1944-54) and John Owen (1977-2004).

Present position: Minister: Rev. Morris P. Morris; 206 members; 13 adults and 25 children in Sunday school.

Further reading: R.H. Evans (ed.), *Hanes Henaduriaeth Dyffryn Clwyd* (1986); J. Meirion Lloyd Pugh, *Dathlu Dwbl, hanes daucanmlwyddiant yr achos 1791-1991* (1991); *Capel Local Information Sheet*, 28, Ruthin, (2005).

Contrasting interiors at Ruthin Tabernacl (*top*) and Bethesda at Mold [34]

34. MOLD, Bethesda (Pw)

OS: SJ 237 638

House-meetings were held by Calvinistic Methodists in Mold before the construction of a chapel in Chester Street, Ponterwyl in 1794. This was the first Nonconformist chapel in Mold. 300 persons were housed here, with benches provided for members near to the pulpit, others for 'listeners' near the rear wall, with empty benches placed in the intervening space to indicate the difference between them. Early members included Thomas Jones, later associated with Capel Mawr, Denbigh, and his wife Elizabeth. There was a membership of 140 persons in 1806, and the chapel was licensed the following year. Following the move to a new chapel, this chapel was sold to the parish priest, and housed for many years a National School, which was attended by the novelist Daniel Owen.

It was decided in 1818 to build a new chapel and this was opened in the following year. It cost £1,000 and the builder was Thomas Hughes, Liverpool. The chapel had an extensive gallery, and the pulpit, placed between two doors backed on to the main road. In 1851 there were 205 free seats, 350 others and space for 120 to stand. There were present on 30 March 240 in the morning service, 230 scholars in the afternoon and 401 in the evening service: the comment was added that many were absent because of the heavy rain, and the corresponding average annual attendance figures were 300 in the morning and 520 in the evening. This information was provided by Roger Edwards, described as one of the ministers. He became the first official minister of the church, serving from 1876 until 1886, and a statue of him stands outside the chapel. He was one of the main leaders of the Calvinistic Methodists, and was the co-founder and co-editor of Y Traethodydd (1845-65) and co-editor (1847-53) and editor of Y Drysorfa (1853-86).

The awareness of the need for new, larger premises resulted in the building, in 1863 on the same site, of a chapel with a striking Classical frontage, designed by the London architect, W.W. Gwyther. The chapel is listed Grade 2* by Cadw, and the gates, gate piers, railings, piers and dwarf walls around the perimeter are listed Grade 2. The chapel is of a Classical style with a Corinthian pedimented portico and tall Grecian columns. The interior has a rectangular, raked gallery with a panelled front, and a coffered ceiling with a central rose. The seats and pulpit have been painted in a light colour which softens the appearance of the interior. A number of items remind one of the influence of Bethesda on Daniel Owen, who was an occasional preacher, and was responsible for organizing the weeknight services following the death of Roger Edwards, who represented a major influence on him. Instalments of the novel Rhys Lewis appeared on a monthly basis in Y Drysorfa. The clock on the front of the gallery is the one which Wil Bryan is said in Rhys Lewis to have moved onwards to deceive Abel Hughes, and the table in the vestry is the one where Daniel Owen sat whilst engaged in his work as a tailor. The lectern in the front of the chapel commemorates Jennie Eirian Davies, the politician and editor of *Y Faner* from 1979 until her death in 1982, whose husband, the crowned bard J. Eirian Davies was the minister of Bethesda from 1962 until 1979.

The chapel has been renewed on several occasions, and an extension, including a schoolroom, was added in 1893. The renovation-work undertaken in 1905-06 amounted to nearly £1,200. Peter E. Roberts, Bromfield Road paid half the cost of the organ, made by Charles Whiteley, and the remaining £250 was paid by Andrew Carnegie. In 1908 electric light was installed in the chapel. A sum of £65,000 was paid on the buildings in the period 1979-84, over £8,000 on the organ in 1986, and £110,000 on the adaptation of the schoolroom in 2004 which has provided the church with modern facilities in the centre of the town.

There has been a close association between the church and the provision of Welsh-language education in a town situated near to the boundary with England. The plaque on the wall of the schoolroom records that the primary school which evolved into Ysgol Gymraeg Glanrafon, the town's Welsh school, was first held in the schoolroom in 1949.

Present position: Minister, Revs. Huw and Nan Powell Davies; 299 members; 45 children and 20 adults in Sunday school, Sunday services, 10.30 a.m. with Sunday school and 5.30 p.m.; weeknight services include prayer meeting, non-denominational children's club, youth club, Cwch Gwenyn society once a month.

Further reading: Rhian Phillips, *Y Dyfroedd Byw* (1987); *Capel Local Information Sheet*, 10 (1995).

35. WREXHAM, Capel y Groes (Pw)

OS. SJ 339 505

The earliest Calvinistic Methodists in the town of Wrexham met in their homes and were members of Adwy'r Clawdd. In 1797 a 21-year lease was signed for a plot of land and a building in Nailor's Yard in Pentrefelin, and this building was then adapted to a chapel for 50 persons. By 1805 a church had been formed but, following the termination of the lease and as the locality was described as "one of the most unhealthy districts in the town", a new chapel was built in Abbot Street in 1821. The land cost £100 and the chapel approximately £1,100, and in 1832 the church had 50 members with 100 to 120 attending services and 60 the Sunday school. In 1845 some of the members left the church to establish a church in Bank Street, and in 1907 Trinity chapel was built. On 30 March 1851, there were present at the Abbot Street chapel 150 in the morning service, 158 scholars in the afternoon, and 218 in the evening service, and at the Bank Street chapel 52 scholars in the morning, and congregations of 65 in the afternoon and 59 in the evening service.

Conditions in this area again attracted criticism as "the most unhealthy street in the town". The growth in the town, and accompanying increase in the congregation resulted in the purchase of a plot of land in Regent Street for £1,085.15s, and the construction of Seion chapel at a cost of nearly £6,000. The chapel, an impressive building designed by the Liverpool architectural firm, W. & G. Audsley, seated 800, and there were at the time 206 members in the church, 80 children and 273 members of the Sunday school. In 1884 a schoolroom was built in Egerton Street on land donated by Edward Williams, Elwy House. A new organ was installed in 1902, and substantial improvements were made to the chapel in 1951.

Concern was expressed since 1972 with regard to the condition of the chapel building, and especially the damaging effects of dry rot, and as a sum of £50,000 needed to be spent, discussions led by the minister, the Rev. Pryderi Llwyd Jones, centred on selling the site and building a new chapel. Another topic of discussion was to unite Seion with Ebeneser, Rhosddu which had been established by Seion in 1880. The Seion site was sold for £310,000 in 1978, and the final service was held at Seion on 27 May, 1979. A new chapel designed by Bowen, Dann, Davies, the Colwyn Bay firm, and built by McAlpine in 1981-82 at a cost of c.£275,000 on a site previously occupied by Llanelwy Home which had been purchased from the Church in Wales, was opened on 13 February 1982. The architectural firm received many awards for its work, including being commended by the RIBA, and awarded the Gold Medal of the National Eisteddfod. The structure comprises a steel frame with brick cladding, and a distinctive feature is the low spreading roof. The windows are stained hardwood, and a free-standing brick tower supports a cross, which is appropriate in view of the name selected for the new chapel. Within the chapel there is a memorial tablet to the Rev. Elwyn Hughes, former minister of Seion, by John

Price, Machynlleth and a slate emblem by Jonah Jones has been placed in the porch.

Present position: Minister, Rev. Robert Parry; 260 members, 70 children; Sunday services, 10.00 a.m. with Sunday school, 6.00 p.m.,11.00 adult Sunday school, weekly devotional, women and children's meetings, literary society, luncheon club, youth club, craft club, Welsh history class.

Further reading: Gareth Vaughan Williams, *Hanes sefydlu'r Capel a'r Chwarter canrif* (2007); *Capel Local Information Leaflet, 38, Wrexham* (2010).

36. LLANFYLLIN, Pendref (I)

OS: SJ 144 193

The present chapel is the third on the site and is associated with one of the oldest Independent causes in Wales, with Vavasor Powell reputed to be the first minister. Meetings were held in local farmhouses, including the home of John Griffith who donated land for the building of the first chapel in 1708. Access was from the lane behind the chapel. In 1715 the chapel was destroyed during a fierce attack mounted by a mob apparently inflamed by the High Sheriff and local clergymen. Nine local inhabitants were indicted for riotous assembly, which represented one of the most dramatic events of the Jacobite rebellion in Wales. The chapel was rebuilt in 1717, and the memorial stone on the exterior wall recorded that "THIS PROTESTANT CHAPPEL" was rebuilt in this year being "the 172 years since the Reformation, the XIX since the Revolution and the IV year of the reign of King George". Beneath this statement, an inscription containing a Latin quotation from Virgil represents a most unusual feature in an early Protestant meeting place. It was during the ministry at Pendref of the Revd. Jenkin Lewis that the hymnist Ann Griffiths had come to Llanfyllin, and been subjected to an intense spiritual experience whilst listening to a sermon preached by the Revd. Benjamin Jones, Pwllheli, either in the chapel or on the High Street. Her new-born daughter Elizabeth was baptized in 1805 at her home, Dolwar-fach, by the Rev. Jenkin Lewis. Dr. George Lewis, a successor as minister during the period 1815-21,was one of the leading theologians in Wales. He was the principal of the Independent Theological College located in the High Street, and one of his students was Samuel (S.R.) Roberts, Llanbryn-mair, where Dr Lewis had previously been minister of Yr Hen Gapel.

The final part of the memorial stone was added and incorporated after the chapel had been rebuilt in local red brick and enlarged in 1829 with the final statement declaring that 'This is none other than the house of God'. The Classical side elevation faces a wide graveyard and the road, and the chapel has a wide interior. In 1851 there were 140 free seats and 350 others, and the average attendance over a 12-month period was 105 scholars in the morning, 200 in the afternoon service and 420 in the evening service. No services were held on 30 March, the day of the Census, as the chapel was being repaired. Of the seven Nonconformist chapels in the town and parish of Llanfyllin, Pendref, recorded as 'Pendu', was clearly the chapel with the most numerous congregation, with the nearest to it numerically being the Calvinistic Methodist Capel Newydd with an average evening congregation of 170. Surviving photographs dated in 1884 and c.1900 reveal that on the intervening period two doors with semi-circular porticoes were added at each end of the façade.

Behind the pulpit there is a slate commemorating the life of the Rev. Susannah (Susie) Rankin (née Ellis) who attended Pendref as a child and was ordained as a minister in the chapel before leaving for Papua New Guinea where, after marrying

Robert Rankin, she stayed for nearly 50 years.

Present position: Minister: Rev. Gwyndaf Richards; 20 members; services are held regularly every Sunday in conjunction with Tabernacl Wesleyan Church, mostly at Pendref but occasionally at Tabernacl, and a united Sunday school is held.

Further reading: A.M. Allchin, *Ann Griffiths* (1976); *Living Stones Heritage Trust Guide*, 10.

Website: www.living-stones.info

37. PONTROBERT, John Hughes Memorial Chapel [Hen Gapel John Hughes]

OS: SJ 109 130

This chapel was built by the Calvinistic Methodists in 1800, and in the early period had been the location of one of Thomas Charles's circulating schools. John Hughes, a local weaver, had been one of the teachers. After his ordination in 1814, he served as minister until his death in 1854, and resided with his wife Ruth in the neighbouring cottage. He composed a number of hymns, and published his sermons. His pulpit, believed to date from 1835, is preserved in the chapel. In his old age, he was unable to move from his bed in the cottage, and preached to the congregation from a hatch placed in the dividing wall. Ruth was Ann Griffiths's maid, and had memorised her hymns. After she had recounted them to her husband, he then recorded them; consequently John and Ruth Hughes, who were both buried in the graveyard next to the chapel, were largely responsible for ensuring the survival of some of the main hymn-writing and literary treasures of Wales.(See [38] Dolanog.)

On 30 March 1851 there were present in the chapel, described as 'Upper Chapel', and with 40 free seats and 66 others, a congregation of 100 in the morning service, together with 140 scholars, 120 in the afternoon and 150 in the evening service. The chapel was closed in 1865 when the congregation moved to a larger chapel in Pontrobert village, and the old chapel was sold to a neighbouring wheelwright. It was sold again in 1939 but continued to be used as a workshop. In 1983 a national appeal was launched by local inhabitants to restore the chapel and cottage, and in 1995 the vision of Nia Rhosier, who had moved to the cottage in 1993, was realised when the chapel re-opened as a non-denominational Centre for Christian Unity and Renewal.

The restoration work, aimed at providing the chapel's appearance before the alterations of the late-nineteenth century, was designed by Merfyn Roberts and Donald C. Jones. The symmetrical front elevation consists of a pair of high level windows flanked by entrances for men and women. The pulpit has been retained at the centre of the rear wall but on a low dais. The partition between the chapel and cottage is timber framed, and on a high level may be seen the preaching hatch used by John Hughes in his old age.

The chapel has been listed Grade 2* by Cadw as a well-restored early chapel which also respects its later history as a wheelwright's shop, and with a significant association with John Hughes and Ann Griffiths.

In 2010 the chapel was included as one of the fifteen churches and chapels in north Montgomeryshire featured on the newly-launched Heritage Trail, 'Living Stones' (www.living-stones.info) which encourages pilgrims and visitors to explore the Christian heritage of the area.

Present position: Nia Rhosier welcomes hundreds of pilgrims annually, many of whom continue the tradition of visiting Dolwar Fach, Ann Griffiths's home, and also visitors who seek spirituality, renewal and unity. A programme of day retreats is regularly arranged at the Centre from Easter to the end of September, and the Centre is open from Tuesday to Thursday, from 2.00 p.m. and 4.00 p.m.

Further reading: Edward Griffiths, *Hanes Methodistiaeth Trefaldwyn Isaf* (1914); Nia Rhosier, series of articles in *Cristion* (September/October 1995; November/December, 1997), and in *Capel Newsletter*, 20 (Autumn 1993); 38 (Autumn, 2001); E.Wyn James, *Rhyfeddaf Fyth...* (1998); A.M. Allchin, *Resurrection's Children* (1998); *Living Stones Heritage Trust Guide*, 12.

Website: www.living-stones.info

38. DOLANOG, Capel Coffa Ann Griffiths Memorial Chapel (Pw)

OS: SJ 067 126

The Memorial Chapel stands in the village of Dolanog on the site of Salem chapel which was built in 1828. Its condition had deteriorated by the end of the century, and in 1904, following a national appeal for contributions towards the construction of a new chapel in the neighbourhood of Dolwar-fach, the home of Ann Griffiths, described by Tony Conran as "the greatest of Welsh women poets" and by A.M. Allchin as a "central figure in the Christian tradition of vision and song", the Memorial Chapel was opened in September 1904. A large congregation assembled and the services had to be held in a neighbouring field.

The chapel measured 32' by 26' and was built by the W.H. Thomas firm, Oswestry. The architect was G.E. Dickens-Lewis, Shrewsbury and Aberystwyth, the grandson of Lewis Edwards, the principal of Bala Theological College and the great-grandson of Thomas Charles, Bala. He was the main architect employed by the Davies family, Llandinam. He, together with R.E. Haymes, designed a number of buildings sponsored by the family, including the Owain Glyndŵr Parliament building and Public Institute, Machynlleth, the Public Hall Institute Llanfair Caereinion, and the adaptation of the Cambria Hotel, Aberystwyth which became the United Theological College (following the closure of the Theological College, the building, again utilised as a hotel and again named the Cambria Hotel, was offered for sale at £2,000,000 in June 2011). He also designed several schools in Ceredigion whilst he was the County Architect for Cardiganshire (1907-19) and various chapels, including Peniel, Trefriw.

The Memorial Chapel was built in the Arts and Crafts style with the furnishings reflecting the Art Nouveau style. The front is buttressed with a porch, bellcote and turrets. Inside, the white-washed walls and the dark-coloured wooden pews correspond to the timber ceiling. Four corbel heads have been placed in the chapel with those of Ann Griffiths facing Dolwar-fach, and John Hughes on the eastern wall facing Pontrobert. The other two were of prominent individuals in the former Salem chapel. A tablet on the pulpit commemorates Ruth Hughes, Ann's maid with the inscription stating that she was responsible for ensuring the survival of Ann Griffiths's hymns (see 37, Pontrobert). Two chairs in front of the pulpit had belonged to the hymn-writer and which had been presented to the Calvinistic Methodist chapel in Pontrobert by the family of the Rev. E. Griffith, Meifod.

The centenary of the chapel was celebrated in 2004 with a lecture on the 1904-05 revival, a hymn-singing festival and an exhibition mounted in the Community Centre of photographs illustrating the history of the chapel.

Recent developments, largely funded by the denomination but with some financial assistance from Cadw, include the re-roofing and re-wiring of the chapel, and

the provision of a ramp to improve access for disabled persons.

Present position: Minister, Rev. Peter Williams; 36 members, Sunday services at either 2.00 or 6.00 p.m., some united services with Saron Wesleyan chapel, some joint pastorate meetings.

Further reading: Edward Griffiths, *Hanes Methodistiaeth Trefaldwyn Isaf* (1914); A.M. Allchin, *Ann Griffiths* (1976); *Living Stones Heritage Trust Guide*, 13.

Websites: www.living-stones.info   www. Anngriffiths.cardiff.ac.uk

39. ADFA, Capel Coffa Lewis Evan a Charmel (Pw)

OS: SJ 060 010

The chapel at Adfa was built c.1790 following approximately fifty years of holding services in local farmhouses such as Llwyncoppa, and was enlarged c.1820 when a timber-framed schoolroom was added.

A prominent figure among the local Calvinistic Methodists was Lewis Evan (1719-1792), who, born in Trefeglwys, trained as a shuttle weaver whilst residing with his grandparents at the Coegnant woollen mill, Llanllugan. He was converted in 1738 after hearing Howel Harris preach at Trefeglwys, where he had been born, and learned to read at one of Griffith Jones's circulating schools, which developed into a Methodist society. He then devoted himself to preaching, serving as a counsellor and organising the activities of Methodists in north Wales. He travelled widely, preaching in Anglesey and Caernarfonshire and after being imprisoned in Dolgellau, was only released as a result of the intervention of Howel Harris. The chapel had been built before his death in 1792, and a memorial to Lewis Evan, raised by his nephew John Lewis, Felin Uchaf, stands outside the chapel.

One of the early members of Adfa was Humphrey Gwalchmai (1788-1847) who had been taught at the Adfa schoolroom by John Davies, who later became a missionary in Tahiti; he was elected an elder here when he was 17 years of age. Within two years he had been accepted as a regular preacher by the local presbytery and, having moved to Llanidloes, he became the first full-time minister with the Calvinistic Methodist denomination. He was buried in the Adfa graveyard in 1847, where another gravestone commemorates Owen Brown (1748-1835), whose father, also named Owen Brown, was closely involved with the growth of Sunday schools in this area. A number of these developed into churches, whilst others which experienced problems were assisted by the Adfa church, which has been described as "the base of operations" in this area for "Christianity in its Methodist forms for many years".

Robert Davies, classified as 'Minister', recorded in the 1851 Census that the chapel comprised 39 feet by 21 feet 'free space' and 37 others. There were present on 30 March 175 in the morning service, 193 scholars in the afternoon and 235 in the evening service.

A number of events were held in 1992 to celebrate the 250th anniversary of Adfa Chapel, including a *Gymanfa Ganu*, a lecture by R. Gerallt Jones on Lewis Evan, which was published together with a celebration booklet. Following extensive damage caused by lightning in 1995, a considerable amount of restoration work was undertaken.

Present position: Minister, Rev. Peter Williams, 18 members, 4 adults in Sunday school, Sunday service at 2.00 or 6.00 p.m.
Further reading: *Capel M.C. Adfa C.M. Chapel 1742-1992* (1992); R. Gerallt Jones, *Lewis Evan a'i Gyfnod* (1992).

40. PENTRE LLIFIOR (Me)

OS: SO 147 978

This chapel is located between Berriew and Bettws Cedewain on what was the main road in the eighteenth century from Welshpool to Newtown. John Wesley is believed to have travelled along this road in 1769 on his way to Newtown having been turned away from Welshpool town hall, and several other itinerant preachers visited a large number of towns, villages and homes in mid and north Wales.

The first Wesleyan Methodist cause was established at the Pentre farm and John Evans, a carpenter and builder, was appointed leader of the small society which met there. Itinerant preachers invited to the farm included Thomas Carlill (1730-1801), the Lincolnshire pipe-maker, and Cleland Kirkpatrick (1763-1834), born at Bangor, Northern Ireland, an ex-Royal Navy seaman who had lost his lower left arm in a naval encounter. Other preachers associated with the early history of the church were William Warrener, who became a missionary to Antigua, William Fish, a missionary to Jamaica, and Richard Whatcourt, who became one of the leaders of the Methodist Church in America. Land for the chapel at Pentre Llifior was provided by Evan Nock, who resided at the Penney farm, and received on 11 April 1798 a sum of 10 shillings from the Rev. James Buckley (1770-1839), who, as the Assistant (Superintendent Minister) at Brecon, headed the trustees. He and James Gill (1770-1844), another itinerant preacher who had been sent to Brecon in 1797 to assist James Buckley, and who was an early missionary to Gibraltar, collected money for the building of the new chapel, whose total cost was £211,7s.7d. The building-work had been completed by the autumn of 1798, and James Buckley soon afterwards married the daughter of Henry Child, a prominent Methodist and malster of Llanelli, whose brewing business he later inherited.

The chapel is a simple, rectangular Georgian brick building, constructed of local bricks. It has eight rounded Gothic windows and a part-enclosed stairway leading to a small gallery mounted on two slender cast-iron pillars. Fifteen pews downstairs include four in front of the great pew and the communion table, and replica candle-sticks and the original blue/white enamel pew number plates and hat pegs are notable features of the interior, which is largely original. Innovations in recent years include the installation of new pendant lights, under-seat heaters and carpet. Also, the addition of a lean-to structure in the 1960's provided a comfortable vestry and vestibule. Parts of the stable across the road date from 1805, when it was built in readiness for a visit by either Owen Davies, the leader of the Welsh Wesleyan mission to north Wales, or 'Bishop' Thomas Coke (1747-1814), one of John Wesley's closest followers and described as 'father' of the Methodists' overseas missions.

Present-day developments include the replacement of a 'lean-to' by a Georgian-style porch; the construction of a new building on the other side of the road, costing £105,000, which houses a meeting-room, museum, kitchen and toilet, and

improved parking facilities.

Pentre Llifior has been listed Grade 11 by Cadw, and has also been registered as a Methodist heritage site.

Present position: Minister, Ian Waugh; weekly afternoon Sunday service; monthly prayer meeting.

Further reading: *Information Leaflet, Pentre Llifior*; Heritage Leaflet 1; *James Buckley, Wesleyan Methodist Minister (1770-1839)*; Heritage Leaflet 2: *Thomas Carlill (1730-1801)*; Heritage Leaflet 3: *James Gill, Wesleyan Methodist Minister (1770-1844)*; Heritage Leaflet 4: *Cleland Kirkpatrick, Wesleyan Methodist Minister (1763-1834)*.

41. NEWTOWN, Crescent Christian Centre (UN/Pe)

OS: SO 110 915

English and Welsh-language services are held in this Presbyterian Church of Wales chapel which houses three churches, the Crescent English and Bethel Welsh Presbyterian Churches, and the Capel Coffa Independent church. This development had been significantly proposed in 1872 by the Rev. Thomas Jones Wheldon, minister of the Welsh Calvinistic Methodist church in Newtown who was offered the position of minister of the corresponding English church, but his suggestion that the two churches should unite and build one chapel was rejected and only realised after a period of a hundred and thirty years.

Edward Chapman, a flannel manufacturer and elder in the Welsh church, had been among those who sought to organise regular English-language services in Newtown and served as treasurer of the new English church established after early meetings had been held in various buildings, including a house and stable loft. Following the purchase in 1844 of a plot of land in Penygloddfa in the area later known as Chapel Street, a chapel built at a cost of £841 was opened in August 1845. The Sunday school flourished during the pastorate of Dr. Owen Thomas (1846-51) and congregations of between 400 and 500 attended the services. In 1856 the church had 70 members, 259 scholars in the Sunday school, and a congregation of 160.

The need for larger premises was appreciated, and another impetus was the opening of Bethel, the third Welsh Calvinistic Methodist chapel in the town which, designed by Richard Owens, the Liverpool architect, and seating 450 persons, was built between 1875-76 at a cost of £2,300. The same architect designed the English chapel, and he described the site, on a plot of land generously donated by Lord Sudely, Gregynog, the Member of Parliament for Montgomeryshire, near the junction of Crescent Road and Milford Road, as "a very prominent... position". Morgan Morris, a local builder who traded as Morris & Sons was described at the opening of the chapel on 16 May 1879 as "our excellent contractor". The cost of the building exceeded the estimated sum of £3,000 and whilst £1,275 had been collected before the opening, and another £440 collected at the opening services, with a substantial donation by David Davies, the industrialist and Member of Parliament for the Cardigan Boroughs, the remaining deficit was eventually cleared in 1900. Richard Owens described the Crescent's style as "geometrical Gothic in a planned parallelogram", with the schoolroom and vestries at the back in the form of a Cross "so as to give a transept appearance". The entire internal woodwork was pitch pine worked clean and varnished. All the windows were glazed with cathedral tinted glass and coloured borders, and a very large three light window was placed in the centre of the front, facing Crescent Street. The tower and spire were of a combined height of 90 feet, with a parapet at their junction. Both the chapel and schoolroom were intricately detailed in the decorative style with buttresses at the

front corners of the chapel. Seating was provided for about 450 people, 350 on the ground floor and about 100 in the gallery.

Demand for additional space resulted in the construction in 1897 of another schoolroom, designed by F.H. Shayler and built by John Swain, a local contractor. In the same year, the earliest surviving report of the Crescent lending library, which operated for many years, recorded a total of 1,233 books at the beginning of the year, the addition of 84 titles during the year, and that 84 members borrowed 902 books. A significant development in 1903 was the installation of an organ built by Bishop & Son, London & Ipswich, for £45,11s.6d, and the total cost, including ancillary work, amounted to £642,11s.0d. The new organ was opened by a recital given by Dr. H. Walford Davies, organist of the Temple Church, London, and organ recitals were regularly held over the years. Extensive remedial work on the organ was undertaken in1958 by Bishop & Son for the sum of £318. Substantial payments for renovation over the years have included those on general repairs and maintenance in 1974, and on efforts to counter the damage caused by dry rot undertaken in 1983 and 1984.

A critical report presented in 2000 by the denomination's estate managers on the chapel's condition and health and safety provision led to a decision to vacate the chapel, sell the building and site and use the revenue to ensure that Bethel satisfied the necessary requirements. Before any action could be taken, a fierce storm in October 2002 caused extensive damage to the roof and interior of the chapel. Further discussions with the officials of Bethel eventually led to an agreement to sell

Bethel for redevelopmemt into flats and/or offices, and for each congregation to re-assemble in a new building on the site of the Crescent chapel, and thereby activate the vision expressed by the Rev. Thomas Jones Wheldon in 1876.

The chapel today accommodates the Crescent, Bethel and Capel Coffa Welsh Independent churches. Capel Coffa had also been built on land gifted by Lord Sudeley, and was constructed in 1863 as a memorial chapel commemorating the events of '*Cae Bendith*', the Field of Blessing which provided for Henry Davies and his family following cruel persecution during the seventeenth century. An auditorium type chapel with a gable-end façade, typical of the 1830s, the chapel was refurbished in 1885, and again in 1909.

The three churches worshipped at Capel Coffa whilst the Crescent chapel was being repaired following the storm damage of 2002, but the three now co-operate in sharing the facilities of the Crescent Christian Centre – Canolfan Gristnogol y Cilgant which has set itself out to be a pivotal point for the community.

Present position: No minister, since the retirement of the Rev. Edwin O. Hughes; Crescent 26 members, Bethel: 29 members, Capel Coffa 35 members; Sunday English services, 9.30 a.m., Welsh services, 11.00 a.m. The building is active almost every day. The church has a monthly service for Welsh learners, and each Friday, there is a successful coffee morning. Meetings of the Presbyterian Church of Wales and Welsh Independents are held here. Outside organisations which use the building include Yoga, Weight Watchers, Welsh classes from Aberystwyth University and various local societies: an annual Open Day is held for local societies and organisations to show the community what is available for them.

Further reading: David Peate, *A History of Crescent Chapel Newtown* (2004); *CAPEL Local Information Sheet*, 34, Newtown (2008).

42. NEWTOWN, Zion (Be)

OS: SN 109 915

Groups of Baptists, Congregationalists and Calvinistic and Wesleyan Methodists met in various premises in Newtown in the eighteenth century. A dramatic increase in the population of the town in the early nineteenth century as a result of the expansion of the woollen industry, with Newtown becoming known as 'the busy Leeds of Wales', was accompanied by the building of chapels by these Nonconformist denominations. The first chapel was built by the Baptists in 1801, followed by the Wesleyan Methodists in c.1806 and the Calvinistic Methodists in c.1810. Three larger chapels were built by the Baptists on the same site, in 1814, 1821 and 1836. The 1851 Census recorded that the fourth chapel had 454 free seats and 632 others, and that 373 were present in the morning service on 30 March, and 731 in the evening with 390 scholars. A site on New Road was purchased in 1880, on which was built Zion chapel, designed by George Morgan, Carmarthen, apparently based upon the Metropolitan Tabernacle in London.

Zion, described as one of Wales's finest chapels, was built of brick and sandstone by Griffiths & Williams of Knockin between 1881 and 1882, at a cost of £8000, in the Beaux-Artes Baroque High Classical style. Impressive pillars were placed at the front and in the interior adjacent to the organ. A broad flight of stone steps leads to five bays in red brick on an ashlar base. This is surmounted by a giant order of Corinthian pillars above which is a shaped brick and stone gable and over which projects a portico and pediment. The inside is similarly lavish with serpentine iron gallery fronts, supported on iron columns, with arcades above. A large organ, built by Peter Conacher & Co (the old firm), Huddersfield, is contained in a Serliana recess with marble columns. The schoolrooms are located below the chapel, which, when it opened, provided accommodation for 1,334 persons.

Present position: No minister, 25 members; Sunday services, 10.30 a.m. and 6 p.m. monthly lady's guild.

Further reading: *Capel Local Information Sheet, 34, Newtown* (2008).

(*Top*) Newtown, Zion and (*right*) the memorial to Humphrey Gwalchmai at China Street, Llanidloes

43. LLANIDLOES, China Street (Pw)

OS: SN 954 845

The first Calvinistic Methodist chapel in Llanidloes, named 'Bethel' was built in 1770. Whilst visiting one of his Sunday schools in the Llanidloes area, Thomas Charles was so impressed by the singing voice of Henry Mills that he proposed that Mills be put in charge of the congregational singing in Bethel, where the singing was apparently of a low standard. It seems that some of the elders viewed with apprehension Henry Mills's ability to play two or three musical instruments such as the fiddle, especially as they were opposed to the use of musical instruments in religious services which they considered should be plain and unaccompanied. However, despite this, Mills served as precentor at Bethel until his death in 1820. He was succeeded by his son James in his post at the chapel where a choral society was established, as well as a weeknight class where the rudiments of music were taught to approximately 60-70 young people who attended this class after working in the town's flannel factories. James Mills also composed a number of anthems and hymn tunes, many of which appeared after his death in a volume entitled *Y Cerddor Eglwysig* ['The Church Musician'] which was published by his nephews John and Richard Mills. This is where Humphrey Gwalchmai served as the first official full-time minister of the Calvinistic Methodists (see 40, Adfa).

On 30 March 1851 368 were present in the morning service, 475 scholars in the afternoon and 614 in the evening service. The chapel had 250 free seats, 460 others and room for 190 to stand. The need for a larger chapel resulted in the construction of two chapels to replace Bethel in 1872-73: the Welsh-language China Street chapel and the English-language Bethel seating 240, which closed in 2004, when the congregation united with Zion U.R.C. church to form the Trinity Church. Zion chapel was designed by John Humphrey, Swansea (see 90, Morriston, Tabernacl).

The chapel, seating 900, was designed by Richard Owens, Liverpool and built in 1872 by Rhydwen Jones, Rhyl at a cost of £4,000. The façade comprises contrasting stonework and the sides have a glazed brick base with slate hung above. The single storey portico was built the following year, and contains a memorial to the Rev. Humphrey Gwalchmai. The interior of the chapel has a three-sided gallery and a fine plasterwork ceiling. The *sêt fawr* and organ are of a composite design. The raised schoolroom to the rear, built in 1876, is also slate hung and the extensive interior space has been frequently used for various local functions. An organ, built by Wadsworth and Bro., was installed in 1896.

Present position: Minister, Rev. Jenny Garrard; 34 members; Sunday services, 10.00 a.m.

Further reading: Ronald Morris, *Llanidloes Town and Parish, an illustrated account* (1993), and 'Chapels in Llanidloes and District', *Capel Newsletter*, 26 (1995); *Capel Information Sheet*, 27, Llanidloes [2005].

44. LLANBRYN-MAIR, Yr Hen Gapel (I)

OS: SH 913 020

The activities of a number of the early Puritan leaders in the seventeenth century, such as Walter Cradoc, Morgan Llwyd and Vavasor Powell formed part of the early history of Yr Hen Gapel [The Old Chapel]. Lewis Rees became minister of Llanbryn-mair in 1734, having been recommended by Edmund Jones, Pontypool. He extended an invitation to Howel Harris to visit Bala, and in 1739, when this chapel was built, a thanksgiving service was held here when Howel Harris was released after he was prosecuted at the Monmouth Assizes in August 1739. The three shires in north-west Wales represented a mission field for Lewis Rees, and in his address in 1934 when the 200th anniversary of the church was celebrated, R.T. Jenkins emphasised the contrast between the condition of the church in 1734, when it was merely a branch of the Llanfyllin church, and the thriving one in 1759 when Lewis Rees departed.

Further periods of success were experienced, especially in 1778 and in 1787 during the pastorate of his successor, Richard Tibbott (1762-98) who had been born in the locality, and educated in one of Griffith Jones's circulating schools before he served as a minister with the Calvinistic Methodists for 25 years. The chapel was extended in 1778, and then rebuilt in 1821 during the pastorate of the third minister, the Rev. John Roberts (1796-1834). R. Tudur Jones considered that he was the most gifted student of Dr. Edward Williams, who had been principal of the Academy in Oswestry before he was appointed the head of Rotherham Academy. He ordained as co-minister his son, Samuel 'S.R.', the author, editor of the periodical *Y Cronicl*, and supporter of progressive contemporary movements and radical causes; and his younger son John 'J.R.' assisted him during the period 1835-48. The father and two sons were buried in the graveyard. In 1851 Samuel Roberts, as the minister, was responsible for presenting data for the 1851 Census, and it was reported that 410 were present in the morning service, 98 scholars in the afternoon and 430 in the evening service. It was added that seven separate Sunday schools belonged to the 'Old Chapel', and that the evening congregation would "meet for worship in the Chapel, or in their School rooms, as may best suit their convenience".

The direct association of this family with the pastorate came to an end in 1857 when 'S.R.' emigrated to the United States to escape the wrath of the steward of the Wynnstay estate which owned his farm, Diosg. He unsuccessfully attempted to establish, with the aid of other persons hailing from Llanbryn-mair, a Welsh colony in Tennessee.

Following the ordination of his successor, David Rowlands, the chapel was renovated in 1861 when the ceiling, pulpit and railings surrounding the chapel were added at a cost of £300. A year later a harmonium was provided through the efforts of Richard Davies, 'Mynyddog', the poet and eisteddfod leader. New seats were installed throughout the chapel during the pastorate of the Rev. Dr. Owen Evans (1876-81), and when the Rev. Samuel Roberts was the minister, from 1902 until 1920, a new roof was placed on the chapel and two new porches were built above the doors at the entrance in 1904. Also, two stained glass windows by A.L. Moore, one depicting The Good Shepherd and the other The Light of the World, were donated in 1906 and 1907: these were later denounced by Iorwerth C. Peate, founder of the Welsh Folk Museum, now re-named the St.Fagans: National History Museum. Dr Peate, who had been brought up in the Old Chapel, composed a sonnet in praise of the chapel: 'Yr Hen Gapel, 1739-1939', and, recounting his reminiscences in his autobiography, *Rhwng Dau Fyd*, often referred to *traddodiad Llanbryn-mair* ['the Llanbryn-mair tradition'] when emphasising the Welsh person's emphasis on one's independence and the right to express an opinion.

The chapel was renovated during the early years of the ministry of the Rev. Robert Evans (1933-57), new heating equipment was provided and electric light introduced. His successor, the Rev. Dr Dewi Eirug Davies (1959-65) discussed some of the main personalities involved in the events of the period 1939-89 in the collection of essays which he edited with Iorwerth C. Peate.

Recent developments have included improving the car park and the graveyard, and facilities for the disabled.

Present position: No minister following the departure of the Rev. Marc Morgan; 160 members; Sunday service at 10.00 a.m., bi-monthly youth and children's service.
Further reading: *Hen Gapel Llanbrynmair 1739-1989,Ysgrifau*, ed. Iorwerth C. Peate and Dewi Eirug Davies (1989); *Llanbrynmair in the Twentieth Century*, ed. Marian Rees (2005).

45. MACHYNLLETH, Tabernacle

OS: SH 747 009

John Wesley travelled through the town in 1747, 1750 and 1755 but there is no evidence that he preached in Machynlleth. Two Wesleyan Methodists, Edward Jones, Bathafarn and W. Parry, preached in the town in 1804 and in 1806 local Wesleyans met for worship in an old barn in Doll Street. The first Wesleyan chapel was built in Graig-fach in the following year, and William Owen, who had ministered in a number of circuits in north Wales since 1807, assumed responsibility for the church in 1821-23. By this time the church was considered to be too small, and it was renovated, with the addition of a gallery, during the pastorate of the Rev. Lot Hughes. Tabernacl chapel was re-opened in October 1843 and at approximately the same time English-speaking Wesleyan Methodists, led by the local bank manager W.H. Larkin, built another chapel. This building, at the eastern end of Maengwyn Street, has been converted into two dwellings.

On 31 March 1851 80 scholars were present at Tabernacl in the morning, there was a congregation of 160 in the afternoon and 300 in the evening service. There were in the chapel 72 free seats and 456 others. The church continued to thrive and in 1878, during the ministry of the Rev. John Hughes, Glanystwyth, the trustees decided to build a new chapel beside the existing chapel. The new chapel, with a Classical façade, was opened in June 1882.

Following the closure of the Tabernacl, it was bought in 1984 by Andrew Lambert who established a charity company, The Machynlleth Tabernacl Trust, to be responsible for it. After extensive renovation, Y Tabernacl was re-opened on 11 October 1986 as an impressive centre for the performing arts. The Trust owned the adjoining land, that is, the site of an earlier chapel, and a free-standing structure was built here to provide additional toilet and green room facilities for the Tabernacl. A neighbouring building, Harvey House, which had previously been a grocer shop with a residence above it, was bought by the Trust and this provided much-needed street frontage on the main north-south Wales road. After five years sufficient funds had been raised to convert Harvey House into Art Galleries and the first art exhibition was held in May 1992.

Further substantial grants from public and private funds enabled the provision of considerably enhanced facilities for visitors to the auditorium and galleries of the sensitively-adapted former Wesleyan Tabernacle chapel.

Throughout the year a series of constantly changing exhibitions feature the finest exponents of modern Welsh art and works from the growing Tabernacle Collection are shown in rotation. In July every year artists are invited to enter a new work in the Tabernacle Art Competition. 350 persons may be seated in the auditorium which, containing pitch-pine pews, has excellent acoustics. Chamber and choral music concerts are held here, and also dramatic performances, lectures and conferences. A

Steinway grand piano is available, translation booths, recording facilities and a cinema-screen have been installed, and a lift provides access for the disabled. Events are organised throughout the year, but the annual highlight is the Machynlleth Festival held in the auditorium in late August, with the varied performances including choral singing, chamber music, jazz and poetry readings, together with the Hallstatt Lecture on Celtic culture and the Glyndŵr Award for an outstanding contribution to the arts in Wales.

Further reading: David Wyn Davies, *The Goodly Inheritance / Yr Etifeddiaeth Deg* (1988); *Capel Local Information Sheet, 15 , Machynlleth* (1999).
Website: www.momawales.org.uk

46. LLANDEGLEY, The Pales (So)

OS: SO 137 641

This is the oldest Quaker meeting house in Wales which continues to be in use, and is one of only two thatched meeting houses in Britain. It has seating for 24 persons, and has been listed Grade 2* by Cadw because of its exceptional historic interest for the Quaker movement in Wales.

An extremely well-attended meeting had been held in 1657 on a common, possibly Pen-y-bont Common, addressed by George Fox, the Quaker founder, who requested John ap John to address the crowd in Welsh. Despite persecution, services were held in local homes, and the greatest need in this period was to gain possession of a graveyard for Quaker burials. A plot of land was secured at Llandegley on 17 June, 1673 on the site later known as 'the Pales', on a 1,000-year lease from David Powell, the elder, and David Powell, the younger. Considerable persecution continued, and in February 1683 a meeting held somewhere in the parish of Llandegley (probably at the Pales) was interrupted by the High Sheriff, and several members of the congregation were forced to walk a considerable distance, described as being over 'bleak hills', to the nearest prison, probably Presteigne. In 1716, one of them, Edward Jones joined others to become trustees at the Pales of the "dwelling house with all the houses and outhouses, garden and woods growing at the lower end of the dwelling house,... with a piece part of close called Kay yr Pales" [the Pales Field].

Whilst this building was licensed in 1716, the surviving single-storey structure probably dates from c.1745. It has thatched roofs, a central enclosed porch and from the porch separate six-panel doors, one marked 1745 and the other 1825, provide access to the meeting room and the former schoolroom. The two rooms are divided by a partition wall, and the meeting room has a raised dais with elders' and overseers' benches.

As a result of persecution many Quakers emigrated to America, and especially to the Quaker colony in Pennsylvania, and it is significant that the first American meeting house was called 'Radnor'. By the mid-nineteenth century, it was commented that the Pales meeting house "hardly continued to exist", but a new and unlikely impetus came from what has been described as 'Victorian evangelism'. A school serving the entire community was held in the meeting house from 1867 until 1889, where one of the teachers was Yardley Warner, a prominent American campaigner for the rights of slaves. He was responsible for greater activity at the Pales, which organised a tent meeting at Pen-y-bont in 1879. At this meeting John Owen Jenkins, one of the earliest pupils at the school, had been profoundly influenced by a religious experience, and he then became a prominent preacher in Radnorshire during the Religious Revival of 1904-05.

Considerable restoration work was undertaken at the Pales during the last quarter of the twentieth century when Quaker wardens were re-established. The

graveyard was restored, the meeting house re-thatched and a new water supply provided.

Present position: Wardens, Martin and Lynda Williams. Meetings for worship held at 3.00 p.m. every third Sunday. Also, open all day, every day, all the year round for visitors, at no cost, and available for letting to groups who value the peaceful spiritual atmosphere. Whilst a highly-regarded venue for meetings and retreats, it is emphasised that "its primary function continues to be, as always, a place of worship at which all are welcome".

Further reading: Martin Williams, *Early Quakers in Mid Wales* (1993); Martin Williams, *Radnorshire Quakers and the Welsh Revival of 1904* (2004).

Website: www.hmwquakers.org.uk/html/pales.html

47. LLANDRINDOD, Cae-bach (R)

OS: SO 059 623

Cae-bach was founded in 1715 by the Rev. Thomas Jones of Trefonnen, who had also established in 1710 the Independent chapel at Tetbury, Gloucestershire. The chapel, built by its founder at his own expense, was known as 'Mr. Jones's meeting house' and was described in 1744 as "large as an ordinary barn... At the east end of it is a pulpit. Under that is Mr. Jones's pew, the only one there, all the congregation besides sitting down on benches". Howel Harris is believed to have been entertained at Trefonnen and to have preached at one of the farms owned by the Trefonnen family, and it it is probable that he also preached at Cae-bach.

The chapel has a side entrance with semi-octagonal pulpit, placed at the centre of the short wall, box pews, raked at the rear, a gallery also at the rear, and a coved plaster ceiling. The chapel was considerably rebuilt in 1804 when the gallery was added so that as many as possible could attend the services. A further adaptation of the chapel was undertaken in 1840 when the present box pews were installed, and the open grate at the rear of the chapel was covered. The stable opposite the chapel would accommodate the horse of the minister or a visiting preacher.

A notable feature in the chapel is the large tablet made in 1810 to the Jones family of Trefonnen which has two marbles, grey for the flanking pilasters and white

for the urn. Several members of the family were buried here, with the most famous person being Thomas Jones (1742-1803), the renowned artist. A student of Richard Wilson, his Welsh and Italian landscapes, and especially his series of views of Naples which he painted from 1782 to 1783, have enhanced his reputation, especially in the late-twentieth century.

The 1851 Census recorded 200 free seats and standing space for another 50 persons. On 30 March 37 were present in the morning service and 52 in the afternoon, and whilst it was stated that occasionally 60 were present in the evening, an additional note described the chapel as the nearest dissenting place of worship to the spa resort of Llandrindod Wells, and referred to an average morning congregation of 70-80 in the summer months, and 100-180 in the evening. The chapel continues to be used for services by the local United Reformed Church.

Present position: Minister: Rev. Stephen Gilbert; Sunday service, 2.30 p.m.
Further reading: R.C.B. Oliver, *The family history of Thomas Jones the artist, of Pencerrig, Radnorshire* (1987); J.B. Sinclair & R.W.D. Fenn, *Marching to Zion, Radnorshire Chapels* (1990).

48. BRECON, Plough (R/I)

OS: SO 046 285

The origins of the church extend to the history of the Independents or Congregationalists in the Brecon area in the seventeenth century. Meetings were held in many places in the county, including Aberllynfi, 10 miles north-east of Brecon, but adherents moved to the town in the last decade of the century following the purchase of the 'Plow-house', a building which may well have previously been an inn, and which was licensed as a place of worship in 1699. The first chapel was built here between 1728 and 1733, with much of the work undertaken by members, most of whom were local farmers but also including Benjamin Tanner, founder of the first ironworks in the area. A new chapel was built in 1841 and this had a seating capacity of 700.

On 30 March 1851 it was recorded that 550 were present in the morning service and 800 in the evening service, and that there were in the chapel 900 free seats. Benjamin Jenkins, whose joinery workshops were considered to be the finest in Wales, and whose descendants continue to operate in Brecon in the local building trade, was largely responsible for the extensive adaptation of this chapel in the late-nineteenth century, and the state of the chapel today reflects the skill and craftsmanship of local workers. The installation of fixed pews resulted in a reduction in the seating capacity to 550, with 50 seats placed in the choir pews between the organ and the pulpit. The renovation work completed in this period cost £1,750 and

the organ another £355. The last thirty years have again witnessed considerable renovation work, with the buildings re-roofed, the organ overhauled and the ground floor of the neighbouring property converted for the use of the church.

The church had a close connection with the theological college, which, originally founded in 1838 but reconstituted as the Memorial College in 1869 to commemorate the ejected Dissenting ministers of 1662, continued to train students for the Congregational ministry until it moved to Swansea in 1959. The College provided many members of, and preachers at the Plough chapel and some of them are commemorated in the memorial tablets in the deacons' room.

Services were held entirely in the Welsh language until the end of the nineteenth century, but gradually English was increasingly used. There was already an English-language Congregational church in Brecon, the Glamorgan Street Church established in 1836, but the two churches were united in 1923, and since that time services once a month have been held in Welsh, and in English at other times.

An oratorio was presented by the choir on Good Friday from the 1920s until 1969, and the conductor for many years was Rhys Jones who is commemorated in a tablet placed on the organ. Since 1984 the chapel has annually attracted large numbers of visitors to the annual Flower Festival held in August. This coincides with the Brecon Jazz Festival, when a Jazz concert is held in the chapel on a Saturday evening and on the Sunday evening a 'Songs of Praise' (*Gymanfa Ganu*) is held on the Sunday evening.

Present position: Ministers: Revs. Michael Hodgson, Greg Thompson; Sunday service, with Junior School/ Sunday school, in English and Welsh, at 11.00 a.m. (On the 2nd Sunday of the month the service is held in Welsh).

Further reading: *The Plough United Reformed Church, Lion Street, Brecon, Powys, A Short History* (n.d.).

Website: http://brecon.urc.org.uk

49. MAESYRONNEN, Glasbury-on-Wye (R)

OS. SO 177 411

Maesyronnen is of the greatest importance in the history of Welsh chapels as the oldest chapel to be in continuing use in Wales today. Very few changes have been made to the chapel since it was constructed c.1696. It is possible that an earlier farmhouse and barn had been adapted with the former becoming a meeting house and the latter a home for the minister. Early developments in the locality were associated with the start of Vavasour Powell's ministry in 1640, and the origins of the church at Maesyronnen lay in the 1649 Act for the Better Propogation and Preaching of the Gospel in Wales, which allowed the formation of licensed non-conforming groups. Henry Maurice, an unlicensed preacher (1672-1682) is believed to have used a longhouse-derived farmhouse, known as 'Y Beudy' [the cowshed] for services, and Oliver Cromwell is reputed to have attended a service here. The building was adapted for worship and registered at Presteigne in 1696. The chapel was sited on the land of Charles Lewis Lloyd, Maesllwch, who transferred the land and the chapel from the family to the church in perpetuity.

The rubble stone building has a stone slate roof with a door at each end. The interior comprises one large room, divided into six bays. The raised pulpit with panelled front is placed against the long wall of the building, at the centre of the north side, with on either side a rectangular panelled boxed pew with angled book-rest, a similar boxed pew opposite and another late seventeenth century or early eighteenth century elongated pew in the south-east corner. The communion table and a pew are dated 1722, and the box pews contain seats facing each other to accommodate whole families. There are also rows of bare-backed benches, and a range of wall monuments commemorating individuals, many of whom were children, associated with the church in the nineteenth century.

Maesyronnen has inspired visitors over the years, and R.S. Thomas described it as 'The Chapel of the Spirit', prompting a vision of "a single fountain welling up endlessly from immortal God".

The chapel and adjoining cottage have been listed Grade 1 by Cadw as exceptionally-important surviving buildings associated with early Nonconformity in Wales. The church was formerly an Independent church, but is now part of the United Reformed Church, and is one of the seven churches in the Brecon Beacons Pastorate

Present position: Ministers: Revs. Michael Hodgson, Greg Thompson; Sunday service, 10.30 a.m.

Further reading: M.E. Griffiths, *History of Maesyronnen United Reformed Church and Surrounding Area* (1987); J.B. Sinclair & R.W.D. Fenn, *Marching to Zion, Radnorshire Chapels* (1990).

The interior of ancient Maesyronnen (*top*), and the chapel at Bow Street (*above*)

50. BOW STREET, Capel y Garn (Pw)

OS: SN 627 854

A significant early development was the preaching service held at the Glebe Inn, on the road from Llanfihangel Genau'r Glyn to Tal-y-bont, led by Evan Richardson, born in this area but later associated with establishing the Methodist cause in the Caernarfon area. The first chapel was built in 1793 on Cae Maelgwyn, and given the Biblical name of Jehofa-jire (the Lord has provided), Abraham's designation of the site where he had prepared to sacrifice his son Isaac. Nearby, there was a row of cottages, called Pen-y-garn, and this was the name given locally to the chapel. Membership increased especially after the revivals of 1802 and 1809, and a second chapel was built in 1813 beside the first, which was adapted into a house. The interior of the chapel measured 9 yards by 12, and was known as Capel Mawr Pen-y-garn.

Within twenty years another chapel had to be built. The intention was to use the same site as the second chapel, but because of geological problems a plot of land was secured nearer to the village on a lease of 999 years for a rent of five shillings a year. When the chapel was opened it was reported in *Y Drysorfa*, the denominational journal, that the chapel measured 18 yards long, 15 yards wide and 10 yards high. 900 cart-loads of stones were brought here from Cefnhendre quarry, 12 wagons of wood and 50 cart-loads of lime from Aberystwyth, 100 cart-loads of gravel from Clarach and slates from Aberllefenni. Contributions towards the building costs were made by two local landowners: W.E. Powell, Nanteos and Pryse Pryse Gogerddan. A considerable amount of the building work was undertaken voluntarily by the members. Two stone masons and one carpenter worked on the building, together with a carpenter from Liverpool who was staying in the area. A report for *Y Drysorfa* was prepared by Ebenezer Richard who stated that his admiration for the chapel was so great that he would adopt a similar design when extending his own chapel, Bwlchgwynt, Tregaron. Declaring that the members of Bow Street had been superior to those of Borth, but "*mynnwn ninnau ragori arnoch chwi*" [we are determined to be better than you].

An interpretation of the 1851 Census presents difficulties as it contains two entries for 'Penygarn Calvinistic Methodist'. The first one records that the chapel had been built '20 years', contained 450 free seats and that the average attendance was 400 in the morning, 200 scholars in the afternoon, and 420 in the evening. The second entry, with an appended note stating that this is a duplicate entry for the first one, referred to a chapel built 'before 1800' with 75 free seats, 366 others and space for 100 to stand. There were present on 30 March 329 in the morning service, 262 scholars in the afternoon and 397 in the evening service. One of the consequences of the 1859 Revival was the need to extend the chapel, and in 1866 it was decided to erect a gallery. The builder was William Jones, Dole, father of the Rev. William Jones, minister of Jerusalem, Tonpentre, in the Rhondda Valley for many years, who, having been trained as a carpenter, became renowned not only as a prominent preacher but also as a proficient architect. He was reputed to have designed over 200 chapels in south Wales, including his own chapel, known by his admirers as "the Methodist Cathedral of the Rhondda". His brother Thomas was the builder when further changes were made to Capel y Garn in 1900 with a vestry built, a new pulpit installed and the *sêt fawr* renewed. In 1984 dry rot was discovered in some of the rafters and in the front wall of the chapel. The cost of repairing the damage was over £80,000, and after completing the work the chapel was re-opened in July, 1986.

Capel y Garn has a fine musical tradition. J.T. Rees, a native of Cwmgiedd, in the Swansea Valley, was the precentor for over sixty years, and he was renowned as a composer of hymns, anthems and vocal and instrumental works. The chapel choir performed oratorios and cantatas under his direction, and occasionally an orchestra from Manchester was hired to accompany the choir. His successors included W. Llywelyn Edwards, the hymn-tune composer.

In June 1905, the Association of the Calvinistic Methodists and the Revival Gymanfa Ganu were held here. The impact of the Revival on the locality was so immense that a pavilion had to be hired. Accommodating 2,000 persons, it was installed on Cae Maelgwyn and special trains to Bow Street were organised. The church depended on local ministers to administer the sacraments and the first permanent minister, the Rev. J. Christmas Lloyd was not inducted until 1918.

Present position: Minister, Rev. Wyn Morris; 151 members, 19 children; Sunday Services, 10.00 a.m (with Sunday school for children), and 5.00 p.m., weekly Bible Study for pastorate, Occasional services united with Noddfa Independent church; monthly sisterhood and 'Helping Hand' group, literary society, 'Os Mêts' [youth club].

Further reading: Nerys Ann Jones, *Capel y Garn; c.1793-1993* (1993).

website: www.capelygarn.org

51. ABERYSTWYTH, Bethel (Bw)

OS: SN 584 817

Early Baptist developments in the area centred on the village of Penrhyn-coch, to the north of Aberystwyth. Missionaries travelling from Pembrokeshire to north Wales in the summer of 1787 were welcomed to stay at Plas Gogerddan by Lowry Pugh, who was staying in the mansion with her son, William, the estate steward. Several individuals in the area were baptised, including two men in the town of Aberystwyth, and the first Baptist church in north Ceredigion was established at Penrhyn-coch, where most of the members lived, even though the church was known as 'Aberystwyth'. The few members who lived in the town first met in a house in Queen Street and by 15 January 1794 the 'Bethel meeting house' was registered as a place of worship. By 1797 a new chapel, again called Bethel, had been built on the site of the present chapel, on the corner of Baker Street and Upper Portland Street, and strenuous efforts were made to pay the costs incurred in building the chapel, with collection-trips arranged to Liverpool, Manchester and Birmingham.

The association of Bethel and Horeb, Penrhyn-coch came to an end harmoniously in 1818. Bethel was rebuilt in 1833, and again money towards the building costs was collected in English towns, including Liverpool and Manchester. The 1851 Census recorded that there were 150 free seats and 500 others. On 30 March there were present 205 in the morning service, 244 scholars in the afternoon and 388 in the evening service. The Rev. Edward Williams, a native of Denbigh and minister of Denbigh since 1841, added a note that many members were "seafaring men and cannot attend every Sunday. When they are at home the congregation may be about 500." The chapel was considered to be too small and in 1871, during the visit of Carmarthenshire and Ceredigion Baptists [*Cymanfa Caerfyrddin ac Aberteifi*] services were held in the 'new Market House' (the present-day W.H. Smith store) which was described in the *Aberystwyth Observer* as "crammed to repletion". Another motivating factor was the trend to build large impressive chapels in Aberystwyth, in what was described as 'building mania'. The *Aberystwyth Observer* commented in 1888 that it was "antiquated in design and altogether unfitted for the requirements of the Church and congregation in these days when handsome edifices surround it on all sides". Also, whilst it might have been "a thing of beauty" in 1833, "of recent years it was an eyesore to all who had any taste and an exception to the restored places of worship in the town."

The new chapel, the third to be erected on the site, was designed by T.E. Morgan, a member of Bethel and son of the deacon John Morgan, who became the architect of the University College and later designed many buildings in the town, including Salem chapel [see 52, Aberystwyth, Capel y Morfa], Ardwyn County School and Alexandra Hall of Residence. A detailed description of the 'handsome edifice', which opened in October 1889, was published in the *Aberystwyth Observer*, which referred to the front being "chiefly of the Corinthian order", the walling of Llanddewi Brefi blue stone, the porch with two doorways which were richly moulded and carved, the pediment supported by four massive Aberdeen granite pilasters, and a large lobby. The interior, with 750 seats, contained a rostrum with a baptistry in its floor, a three-sided gallery supported by iron columns painted in two shades of green and a coved ceiling formed into moulded panels. An experienced firm from Abergavenny was responsible for the carving executed in various styles, and local craftsmen also ensured that the standard of the craftsmanship throughout was of a very high order. An American organ was placed in front of the communion pew, and this was replaced in 1924 by a pipe organ, built by Derrick Rothwell, Harrow, Middlesex, and installed in memory of the eleven members killed in the 1914-18 war: their names and that of the member killed in the 1939-45 war appear on brass plates attached to the organ case.

In 1999 a Millennium Project was established to convert the schoolroom so as to provide a large room for formal worship and other meetings; a small committee room and cloakroom, and a new modern kitchen and toilet facilities.

In 2008 dry and wet rot were discovered in the roof timber. A report was commissioned by Bethel's architect so as to establish the extent of the problem and the remedial action required. At the end of 2010, having received financial support from a number of public bodies and charitable organisations work commenced to remove the affected roof timbers and to replace the roof slates. Affected areas of the ceiling, coving and wall rendering were stripped and moulds of ornate corbels, covings and ceiling decoration were prepared from the originals and casts made to replace damaged features. The work was completed in May 2011.

Present position: Minister: Rev. Judith Morris; 48 members; Sunday services: 10.00 a.m., 2.30 or 5.00 p.m., monthly Communion Service and Fellowship Meeting.
Further reading: B.G. Owens, *Bethel Aberystwyth 1788-1889, Canmlwyddiant Tŷ-Cwrdd a Threm ar Ganrif* (1989); *Bethel Welsh Baptist Chapel Aberystwyth, Architectural and Structural Charactersitics of interest* (n.d.); *Bethel Welsh Baptist Chapel Aberystwyth, The Rothwell Pipe Organ* (n.d.).

52. ABERYSTWYTH, Capel y Morfa (Pw)

OS: SN 588 817

Capel y Morfa church was formed in 1989 following the union of Seilo and Salem churches on the site of Salem. Tabernacl, the oldest Calvinistic Methodist chapel in Aberystwyth, together with its branch of Ebenezer, Penparcau, united with Capel y Morfa in 2001.

The background to the establishment of Seilo was the missionary zeal of Tabernacl church, and 300-400 members left Tabernacl voluntarily in 1863 to form Seilo. The fourth Tabernacl chapel on the site was designed by Richard Owens, Liverpool in the 'Italo-Lombard' style and opened in 1880. The church closed in 2001 and though intended to be converted into flats, the building was sadly burned and then demolished in July 2008: fortunately the historic organ, built by Harrison & Harrison had been removed before the fire to Southsea where it will eventually be located in the St. Jude's Anglican church; and the war memorial made by Mario Rutelli, the Italian sculptor survived the fire. Additions to the Seilo chapel, including two towers, were designed by J.P. Seddon, and then significant changes were made before celebrating the chapel's centenary in 1963, when a modern façade was designed by R. Emrys Bonsall and Dewi Prys Thomas. Following the formation of Capel y Morfa, Seilo was demolished and the organ, associated with Charles Clements, the renowned organist, was transported to Sierra Leone and installed in the St George's Cathedral Church at Freetown.

Salem was established following a dispute in Seilo during the period 1891-93, and was opened in 1895 in Portland Street. The architect was T.E. Morgan, who designed Bethel (see 51, Aberystwyth, Bethel) and the builder David Lloyd, Penglais Road who built houses on that road and along Caradog Road, in the town, and also Trefechan Bridge. The architect's intention was to design a chapel with 400 seats, and with an arch behind the pulpit which could accommodate an organ in the future. The façade was to be of rockwork and Grinshill sandstone dressing, the windows Gothic and cathedral glass, and the seats were to be of pitch pine. The rectangular building had a gallery in the rear, and the pointed arch, latticed pattern was a feature in the pulpit, the rear of the *sêt fawr* and in the ironwork of the gallery front. It was soon realised that the chapel was too small, and in 1898 David Lloyd built a schoolroom at the rear of the chapel. This was designed by John Arthur Jones, who was a member of Salem. He presented a number of other suggestions, and in 1906, at a cost of £1,350, two transepts were added, one on each side of the *sêt fawr*, a heating system was provided, and an organ, built by Abbot & Smith, Leeds, under the direction of Stephen Evans, was installed.

Following the formation of Capel y Morfa, further substantial changes were made in 1993. A low platform was introduced, on which were placed a communion table and lectern, instead of the *sêt fawr*, and this ensures greater flexibility in services. One permanent element was the use of the pointed arch motif in the lectern which corresponds to the traditional patterns in the pulpit and gallery front.

The demolition of Seilo resulted in the opening in 2005, on part of the site, of Y Morlan, Faith and Culture Centre, with the objective of creating a bridge between church and society. A full programme of events is organised, the facilities are widely used by a wide range of groups, and some of the church meetings and activities are held here.

Present position: Minister, Rev. Eifion Roberts, 382 members, 60 children, Sunday services, 10.00 a.m. with Sunday school [children and adults], and 6.00 p.m.; weekly children's club, prayer and coffee circle, devotional meeting, youth club, tapestry group, fortnightly cultural society.

Further reading: F.Wynn Jones, *Canmlwydd Siloh Aberystwyth* (1963); Moelwyn I Williams, *Y Tabernacl Aberystwyth, 1785-1985* (1985). Brynley F. Roberts, *Cyfannu'r Rhwyg, Hanes Eglwys Salem, Aberystwyth 1893-1988* (1995).

Website: www.capelymorfa.org

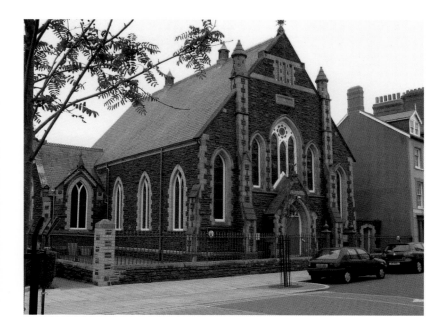

53. ABERYSTWYTH, Seion (I)

OS: SN 583 817

The present chapel was built in Baker Street in 1878. It was known as 'Baker Street' until 1987 when the name of the original Independent chapel, 'Seion', was adopted at the same time as the centenary of the chapel was celebrated. The Rev. Azariah Shadrach was the minister of the small Independent chapels in Tal-y-bont and Llanbadarn Fawr before the establishment in 1819 of the church named 'Seion' and located in Penmaes-glas in Aberystwyth. Seion chapel was used occasionally by the church before it was sold to the Apostolic Church in 1955, and is now the Merched y Wawr Centre. In 1851, 150 free seats were provided and 320 other seats. On 30 March 152 were present in the morning service and 238 in the evening.

Steps were taken to build a new chapel soon after the Rev. Job Miles commenced on his ministry in 1873. A significant influence was the establishment of the University College of Wales in 1872 and there has been a close connection between the chapel and the university over the years. Richard Owens, Liverpool was appointed as the architect, and Thomas Jones, Dolau near Bow Street the builder. The new chapel, costing £4,400, was opened on 1 May, 1878, with the *Cambrian News* describing it as the most handsome of all the town's chapels. The chapel has a two-storey pedimented façade with large paired pilasters. The interior has a curved gallery on thin columns with a thin upper arcade. The ceiling is ribbed and the gallery front has long horizontal panels. Seion has an extensive pulpit and *sêt fawr* with three eisteddfod chairs presented in memory of various ministers by T.E. Nicholas (Niclas y Glais), the poet, minister of religion and Communist Party supporter. The vestry under the chapel contains a number of rooms. The organ, designed by Mr. Leah, organist of the English Congregational Church, Portland Street and built by Messrs. Norman & Beard, was installed in 1903 at a cost of £640 and has been renovated on several occasions. Accompaniment is occasionally provided by an orchestra, and the chapel also has a female choir.

The chapel has been renovated and repainted several times, and in 1977 the roof and window frames were renewed, while the chapel was repainted at a cost of more than £2,000. A programme of maintenance work is regularly undertaken, and the organ pedals were recently renovated.

Present position: Minister, Rev. Andrew Lenny; 226 members, 40 children; Sunday services 10 a.m. and 6.00 p.m.; weekly devotional meeting, cultural society 2-3 per month, monthly coffee mornings.
Further reading: E.D. Jones, *Trem ar Ganrif, yn hanes Eglwys Gynulleidfaol Baker Street, Aberystwyth* (1978).

54. ABERYSTWYTH, St. Paul's Methodist Centre (Me/w)

OS. SN 584 820

The St Paul Methodist Centre, standing on the corner of Queen's Road and Bath Street, on the site of the former English Methodist Church, was opened in 1992. Providing facilities for both English-language and Welsh-language Wesleyan Methodist congregations to worship under the same roof, this represents the only new purpose-built place of worship in the middle of the town of Aberystwyth to be opened during the twentieth century. The English church forms part of the Ceredigion Circuit, and the Welsh church part of Cylchdaith Cymru. The first Welsh-language Wesleyan Methodist chapel, named Salem, had been erected in a courtyard off Queen Street before 1810 and rebuilt in 1842. Provision for the few English speakers was initially made in this church which at a later stage assisted in the establishment of a separate English cause. The first English-language Wesleyan Methodist chapel to be constructed in Aberystwyth was built in Alexandra Road in 1844. This building is at present used by the Salvation Army, with Sunday services held at 10.30 and 6.00, with weekly Bible study, prayer meeting, and over-60s meeting, and a students' fellowship during term-time.

The 1851 Census recorded that the Welsh-language chapel contained 180 free seats, 540 others and standing room for another 500. On 30 March 281 were present in the morning service, 260 scholars in the afternoon and 464 in the evening service. The English-language chapel had 166 free seats with standing room for another 90, and on 30 March 15 were present in the morning service with seven scholars in the Sunday School, and 16 in the evening service and six scholars. An additional note referred to the "general congregation" being larger in the summer "arising from the influx of Visitors".

A new English Methodist Church was opened in Queen's Road in 1870 with seating for 450 but with only 60 members. Ten years later, the Welsh Wesleyan Methodists proceeded to build the imposing St. Paul's chapel in Great Darkgate Street, designed by Walter Thomas, Liverpool at a cost of £5,900. The front was built of blue-grey Llanddewi Brefi stone with beige Stourton sandstone dressings. Three central bays with full length Corinthian columns were surrounded by two winged bays with large arched windows to each floor. A new English Methodist Church was built at Penparcau in 1954. By the late-twentieth century the physical condition of both the English and Welsh language chapels in the town was causing concern, and it was resolved to unite the two churches. The St.Paul's chapel was sold and is at present open as the Academy public house: several distinctive features of its history as a chapel have been retained including the pulpit, organ pipes and wall panels inscribed with the Ten Commandments and The Lord's Prayer.

Cadw was persuaded to withdraw the restriction on demolishing the English chapel, and a new building was constructed on the same site, designed by the

Cornfield, Crook and Walsh firm. The architects sought to make the best possible use of the corner site, with a wide entrance in an octagonal building. The absence of steps, with the ground floor on street level, and the installation of a lift to the first floor provides ease of access for the disabled. The guiding principle was to ensure maximum flexibility and multi-purpose usage. There is no fixed furniture in the main worship hall, and adjoining it is a spacious concourse which may be opened into the main hall if this should be necessary. The hall and concourse are served by a kitchen, and opportunities are provided for social gatherings after the service. A crèche, church office and minister's room are also located on the ground floor. An octagonal hall used for worship and 'quiet activities' occupies the upper floor of the two-storied wing. Several smaller rooms are used for junior church and various other meetings.

By the time that the building was constructed the English-language church was much stronger than the Welsh one, and one of the guiding principles when designing the building was to build a bridge between the two language groups, respecting both languages. It was appreciated that it would be preferable to hold separate rather than bilingual services, and normally on Sunday English services are held in the ground floor hall, and the Welsh ones in the first floor hall. Another original intention, to provide a service for the community, and promote Christian activities in the community, has also been fulfilled in that there has been a constant demand for the use of rooms by outside bodies, with the coffee bar open every day.

Present position: Minister, Rev. Dr. David Easton; English Church, 120 members, Welsh Church, 35 members, 20 children; Sunday services, English service 10.30 a.m. (Creche and Junior Church) and two services at 6.00, of which one, during University term-time, is a modern service with a live band and an interactive format; shared services with Holy Trinity Church on alternate months; Welsh service 10.30 a.m. Activities include house groups, Bible studies, prayer and singing groups, weekends away, retreats and courses.

Further reading: *Capel Local information Leaflet*, 9, Methodism in Aberystwyth; Glyn Tegai Hughes, 'Welsh-speaking Methodism' in *Methodism in Wales, A Short History of the Wesley Tradition*, ed. Lionel Madden (2003).

Website: www.aber.uk.net/methodist/stpauls

55. SOAR Y MYNYDD (Pw)

OS: SN 785 532

One of the strangest aspects of the religious situation in Wales today is that large congregations are attracted in the summer months to one of the remotest areas of Wales, located approximately ten miles from Tregaron and in an area which has suffered severely from depopulation. The continuing appeal of Soar y Mynydd was expressed by R.S. Thomas who described it as 'The Chapel of the Soul' and the type of place where 'the soul of the true Welshman is formed'.

Howel Harris and Williams Williams, Pantycelyn visited this area in the eighteenth century. In 1822 the chapel was built beside the Camddwr river in the parish of Llanddewi Brefi on land belonging to John Jones's Nantllwyd farm. His descendants included the evangelical preacher, the Rev. Dr. Martin Lloyd Jones and also John Crowter-Jones, Devon, who provided me with much of the early history of the chapel.

John Jones paid for building the chapel but practical help was provided by local inhabitants in transporting from Aberaeron building material in carts and on horseback. One of the witnesses to the 999- year lease provided by John Jones, dated 18 December 1822, was the Rev. Ebenezer Richard, father of the Rev. Henry Richard, the political reformer and Member of Parliament for Merthyr Tydfil known as 'the Member for Wales'. The 1851 Census recorded that there were 30 free seats and 126 others in the chapel, and that on 30 March there were present about 50 in the morning service but that the average was about 100.

The chapel and chapel house are under the same roof, with nearby the stable where the horses of the preacher and congregation would be housed, and a well-tended graveyard. The whitewashed chapel is in an excellent condition, with the inside and outside having been painted. On one wall there are two arched windows, and on the other four doors, with the pulpit between the doors. The slightly-raked box pews are a typical feature of Ceredigion chapels in the first half of the nineteenth century. The pulpit was added later in the nineteenth century, and on the wall behind may be seen the words 'Duw Cariad Yw' ['God is Love']. There is no electricity in the chapel, and services are only held in the summer months. There has been very little change to the building or the furniture over the years. In 1983 a new pulpit chair was made by Dafydd Davies, a skilled carpenter, in memory of John Hughes Williams, Brynambor, who had been murdered in his home. The wooden floor was re-set in 1993.

The usual arrangements for many years was for the members who lived in the upland farms to journey to the chapel on horseback, as also would the preacher who often arrived in the locality on the Saturday evening, and be accommodated in one of the farms or in Tregaron or Llanddewi Brefi.

The Sunday service was held at 10.30 a.m. until 1937, but at present the service

is held in the afternoon with a full programme of services arranged in the summer months and well-known preachers attracting large congregations. There is frequently not enough room in the chapel, especially when bus-loads arrive, and a loudspeaker has to be used for the benefit of those who cannot gain entry to the chapel.

The membership has declined in recent years: in 1944 there were 44 members: and the chapel has suffered from rural depopulation and the damaging effects of tree-planting on an extensive scale. This led to doubts being expressed with regard to the future of the chapel, but the threat was averted and the favourable comments in the 'Visitors' Book, and the well-attended Sunday services justify the decision to continue using the chapel.

Present position: 19 members, Sunday services, 2.00 p.m. from May until October, Anniversary services on last Sunday in August, 2.00 and 5.00 p.m. and Thanksgiving Service on last Sunday of season.
Further reading: W.J. Gruffydd, *Tua Soar* (1994).

56. LLANGEITHO, Capel Gwynfil (Pw)

OS: SN 620 958

This was one of the main centres of Calvinistic Methodists in Wales in the eighteenth century on the basis of its association with Daniel Rowland, the eloquent preacher who is reputed to have attracted thousands to Llangeitho every month on Communion Sunday. The white marble statue of him on a high stone pedestal, made in 1883 by Edward Griffith, Chester at a cost of £600, stands near the chapel.

The first chapel was built in 1756 by Daniel Rowland when he was a curate at Llangeitho on land belonging to Peter Davies, his brother-in-law. Another chapel was built on the same plot of land in 1760, and a third chapel in 1764 following the Revival of 1762, after he had been deprived of his curacy. The first chapel had been built of earthen walls and a thatched roof, and measured 30 feet long by 18 feet wide. The third chapel was larger, measuring 45 feet square with a double roof and line of four stone pillars. A few seats were available for women and children, and these were removed when many were present in a service. The pulpit was entered from outside the chapel and Daniel Rowland was said to have allowed the congregation to sing hymns for some time before he appeared in the pulpit. The communion table was lowered on pulleys. The chapel had four doors, one of which was known as '*drws yr allor*' [the altar door] through which the minister would return to the chapel on Communion Sunday after he had departed through the door behind the pulpit. The flagstones in the lobby are believed to have survived from the 1764 chapel.

The present chapel was built in 1813-15 and remodelled in 1861-63 by John Lumley, Aberystwyth. The 1813-15 building measured 60 feet by 36 feet and the cost of £2,000 was exceptionally high for a rural chapel in this period. It contained a gallery but no pews in the centre ground floor. The 1851 Census recorded that there were 96 free seats, 332 others and space for 120 to stand in the chapel. Present on 30 March were 490 in the morning service, 164 scholars in the afternoon and 270 in the evening service.

Llangeitho had a tradition of experiencing revivals, with seven revivals during the time of Daniel Rowland. The Revival of 1859 had a considerable impact on Llangeitho, as also on other areas of Ceredigion, and one consequence was the need for the extension of the chapel in 1861-63. The front was now altered to ensure entry through the pine end, and the greater part of the interior, with the possible exception of the deep coved ceiling and the centre rose, which may date from 1813-15, belongs to the 1861-3 period. Significant features include a high platform pulpit with steps on each side, a plain *sêt fawr*, grained panelled box pews, raked gallery pews, and a three-sided gallery, with plain, flat panels which has been placed on two plain iron columns. The door behind the pulpit reminds one of the entry to the pulpit during the time of Daniel Rowland. A detailed description of the Sunday arrangements associated with the chapel is presented in T.I. Ellis's biography of J.H. Davies, Principal of the University College of Wales, Aberystwyth, who, as a child, had travelled in a trap with other members of the Cwrt-mawr family from their home to the chapel.

The chapel has been listed Grade 2* by Cadw on account of its historical association with Daniel Rowland, and as an exceptionally-large chapel built in 1813-15 with a fine interior dating from 1861-63. Also listed Grade 2 are the statue, chapel house and related buildings.

Present position: No minister, 53 members, Sunday service, 2.00 or 5.00 p.m.
Further reading: J. Evans, *Hanes Methodistiaeth De Aberteifi* (1904); T.I. Ellis, *John Humphries Davies (1871-1926)* (1963); Eifion Evans, *Daniel Rowland and the Great Evangelical Awakening in Wales* (1985).

57. LAMPETER, Brondeifi (U)

OS: SN 582 478

Brondeifi was established as a daughter house of Caeronnen, which, founded in 1654 on a local farm as a Presbyterian chapel, became an Unitarian cause in the 1840s. The first Brondeifi chapel, on a site donated by a local benefactor, was opened in July 1876. It seated about 400 people at a cost of approximately £1,000 with the debt soon cleared. Severe problems were experienced with this building which had to be taken down and replaced by a new building on the site in 1904. The cost of this work was £1,899 and the total expenditure amounted to slightly over £2,043. 1,164 families were claimed to have contributed to the expenditure, which included a payment of £74 to the architect, and the debt was immediately cleared. An illustrated address was presented to the Rev Rees Cribyn Jones, the first minister at the time of his retirement in 1915 and may be seen in the chapel today. He is commemorated by a memorial stone placed in the chapel in 1930; and another memorial stone, placed in 1968, commemorated his successor, the Rev. T. Oswald Williams and his wife. Another notable feature in the chapel is John Petts's stained glass window in memory of Tecwyn Williams who died in Northern Ireland whilst serving with the Royal Regiment of Wales.

In 1996 a new vestry was opened with vastly improved facilities following the demolition of the old one in the previous year. The vestry was designed by the Owen Davies Partnership, Aberystwyth and the building was constructed by J. and E. Woodworks, with a considerable amount of work undertaken by local volunteers. Financial support was received from a number of bodies, including Ceredigion County Council, the Dyfed Churches Fund, and the Lottery Arts Fund, but a substantial sum was also raised by the chapel itself.

From 1876 to the present day, Brondeifi has been served by only three ministers: the Rev. Rees Cribyn Jones (1876-1915); the Rev. T. Oswald Williams (1915 -1965), and the Rev. D.J. Goronwy Evans, 1964 to the present.

Present position: Minister: D.J. Goronwy Evans, 170 members, 25 children; Sunday service, with Sunday school, 10.00 a.m. or 2.00 p.m.

Further reading: D.J. Goronwy Evans, *Hanes Eglwys Undodaidd Brondeifi Llanbedr Pont Steffan, 1874-1974* (1974); D.J. Goronwy Evans (gol,), *Capel Undodaidd Brondeifi, Llanbedr Pont Steffan* (2008); *Capel Local Information Leaflet, 39: Lampeter* (2011).

Brondeifi, on the outskirts of Lampeter (*above*) and Shiloh, in the town centre (*right*)

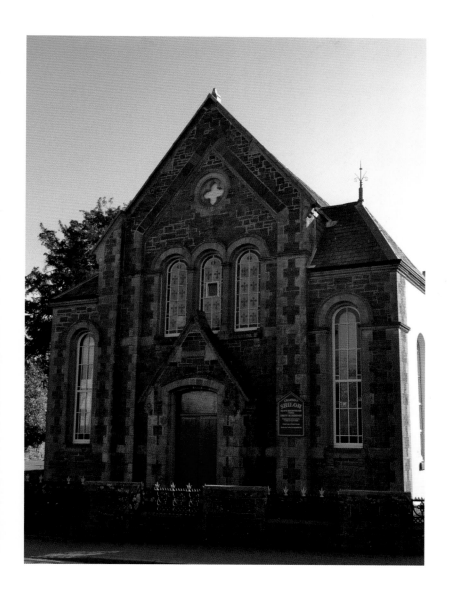

58. LAMPETER, Shiloh (P)

OS: SN 574 481

The early history of the cause may be traced to 1741 when 24 members belonged to a society (*seiat*) meeting in Lampeter, and by 1744 the number had increased to 29. They encountered some opposition and in 1743 a meeting was disrupted by a justice of the peace and his servants who took away as a prisoner one of the members who was at the time offering a prayer. Howel Harris is reported to have preached on a stone in the middle of the town, and Daniel Rowland was associated with the society, and to have supervised the chapel which had been built at Creigiau, located in Cwm-ann at the turning of the road to Cellan. The Tabernacl chapel was built in the town of Lampeter, in High Street, in 1806. The 1851 Census recorded that there were in the chapel 90 free seats, 288 others and room for 120 to stand, and that the congregations on 30 March amounted to 220 in the morning, with 95 scholars in the Sunday School, and 200 in the evening service.

Land for a new chapel was purchased for £450 in 1873, and Shiloh chapel was opened in June 1874. Whilst Hall Caine, Liverpool, was named as the architect, Richard Owens was also probably involved as he was paid on 5 June 1874 a fee of £50. Many farmers were among the early members, and they assisted in carrying building material for the new chapel. The cost of the new chapel was in the region of £2,000, and nearly £1,400 was collected locally with a contribution of £200 from the County Presbytery. Difficulty was experienced in selling the old chapel and chapel house, but the chapel was eventually sold for £170 and the chapel house for £225. Items from the former chapel incorporated in Shiloh included the stone on the front wall, bearing the name 'Tabernacl' and the year of its construction, '1806', which was placed on the wall of the new vestry; and the clock in Tabernacl placed behind the pulpit of Shiloh, and then moved to the front of the gallery in 1892. Also, the old communion cup, jug and plates continued to be used in Shiloh until the acquisition of individual communion cups. To meet the debt, annual preaching services were held, and by 2 August 1890 the debt had been cleared. The surplus collected enabled the purchase of an organ in the following year despite initial opposition from some of the members. This organ was replaced by a pipe organ installed in 1940. The purchase of additional plots of land in 1903 and in 1912 enabled the building in 1913 of a new vestry at a cost of £594. Water pipes were installed to heat the chapel, and it was decided to allow free access to the pews, and thereby terminate the regulations enforced since 1872.

Since the opening of Shiloh improvements have regularly been made to the chapel which has been repainted several times. It was re-roofed in 1950 and 1962, new equipment to heat the chapel was installed in 1968 and the boiler adapted for the use of oil instead of coal. The chapel buildings are now heated by two gas boilers. Extensive renovations during the past fifteen years have included the provision of insulation, and a new ceiling and windows. The damage caused by a storm in late-2010 has been repaired and the chapel has been recently re-painted. A photograph of the chapel, before the removal of its spire, appeared in the *Capel Newsletter*, 38 (Autumn 2001).

Substantial sums have been raised for charity projects aimed at assisting blind children in Africa and children in Brazil.

Present position: No minister, following recent retirement of Rev.J. Elwyn Jenkins (pastorate shared with Soar Independent Church), 65 members, Sunday service, 10.00 a.m., alternate Sundays with Soar.

Further reading: D.D. Richards a J.Trefor Lloyd, *Canlwyddiant Eglwys Shiloh: Llanbedr Pont Steffan 1874-1974* (1974); *Capel Local Information Leaflet, 39: Lampeter* (2011).

59 LAMPETER, Soar (I)

OS: SN 577 480

This church had its origins in the activities of a group of Dissenters meeting in the mid-seventeenth century at Cilgwyn Isaf farm, near Llangybi, which resulted in the establishment of a number of chapels in central Ceredigion.

Members of the Independent church which had evolved at Cilgwyn, Llangybi and who resided in Lampeter held services in the town in 1831. They met in an old brewery, located near Harford Square, for which they paid £5 a year, and where a pulpit and some seating had been placed. A Sunday school was established but soon discontinued and very little progress was made in the early years. David Davies, a schoolmaster at Cellan, was ordained the minister in 1841, when there were 45 members and it was realised that the old brewery was too small. Land was offered by the local squire, J.S. Harford, Falcondale, for a new chapel on the Commons on condition that the members would support him at a parliamentary election. The land measured 32' by 24' and the cost of the chapel was £160. Contributions were received from the county's churches and the debt had been cleared by 1850 when the membership had increased to 120. The chapel had originally only comprised a few pews surrounding the pulpit, with some of the congregation required to stand but the chapel was later extended with the addition of a gallery and pews provided throughout the chapel.

In 1851 there were 180 free seats, 36 others and room for 150 to stand. On 30 March 1851, 53 were present in the Sunday school held in the morning, 350 in the afternoon service and 150 in the evening service. The 1859 Revival resulted in 50 persons admitted to membership on one Sunday, 98 new members were added during this year and the minister's stipend was increased from £5 to £27. The church was evidently in a flourishing state and, following the Rev. David Davies's death in 1871, and the induction as minister of the Rev. John Thomas in 1872, a new chapel was opened in 1873. This cost £700 and special services were held in 1881 to celebrate the clearance of the debt. In 1896 the chapel was extended and renovated at a cost of £1,000 which was repaid by 1901. The purchase of two houses and gardens for £200 in 1900 had enabled the building of a vestry. A pipe organ was purchased for £250 in 1904, and in 1920 Victoria, an inn near to the chapel was bought for £525, and adapted for use as a home for the chapel caretaker.

At the time of the induction as minister of the Rev. T Eirug Davies in 1927 the chapel was painted, which, together with the provision of electric heating and lighting, cost £ 400. This sum was soon paid, and a major expenditure was incurred in 1931 with the building of a new vestry to celebrate the 100th anniversary of the cause at a total cost of over £1,400. Extensive renovation-work has been completed in recent years, but a considerable amount of work requires to be undertaken, especially to remedy the problem of dampness.

An unusual feature here is that the Greek Orthodox Church in Lampeter holds a service every Sunday morning in the vestry.

Present position: No minister since recent retirement of Rev. J. Elwyn Jenkins (pastorate shared with Shiloh Presbyterian Church); 107 members; Sunday service, 10 a.m. alternate Sundays with Siloh.

Further reading: T. Eirug Davies, *Trem ar ganmlwydd Eglwys Soar, Llanbedr, 1831-1931* (1931)); *Capel Local Information Leaflet, 39:* Lampeter (2011).

60. NEUADD-LWYD (I)

SO: SN 474 596

Neuadd-lwyd chapel stands above the main road from Lampeter to Aberaeron, near to the village of Ciliau Aeron. The first chapel, built in 1746 as a branch of the Ciliau Aeron church, was renewed on several occasions. In 1851 there were 72 free seats, 390 others and space for 70 to stand. On Sunday morning, 30 March there were present 367, together with 165 scholars. No statistics were provided for an evening service, but the average attendance was stated to be 500 in the morning with 165 scholars, and 600 in the evening with 200 scholars. The present chapel was built in 1906, designed by David Davies, and had a distinctive pilastered façade with a major arch placed over arched windows.

The monument outside the chapel, unveiled in 1914, commemorates the Rev. Thomas Phillips, who had been responsible for 30 years for the church and academy at Neuadd-lwyd, established in 1810, and who was buried in the graveyard; and also early nineteenth-century ministers and missionaries to Madagascar. The students at Neuadd-lwyd included David Jones and Thomas Bevan, the earliest missionaries to Madagascar. They had travelled there in 1818, but Thomas Bevan and his wife, and also David Jones, had died within a year. David Jones established schools in Madagascar, and translated the Bible into the Malagasy language. He died in Mauritius in 1841 but his work ensured that Neuadd-lwyd would be considered the mother-church of Madagascar Protestants.

Present position: No minister, 73 members, Sunday services, 10.30 a.m. or 2 p.m.

61. LLWYNRHYDOWEN (U)

OS: SN 444 452

There are two 'Llwynrhydowen' chapels today in the village of Rhydowen: the one on the junction of the A475 and B4459 roads, and the 'new' one beside the road leading to Pont-siân. The original chapel was built in 1733, some 300 meters to the south-east of the later 'old chapel, as a result of the foundation of the Wernhir church in 1726, and this was the first chapel to be built in Wales on the basis of Arminian theology. Jenkin Jones, the first minister, had been educated at the Carmarthen Academy, and his descendant was Frank Lloyd Wright (1867-1959), considered to be America's greatest ever architect. When Jenkin Jones died the Llwynrhyowen congregation was estimated to number 400. He was succeeded by his nephew, David Lloyd, who translated several devotional works into the Welsh language, and by Dafydd Davies, Castell Hywel, who established a strong tradition of religious and political radicalism in the area. A number of his friends among contemporary leading Arians, including Iolo Morganwg, Jac Glan-y-gors, Tomos Glyn Cothi and Dr. Richard Price attended services here. Christmas Evans was a member of Llwynrhydowen before he joined the Baptists and preached his first sermon here.

Continual growth resulted in the chapel being extended in 1754. In 1791 another chapel was built on the present site and this was extended in 1834 and renovated in 1862. This is a large rubble stone chapel with a lateral façade and arched openings. The interior has a painted grained gallery supported on thin iron columns with vertical panels, a small platform pulpit with panelled front, plain pews and a *sêt fawr*.

By the middle of the nineteenth century, a number of Unitarian churches had been established in the area between Llandysul, Lampeter and Aberaeron, known as 'Y *Smotyn Du*' ['The Black Spot']. The 1851 Census recorded an attendance of 'about 500' on 30 March of that year, but there were only 42 free seats for the congregation. William Thomas, 'Gwilym Marles', whose name was inherited by his descendant, the poet Dylan Marles Thomas, was inducted as minister in 1860. Following a dispute with John Davies Lloyd, the squire of the local Alltyrodyn estate, who had resented the fiery sermons preached by the radical minister of Llwynrhydowen, and the refusal of the members to support the Tory candidate at the 1868 election, the congregation was evicted from the chapel. A wooden building in the village was used by the congregation before a 'new' chapel was opened in 1879, with funds collected from various areas of Britain. Behind the pulpit there has been placed in a glass case the hammer and trowel used when the foundation stone was laid on 27 June 1878. Also behind the pulpit, on the rear wall there are a number of memorial tablets commemorating several leaders and ministers of the church. This chapel, designed by Watkin Davies, Llandysul, was built of rock-faced Llanddewi Brefi grey stone with beige sandstone dressings. The gabled front has a giant arch and three arched windows, and inside there is a single gallery on fluted iron columns and a coved ceiling.

Before the 'new' chapel was opened, John Davies Lloyd had died and his sister returned possession to the congregation of the 'old chapel', which was used as a schoolroom and library for many years. In 2008, it was acquired by the Welsh Religious Buildings Trust, which will be responsible for the maintenance of the chapel, whose doors were opened to the public in September 2009 and September 2011 as part of the Open Doors European Heritage Day organised by the Civic Trust for Wales.

The 'old 'chapel has been listed Grade 2* by Cadw because of its historical importance in Unitarian history and because it is an unrestored chapel of late-Georgian character. The 'new' chapel has been listed Grade 2.

Present position: Minister, Rev. Wyn Thomas, 47 members; Sunday service, with discussion group, 1.30 or 3.00 p.m.
Further reading: Aubrey J. Martin, *Hanes Llwynrhydowen* (1977); David R. Barnes, *People of Seion* (1995), and 'Yr Hen Gapel, Llwynrhydowen' in *Welsh Religious Buildings Trust, Newsletter*, 3 (2009).

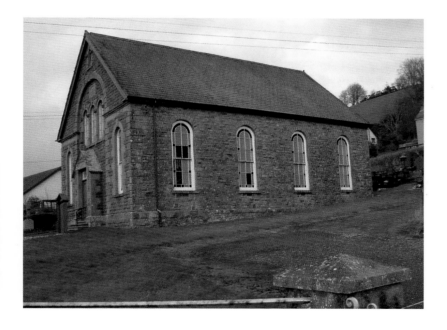

62. RHYDLEWIS, Hawen (I)

OS: SN 346 468

The cause is believed to have commenced in 1747 by members who left Drewen, founded ten years earlier, because of a theological dispute. They met in a house located near to the present chapel. In spite of considering bringing the cause to an end, they built in 1769 a chapel at 'Rhydhawen', again near to the present chapel. This was extended in 1790, and following revivals in the period 1790-1810, the chapel was rebuilt in 1811. The following year it was licensed as a place of worship and although the document refers to a meeting house by the name of 'Rhydmorva' in the parish of 'Troedyroyr' it is evident that this was a lapse and that the word 'Rhydhawen' was intended.

The first minister was the Rev. Benjamin Evans who was also the minister of Trewen. A staunch Calvinist, he succeeded in removing all traces of the Arminian tendencies which had been responsible for the decision to worship in Rhydlewis. A Sunday school was held here during his ministry, and it has been suggested that this was where the Welsh Sunday school originated. The wording on the gravestone of Nathaniel Griffiths, in the graveyard, contains a reference to him as one of the main founders of the Sunday school movement in Wales. The minister died in 1821 and was buried under the pulpit in the chapel, with a slab of marble placed behind the pulpit in his memory. When the chapel was rebuilt in 1838, and assumed its present form, it was moved further away from the road, and the gravestone now stands outside the chapel, between the two external doors.

The 1851 Census stated there were about 400 seats, all free, and on 30 March 200 scholars were present in the morning, 361 attended the afternoon 'sermon', and 198 the evening 'prayer'. The appended note included the comment that a large burial ground belonged to the chapel, 'and all free property'. The chapel was renovated in 1878, and in 1900 a large vestry was built at a cost of £450: this has been on sale for some time. A new Imperial organ was installed in 1959, and Ted Morgan was the guest organist at the meeting held to consecrate the organ. A keyboard has been used since about 1997.

The Rev. David Adams (1845-1923), the author of theological works, was inducted as minister in 1878, and later adopted the bardic name 'Hawen' in memory of his first pastorate. He was severely satirised by Caradoc Evans, who was brought up in Rhydlewis. It is possible that his failure to secure a post at the local school was responsible for the anger of Caradoc Evans, who apparently based upon the minister the characters 'Respected Davydd Bern-Davydd' and the 'Respected Joshia Bryn-Bevan', and referred to "being brought up amongst grinding poverty, always with the background of sanctimonious hymn-singing and hypocrisy". Former members of the church include the popular novelist Elizabeth Mary Jones (Moelona), the author of *Teulu Bach Nantoer* (1913), and John Newton Crowther, the

poet and hymnist, a Yorkshireman who learned Welsh and was headmaster of Rhydlewis school.

Hawen forms part of a pastorate which also includes the six chapels of Glynarthen, Bryngwenith, Capel-y-Wig, Pantycrugiau, Pisgah and Brynmoriah, Recent developments also include the installation of two new double doors at the chapel, the improvement to the path leading through the graveyard, and the sale of two cottages.

Present position: Minister, Rev. Carys Ann; 59 members, Sunday service at either 10.30 a.m., 1.30 or 3.00 p.m.

Further reading: *Eglwys Annibynnol Hawen Ceredigion 1774-1997* (1997); *Fury Never Leaves Us, A Miscellany of Caradoc Evans*, ed. John Harris (1985); Caradoc Evans, *My People*, introd. John Harris (1987).

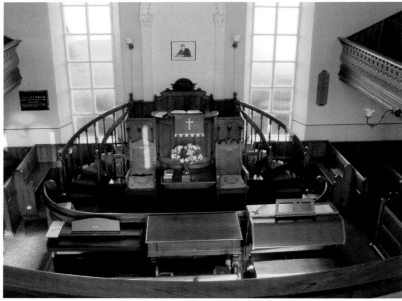

63. BLAENANNERCH (Pw)

OS: SN 247 491

This chapel is largely associated with Evan Roberts's intense religious experience which represented one of the most significant events of the 1904-05 Revival. Evan Roberts was a 26-year old student at a school in Newcastle Emlyn whilst he was a candidate for the ministry with the Calvinistic Methodists. At a meeting held at Blaenannerch chapel on 29 September 1904 the Rev. M.P. Morgan, minister of Blaenannerch recalled that when Seth Joshua was in the middle of a fervent prayer beseeching God to bend him, he heard a commotion, and when he opened his eyes he saw Evan Roberts on his knees and crying repeatedly '*Plyg mi*' ['Bend me']. In another memorable service at the chapel, on 14 March 1905, Evan Roberts named a person in the congregation who was restricting him. The Rev. M.P. Morgan was one of the leaders of a campaign in London in May, 1905. He served as minister of Blaenannerch for 64 years, was buried here and his gravestone is located in front of the chapel.

The first chapel was built here in 1794 and was extended in 1808. The chapel was rebuilt in 1838 and has a stone lateral façade with arched windows. A gravestone records that Dorothy Davies, who died on 2 October 1847, was the first person to be buried in the graveyard. On 30 March 1851, 190 scholars were present in the Sunday school, 332 attended the afternoon service and 288 the evening service. There were 42 free seats and 294 others. The chapel was remodelled in 1896 by James Jones, Rhydlewis, when windows which are typical features of this period were installed, as also was the theatrical gallery with ironwork by W. Macfarlane of Glasgow, whose name appears on the columns. A plaque in the pew where Evan Roberts had sat in the memorable 1904 service commemorates his remarkable experience, and a photograph of Evan Roberts has been placed behind the pulpit. Two eisteddfod chairs in the *sêt fawr* had previously been kept at Tanygroes chapel.

A number of events held here in 2004 to celebrate the centenary of the Revival included special services and party for the pastorate, concert, lectures, day school organised by the Ceredigion Historical Society, a hymn-singing television programme, and a Flower Festival on the theme of 'Darlunio'r Diwygiad' ['Illustrating the Revival'].

Renovation-work costing a sum of £80,000 was undertaken on the chapel and manse in 2008.

Present position: Minister; Rev. Llunos Mai Gordon; 63 members, seven children; Sunday service, 10.30 a.m.
Further reading: Mair Davies, *Hanes Eglwys Bresbyteraidd Cymru, Blaenannerch 1794-1994* (1994).

64. CARDIGAN, Bethania (Bw)

OS: SN 179 462

Churches, such as Cilfowyr (1704) (see 65, Cilfowyr) had been established in the surrounding area in the early-eighteenth century, and it is recorded that Baptists resided in the town of Cardigan in the mid-eighteenth century. The first chapel in the town was built in 1775-76 in Pen-dre and this was described as a large and convenient chapel. The first minister was the Rev. William Williams, the minister of Ebeneser, Dyfed, who had moved to live in the town shortly before the opening of the chapel. He served as minister of Bethania until his death in 1799, and during this period Bethania was a branch of Ebeneser. Bethania was constituted as a separate church in 1800, and the chapel was extended in 1819 during the ministry of the Rev. John Herring (1811-32).

It was decided to build a new chapel during the pastorate of the Rev. David Rees (1837-50). A lease for 999 years was secured in 1846. A new chapel was opened in William Street in October 1847 at a cost of approximately £2,000. This chapel was designed by the architect Daniel Evans, Cardigan, who was paid a sum of £12 for his work in supervising the construction-work. It has been listed Grade 2* by Cadw as one of the finest Classical chapels in Wales, and it was described as the finest chapel in Wales when it was built. A comparison has been drawn between this chapel and Hermon, Fishguard which had been designed by either Daniel Evans or his father, David Evans (see 66, Fishguard, Hermon). The open pedimental gable is above a large Doric porch and broad segmental arch, and there are three arched upper windows. The words 'Baptist' and 'Chapel' in raised letters appear on the external wall, and a plaque bearing the words 'Bethania 1847' beneath the main centre arch. The interior has box pews and a panelled three-sided gallery on Roman Doric iron columns made by T. Lloyd, Cardigan. Decorations on the ceiling are of Classical plant motifs around a centre domelet. The ornate plaster work is the work of Thomas Rees of Fishguard. In 1851 Hermon contained 500 free seats and 400 others, and it was recorded that the chapel measured 61' long by 47' wide. On 30 March, 560 were present in the morning service, 353 scholars in the afternoon and 781 in the evening service.

A schoolroom and vestry in grey stone, designed by John Owen, Liverpool, were added in 1892. The Cardigan and District Baptist Gymanfa Ganu [Singing Festival] was held for the first time in 1885, and this has proved to be a popular function over the years. In 1900 a pulpit and *sêt fawr*, together with an organ by P. Conacher & Co. Huddersfield, were installed at a cost of £440. The organ was formally opened and consecrated on 16 May, 1900 with a recital by Dr. Roland Rogers, former organist of Bangor Cathedral Church. These developments occurred during the pastorate of the Rev. John Williams (1880-1929). A powerful and eloquent preacher, he is said to have baptised nearly 700 persons during his long ministry, and the highest number of members, 542, was recorded in 1905. He was also a prominent figure in the public life of the town and as a county councillor for many years. Following his death in 1929 his widow received a telegram from David Lloyd George, and, commiserating with her, he referred to the death of his good friend and to the loss to Ceredigion and the Liberalism in Wales.

The chapel was renovated and repainted several times in the twentieth century, as in 1936, whilst preparing for the visit of the Union of Welsh Baptists, when the organ was also renovated and cleaned: the total cost was £337. The chapel was also renovated and repainted in 1975, when the work was supervised by specialists. The chapel has also been recently painted.

Present position: Minister; Rev. Irfon Roberts; 85 members, Sunday service, morning or evening every other week; monthly united prayer meeting with other churches.
Further reading: R. Edwards, *Bethania, Aberteifi* (1947); William H. Howells, *Canrif o Fawl, Cymanfa Ganu Bedyddwyr Aberteifi a'r Cylch, 1885-1985* (1995).

65. CILFOWYR, (Bw)

OS: SN 221 421

Cilfowyr was the 'eldest daughter' of Rhydwilym Church, as the history of the cause commenced with the visit of Lettice Morgan, Cilfowyr, together with Margaret Nicholas, to Rhydwilym on 12 May 1668. Services were held for a time in Cil-cam, in the parish of Eglwys-wen-yng-Nghemais, and afterwards in Cilfowyr farmhouse, that is, the home of the Morgan family, in the parish of Maenordeifi. The church was established in 1704, and Samuel John, a local member of Rhydwilym, served as the minister until his death in 1736 at the age of 80. The first chapel, named Tŷ Gwyn [White House] was built c. 1716 on land belonging to the farm, on a site overlooking Llechryd and the Teifi river. James Morgan leased the land for a Baptist meeting-house for one thousand years or 'as long as water shall run or be running or be in the River Tivy', and also a baptistry. The church grew and branches were established in Newport, Blaen-waun, Pen-y-parc, Blaen-ffos and Fronddeiniol. By 1783 there were 387 members and the chapel was extended in 1795.

The 1851 Census recorded that there were 9 free seats and 31 others, together with another 60 free seats and the gallery. On 30 March there were present 475 in the morning service, and 66 scholars in the afternoon. The chapel was clearly too small, and was rebuilt in 1877-79 by C.J. Davies, Cenarth. The vestry was built in 1896-97, and buildings outside the chapel were used as stables.

The present minister is the forty-first of the church, and other long-serving ministers have included the Revs. Rees Price (1850-1896) and Dafydd Henry Edwards (1960-4) and (1982-2000)

Present position: Minister, Rev. Richard Gareth Morris, 49 members, Sunday service 10.30 a.m. 2nd Sunday every month.

Further reading: William R. Bowen, *Hanes Cilfowyr 1704-2004* (2004).

66. FISHGUARD, Hermon (Bw)

OS: SM 957 369

Services were held in local houses until a chapel was built in High Street, or Penucha'r Dre, which continues to be occupied by the present chapel. Ministers from the Llangloffan church often preached in Fishguard, and the Rev. John Williams, Llangloffan was closely involved in the construction of the chapel, with financial backing from Henry Morgan, Tregroes. Measuring 47' by 27', this was the largest chapel in the county at the time. Communion was administered every other month in 1777, and then monthly from the following year. The church was incorporated in 1807, when 128 members were released from Llangloffan, and the name 'Hermon' was adopted instead of 'Penucha'r Dref'.

An increase in membership resulted in the building of a new, larger chapel on the site in 1832, designed either by Daniel Evans, Fishguard and Cardigan, in view of the similarity to Bethania chapel, Cardigan; or possibly his father, David Evans. (see 64, Cardigan, Bethania).

This chapel is regarded as being of considerable architectural interest in view of its exceptionally early Classical façade, and probably the earliest use in Wales of the giant arch breaking into an open pediment. The doors and windows have elegant blind fan-heads, and gallery stairs rise each end, rather than from within the chapel. The three-sided gallery has plain vertical panels and there is a fine ceiling rose. In 1851 there were stated to be 16 free seats, with long seats at the back for 66, and another 87 seats. Many, presumably, had to stand, and on 30 March there were present 308 in the morning service, 118 scholars in the afternoon and 286 in the evening service. A note was added that congregations were more numerous in the winter when sailors were at home. The Rev. Dan Davies (1899-1934) baptised 750 persons in Hermon during his pastorate, with 92 persons remarkably baptised in 25 minutes on one day, 15 January, 1905. The considerable increase in the congregation resulted in the extension and re-modelling of 1906-07, designed by George Morgan & Son, and this involved the installation of a gallery for the choir, a pulpit, and an organ built by Grey & Davison, Shrewsbury, and a hall and various rooms were built in the rear of the chapel. The membership peaked at 748 in 1934, the last year of the pastorate of the Rev. Dan Davies.

Present position: No minister, since retirement of the Rev. Carl Williams. 141 members, ten children, Sunday service, 10.00 a.m., united prayer meeting every two months, monthly women's meeting.

Further reading: Undeb y Bedyddwyr, Llawlyfr yr Undeb (2000); Capel Local Information Leaflet 37: Fishguard (2010).

67. SOLVA, Caerfarchell (Pw)

OS: SM 795 270

The history of the Caerfarchell church may be traced to the winter of 1737/8, and in the following year one of the Rev. Griffith Jones' circulating schools was held in the village. At approximately the same time Howel Harris visited this area, and it is possible that there may have been some Moravian influence involved in the establishment of the cause here. Other early Methodist leaders who preached here included William Williams, Daniel Rowland and Howell Davies, who led the revival in Pembrokeshire from the 1740s until his death in 1770, and also John Wesley and George Whitefield.

The first chapel was built as a long narrow building in 1763. This was followed in 1827 by the present building, which has a five-sided panelled gallery. In 1851 there were180 free seats and space for 150 to stand. On 30 March 40 scholars were present in the morning, and 200 in the afternoon service. The chapel was expensively refurnished in the late-nineteenth century. The ground floor pews dating from 1827 were removed in 1912 and replaced with the current arrangements. The original pews remain in the gallery however, and the open-backed seating in the gallery corners are reputed to have been re-used from the 1763 structure. The vestry was added in 1933. Some of the planks and framed panels from the original 1827 pews may be seen as pink-painted dividing panels under the present seating. Four horses' skulls are reported to have been buried, one in each corner of the building in order to improve the building's acoustics, and the chapel is certainly an excellent auditorium. A memorial stone to Albert Prance who was killed during the final weeks of the First World War is displayed next to the pulpit.

Provenance for the arrangement of the pews and their occupants in the earlier chapel dating from about 1820 is available. Other early records include a legal document from 1766 appointing about ten trustees including three women for the chapel, a letter from the Carvarchell Society to Howel Harris at Trefeca in 1770, and a series of indentures appointing trustees (men only) dating from 1827 and 1866. Twentieth-century documents are more numerous, and the role of women in the administration of the chapel becomes prominent during that century. Extensive photographic evidence of the building and some of the people who were active in the cause exists from the late-nineteenth century onwards.

The chapel has been listed Grade 2* by Cadw, largely on the basis of the fine rural vernacular architecture and the quality of the interior furnishings, which include the rare five panelled gallery. It is located within the Caerfarchell village, which is designated as a conservation area.

Present position: Minister, Rev. Wiliam T.E. Owen. Public services are regularly held each Sunday afternoon and all are welcome to visit the chapel by prior arrangement.

68. PEMBROKE DOCK, Zion Free Church

OS: SM 967 034

Zion, seating approximately 1,300, is considered to be the largest chapel west of Swansea. The Wesleyan Methodists had established a meeting house at Pembroke Ferry, and built a small chapel called Ebenezer in 1820 before moving to the present site. The present Zion chapel was built as the Tabernacle Wesleyan chapel between 1846-48, probably by John Road, who provided the data for the 1851 census where he was described as a steward, and as a shipwright. He also designed the Trinity Congregationalist chapel, presently the Trinity United Reformed chapel, Meyrick Street, which opened in 1852. The 1851 Census stated that there were 346 free seats and 574 others, and that on 30 March 389 were present in the morning service, together with 191 scholars, and that 545, with 80 scholars, were present in the evening service. John Road added the comment that the chapel and schoolroom were in one building, with the schoolroom under the floor of the chapel.

The chapel has a high five-bayed Classical front with arched small-paned windows and three arched doors. The interior has a plaster ceiling with two large roses and several smaller ones, and the galleries all around, supported by painted timber columns. Curving timber stairs on each side lead to the pulpit standing high on painted columns. The organ gallery, designed by K.W. Ladd, Pembroke Dock, was installed in 1865-7.

The physical condition of the chapel had deteriorated over the years, but a considerable amount of restoration work was undertaken in the period 1986-90. The chapel may be said to have been rescued as a place of worship from dereliction, despite immense difficulties, as a result of the dedication of the Rev. Hugh Michael, and a faithful congregation.

Present position: The church constitution does not have membership. It is open to all who are like-minded believers with a generally broad centre path of Christian faith but the trustees and officers only are required to sign their acceptance of the basis of faith set down in the trust deed. There is a congregation of approximately 60 on a Sunday morning, 40 on a Sunday evening, 20 at the midweek prayer meeting, and up to 24 children at the Sunday school.

Further reading: Phil Carradice, *Pembroke Dock, The Town Built to Build Ships* (2006); *Capel Local Information Sheet*, 33, Pembroke Dock (2008); a volume on the history of the church is at present being prepared.

69. Woodstock (Pw)

OS: SN 022 257

This was the first chapel where Communion was given to Methodists in a building not consecrated by the Anglican Church. Woodstock was founded by Howel Davies in 1754 in the middle of the county and was regarded as a meeting house for a wide area, rather than as a local place of worship. Howel Davies used the Anglican service for the Communion, and for many years members continued to refer to the Communion as '*Cwrdd Mawr*' [Great Meeting]. Large crowds assembled to listen to sermons preached by Howel Davies, George Whitefield and other leaders of the Calvinistic Methodists. A native of Monmouthshire, Howell Davies had been a schoolmaster at Talgarth, where he was converted whilst hearing Howel Harris preach. His preaching had a significant influence on Pembrokeshire, and he was known as 'the Apostle of Pembrokeshire'. His usual congregation was said to vary from 7,000 to 10,000, and Howel Harris estimated that 12,000 were present to hear George Whitefield preach at Llys-y-fran.

The chapel was renovated in 1808 and it is probable that the long façade, with its brick eaves and hipped roof dates from this period. In 1851 there were 11 free seats and 28 others, and there were present on 30 March 230 in the morning service and 52 in the afternoon, the majority of whom were probably unseated.

The chapel was rebuilt in 1890 when the render and timber detail were added. Two parallel roofs result in a square interior, and two iron columns, and also the fittings probably date from 1890. However, the general impression resembles that of an early chapel form, and a comparison has been drawn between this chapel and Daniel Rowland's second chapel of 1764 at Llangeitho. The chapel's connection with the early Methodist leaders is also emphasised by the marble memorial tablet to Howel Davies which was installed in 1895.

Present position: Minister, Rev. Wiliam T.E. Owen, 33 members, Sunday services, 10.30 a.m., 2.00 or 5.00 p.m.

Further reading: Wiliam T.E. Owen, *250 o flynyddoeddyn hanes Capel M.C. Wystog, Sir Benfro o 1754-1755 hyd at 2004-2005* (2005).

70. HAVERFORDWEST, Tabernacle (C)

OS: SM 951 157

Tabernacle church was established by the Calvinistic Methodists, who established a society in a house in Cokey Lane (City Road) following a sermon preached by Howel Harris in the town in 1743. The leader of the society was the Rev. Howel Davies whose influence in the locality is described in the entry for Woodstock [69], and whose daughter Margaret was married to the Rev. Nathaniel Rowland, the son of Daniel Rowland, Llangeitho. The preaching tour of George Whitefield in 1768 resulted in the construction in 1774 of the first chapel on a plot of land next to the site of the society meeting. Although a powerful preacher, the Rev. Nathaniel Rowland had an arrogant personality, and opposed appeals from congregations to administer the sacraments and support efforts to build new chapels. As a result, many persons who had belonged to Methodist societies joined other denominations. In 1790, following a dispute concerning a layman administering Communion, Tabernacle church, with Rowland Hill, a native of Shropshire, one of the more prominent members, decided to join the Congregationalists.

The earliest chapel had a pedimented façade and a similar design to the present one, but with a plainer ceiling. The interior was restored in 1819, and iron gates added *c.*1835. In 1851 there were 200 free seats and 500 others, and standing space in '2 Passages'. On 30 March 700, together with 116 scholars, were present in the morning service, and 222 in the afternoon.

The chapel was extensively remodelled and enlarged in 1874, with the work designed by Lawrence and Goodman, Newport (Monmouthshire). The chapel has been described as one of the most attractive Classical chapels in south-west Wales, and has been listed as Grade 2* by Cadw. It is probable that the builders were James & John Allen , Pembroke Dock, which submitted the lowest estimate of £1,541,10s.

The stuccoed and coloured building, similar to a Roman basilica, has a middle projecting as a half-drum with Ionic columns on high bases. Arched doors on the ground floor extend into an open vestibule. The large interior, based upon the plan of the original chapel, is divided into nave and aisles of five bays by tall iron columns. The gallery is three-sided, the coved, cast plaster ceiling is elliptical and coloured windows have been placed behind the pulpit.

The restoration of the interior in 1903 was designed by A.H. Thomas and a memorial window commemorating nine members who had lost their lives in the 1914-18 war was unveiled in 1920. An organ built by W. Sweetland, Bath, which had been installed in 1879, was rebuilt in 1936, and again in 1984, and the builder this time was Peter Jones, Douglas , Isle of Man. The chapel was again renovated in 2000 when the large schoolroom adjoining the chapel, originally built in 1864, was substantially refashioned, and this now houses many of the church's activities.

The church's ministers included the Rev. Edward Nicholson Jones (1902-37), who was a chaired bard, and a chair which he won at the Llangernyw Eisteddfod in 1903 has been placed in front of the pulpit. He co-operated with Dr Joseph Parry and provided the words for several of his operas.

In 1972 the church decided not to join the United Reformed Church, but preferred to remain independent, and in 1983 it joined the Congregational Federation.

The old Sunday School building has been completely refurbished and provides a modern and comfortable community centre. Outside bodies who use the Centre include the Haverfordwest Male Voice Choir, the Friends in Harmony Choir, and the Cymmrodorion Society.

Present position: Ministers, Revs. Christopher Gillham (since 1985) and Stephen Skibniewski-Woods, 99 members, 23 children (12 under 10), 30 adherents. Sunday services, 11.00 a.m. and 6.00 p.m.(4.00 p.m. in the winter), Communion Service on Tuesday morning at Withybush General Hospital, Haverfordwest, and Welsh-language service on second Sunday of month. Quiet morning / Bible Class, Men's Fellowship and Ladies Guild meetings once a month; Boys' Brigade and Girls' Association; and the Church also provides a short mat bowls club, over-fifties aerobics, and a drop-in coffee morning.

Further reading: W.L. Richards, *A Well-Found Ship, History of Tabernacle Congregational Church, Haverfordwest* (1988); Robert Scourfield, 'The Churches and Chapels' in *The History of the Town and County of Haverfordwest*, ed. Dillwyn Miles (1999).

Website: www.tabernacle-haverfordwest.org.uk

71. MARTLETWY, Burnett's Hill

OS: SN 024 098

This chapel was built in 1812 in south Pembrokeshire by the Calvinistic Methodists. It was renovated c. 1850 but as the membership had decreased substantially, the church was closed in 1984. The condition of the chapel then deteriorated significantly, and the Friends of Burnett's Hill Chapel was formed by a group of local residents concerned with regard to the future of the chapel. They then secured the chapel on a lease from the Pembrokeshire Coast National Park Authority which had bought the chapel from the Presbyterian Church of Wales. With the assistance of a Heritage Lottery Grant the chapel was restored and the chapel reopened with a special service held on 31 July, 2001.

The location today may seem remote, yet when the chapel was built it was in the middle of a thriving industrial area, within reach of the dock of Cresswell Quay, the limestone quarries of Coedcanlas, ship-building yards at Lawrenny Ferry and the anthracite colliery at Landshipping, which, at its height, employed 160 colliers. By the end of the eighteenth century the industrial village of Landshipping was an important centre for the Calvinistic and also the Wesleyan Methodists, with coalminers from Carmarthenshire and south-east Wales attracted here. The two denominations at first shared a small meeting-house about a mile outside Lawrenny, but doctrinal differences led the Calvinistic Methodists to decide that they should build their own chapel. They selected the site at Burnett's Hill because it was near the home of one of their adherents, known as 'Reesey of Burnett's Hill'. Travelling preachers often stayed at 'Reesey's cottage', and preached at a nearby field. One of those prominently involved in the work of building the chapel was John Allen, an elderly farmer from Lawrenny who in his youth had travelled to hear John Wesley preach in Haverfordwest. He offered to supply and deliver free of charge all the lime and stone needed for the new building, and also assiduously collected funds locally for the necessary fittings and furnishings. As a result of the enthusiastic support of the local community, the chapel constructed by rural craftsmen was a simple, finely-proportioned, cottage-style building.

The guest preacher at the opening of the chapel in January 1813, was the Rev. Theophilus Jones whose sermons are reported to have caused congregations to shake and tremble "and end up weeping like children". The church was without a minister for 50 years. In 1851 there were 170 free seats, 18 others and room for another 50 to stand. On 30 March 170 were present in the afternoon, in the only service held on the Sunday.

The other denominations had also built chapels in Martletwy by the middle of the nineteenth century. The locality had experienced industrial growth up to 1844 when 40 coalminers were drowned in a mining disaster at Landshipping. The damaging effects of this disaster could not be overcome, and in 1867 coalmining at

Landshipping came to an end. Many families subsequently left the area, and one result was that the Baptist church, which had recently extended its chapel at Martletwy, faced a heavy debt in order to pay for a chapel that was by now too large for its members. On the other hand, the Burnett's Hill chapel was of a sufficient size for its rural congregation, and, as it was neither extended nor rebuilt, it has, to a considerable degree, retained its original character.

The only significant change after the disaster was that the interior was remodelled. The original gallery facing the entrance was taken down, the seats were moved to face the east, and the pulpit, previously placed against the rear long-wall, now faced the door which had been re-located on the western end, thereby providing an entrance on the gable end. The original thatched or slate roof was replaced in 1890, reusing pine trusses from another building. A plaster ceiling provided greater warmth as the original fireplace, located on the gable wall, had been removed. Electricity was not introduced until the twentieth century and replaced the oil lamps. There was no organ, and the tradition persisted of pitching the first note of each hymn. Another old custom which continued to the very last service, was for the men and women to sit separately, and this is indicated in the present building by the wooden rails on each side with one bearing pegs for bonnets, and the other one with bowler hat pegs.

The first full-time minister, the Rev. William James, was inducted in 1867 when the chapel was linked to the recently-opened Millin chapel near The Rhos, on the other side of the Cleddau river. The normal practice was for the preacher to hold a service at Millin on a Sunday morning, then walk a couple of miles to Picton Point where he would cross the river by rowing-boat ferry to Landshipping Ferry and then walk two miles to Burnett's Hill. After the service, he would follow the same route and return to Millin for the evening service.

The Friends of Burnett's Hill Chapel have been responsible for maintaining and managing the chapel since it was re-opened in 2001. The success of the work that has been undertaken here may be attributed to the enthusiasm of the local residents, and especially to the guidance of Robert Scourfield, the specialist chapel architectural historian who is the Treasurer of the Friends.

Present position: The chapel is used for occasional services as well as for concerts and local history exhibitions.

Further reading: Robert Scourfield & Keith Johnson, *Burnett's Hill Calvinistic Methodist Chapel, Martletwy, A Brief History* (2001).

72. RHYDWILYM (Bw)

OS: SN 114 249

Rhydwilym is one of the earliest Baptist chapels in Wales, and is the mother church of many Baptist churches in west Wales. It is located in a remote area of west Carmarthenshire, near to the boundary with Pembrokeshire. The church was incorporated on 5 July, 1668 in the middle of a period of persecution. The main founder was William Jones, the curate of the neighbouring parish of Cilymaenllwyd. He had been baptized at Olchon, Herefordshire, having previously been imprisoned at Carmarthen, and later at Haverfordwest. Thirty persons were baptized at Rhydwilym in 1668, when there were 33 members, and by the following year the membership had increased to 55, and to 113 in 1689. The church register records that the members came from 40 parishes in the counties of Carmarthenshire, Pembrokeshire and Ceredigion, and the usual practice was to meet locally on Sundays but to assemble together for Communion one Sunday a month. In 1696 Glandŵr church was formed by members of Rhydwilym, and this represented the beginning of the process whereby individual churches were established by the mother-church.

The first chapel was built in 1701, and this is recorded on a stone which may be seen in the chapel porch. A local landowner, John Evans, Llwyndŵr, paid for the chapel, but T.M. Bassett, in *The Welsh Baptists*, has suggested that there were fewer wealthy members at Rhydwilym than there were in many churches. Members were baptized in the river beside the chapel from that time onwards. The membership increased to 220 in 1722-3, and the chapel was refurbished and extended in 1763. The third chapel was built in 1841, and on 30 March 1851 275 were present in the morning service and 89 scholars in the afternoon. The average attendance was stated to be 370 in the morning and 105 in the afternoon.

The present chapel was built in 1875 in the Classical style at a cost of £1,300. Local stone and grey limestone were used in the construction, and they blend well with the surroundings. Anthony Jones has suggested that the same architect was responsible for designing both this chapel and the nearby Bethabara chapel built two years earlier. The atmosphere within the chapel is light, with the pine wood restored, and seating provided for 600 persons. The three-sided gallery is supported on iron columns made by the Priory Foundry, Carmarthen. One of the eisteddfod chairs won by the Rev. E. Llwyd Williams, the chaired bard and writer, (1906-1960), brought up at Rhydwilym, has been placed in the pulpit. He was buried in the new graveyard, and a number of former ministers, including the Rev. Thomas Jones, minister from 1808 until 1850, have been buried in the old graveyard.

A baptismal service in the river conducted by the Rev. Peter Thomas, Aberystwyth, whilst he was the minister of Rhydwilym, was filmed for the television programme, *The Dragon has Two Tongues*, presented by Wynford Vaughan Thomas

and Gwyn A. Williams, in 1985.

In 1987 Rhydwilym joined a pastorate comprising of Bethel, Mynachlog-ddu and Horeb, Maenclochog, and in 2003 Calfaria, Login joined the pastorate.

Present position: Minister, Rev. Eirian Wyn Lewis, 77 members, Sunday services, morning or afternoon, Gymanfa Bwnc [Congregational Scriptural recitation and responses festival] held at Whitsun.

Further reading: E. Llwyd Williams a John Absolom, *Rhamant Rhydwilym* (1939).

73. TRE-LECH, Capel-y-Graig (I)

OS: SN 281 303

The first meeting-house on this site was built in 1703. Before that time, during the period 1660-89, inhabitants of the parish of Trelech a'r Betws attended meetings in the Pal Mawr, in the parish of Ciffig, where Stephen Hughes preached and administered the sacraments. Services were then held at the large farm of Dinas in a lonely valley about three quarters of a mile from the chapel and nearer to the boundary with Pembrokeshire. The chapel, believed to have been a white-washed, thatched building, was sited in a more convenient location near the road from Meidrym, and became the focal point of a cluster of houses and eventually a village.

The chapel was rebuilt between 1750 and 1765, and again enlarged and rebuilt in 1791. The final extensive changes, made in 1827 and probably including the installation of part of the gallery, were paid for without incurring a debt. They were required because of the population growth of the late-eighteenth century and the early-nineteenth century, and the increased membership, from c.140 in 1790 to c.410 in 1835 during the pastorate of the Rev. Morgan Jones (1790-1835). He is reputed to have accepted 2,400 members, and he also established a number of churches, including Ffynnon-bedr and Pen-y-bont, in the same parish, and Blaen-y-coed, Llwyn-yr-hwrdd and Bryn Iwan in neighbouring parishes. He also contributed significantly to the founding of the churches of St Florence, Sardis, near Saundersfoot, Rosemarket and Tyrhos in Pembrokeshire; and also the first Welsh Independent Church in London. On 30 March 1851, 381, 586 and 198 respectively were present in the morning, afternoon and evening services, but for some reason no scholars attending the Sunday school were recorded. A note was added that there was an average of 200 scholars during the year, and that the congregation varied from 200 to 1,000, depending on the weather. 416 free seats were provided, and 188 others.

The six-bay stone front with large hipped front has two arched centre windows, doors with gallery lights above and an outer window each side to light the pews under the gallery. An unusual feature is the survival of outside stone stairs to the gallery. The large interior has box pews and a panelled gallery on three sides, supported by cast iron columns, with the date '1827' on one of them. The large pulpit with sweeping stairs and the woodwork belong to the second half of the nineteenth century, and the two front windows date from the period of the Second World War.

The chapel has been listed by Cadw Grade 2* as a large chapel dating from the early nineteenth century. It has been an important religious and social centre over the years, and this is reflected by the adoption of the name 'Tre-lech' for the village which has grown around the chapel: the name 'Tynewydd' was an alternative name used at one time.

Present position: Minister, Rev. Felix Aubel, 132 members, 15 children, services, morning or afternoon, Sunday school in the morning, no regular weekday meetings but seasonal activities include preparations for Gymanfa Ysgolion [Schools Festival] and Gymanfa Ganu, drama company, youth club.

Further reading: *Capel-y-graig, Tre-lech 1703-2003*, ed. Muriel Bowen Evans (2003).

74. BLAEN-Y-COED (I)

OS: SN 307 271

The church is associated with the Rev. Howell (Elfed) Lewis, the hymn writer, chaired bard and Archdruid (1860-1953) who was brought up here, with his father a deacon and precentor. When Elfed was a child he would walk to services from his home, Y Gangell, a small cottage a mile and a half to the north from the village of Blaen-y-coed. Following the renovation of the cottage, a museum was opened in 1964, and many visitors are attracted here, and also to the chapel and the graveyard, where Elfed was buried.

The church was established in 1803 by members of Capel-y-Graig, Tre-lech (see 73, Trelech, Capel-y-Graig), who had held services in a barn which was adapted into a meeting-house, and which was later used as a cowshed. The first chapel was built in 1807 near to the barn and on a plan which corresponded to that of a barn. The leader was Dafydd Bowen, and a tablet placed on the wall inside the chapel refers to him as the founder of the Independent cause. Practical assistance was provided by local inhabitants who volunteered to carry the required materials. The seating was provided by the members themselves, and in the meeting-house four pews and twelve backed benches belonged to specific families, and other benches were freely available for others. The custom of reciting the *Pwnc* [Scriptural congregational recitation and responses] commenced in 1818 and soon spread. The Gymanfa Bwnc festival continues to be one of the main activities of the local church and is held on the last Saturday of April, with the Blaen-y-coed, Bryn Iwan and Hermon Sunday schools participating.

An awareness of the need to renovate the meeting-house resulted in it being demolished and a new one built in 1837, with the members again assisting by carrying materials. This chapel faced eastwards, in contrast to the south-facing previous chapel, and stairs leading to the gallery were placed outside the chapel. In 1851 there were 136 free seats, 240 others and standing-room for another 68 persons. On 30 March there were present 226 in the morning service and 124 scholars in the afternoon: the average attendance over the year was considerably higher: 348 in the morning and 155 in the afternoon. The interior was renovated in 1895. The architect was D. Davies, Penrhiwllan and the builder John Evans, Llanybydder. The money to pay the expenditure of £450 had been collected by the opening service in 1896. Further improvements have been made since then to the chapel and the vestry, located behind the chapel. A new wooden floor had been laid in the chapel, the ceiling and electricity system were renewed in 1957, and the steps leading from the road to the vestry and graveyard were realigned in 2001.

Following the closure of King's Cross Independent Church, King's Cross, London in 2006, the stained glass window in that chapel was moved to Blaen-y-coed, installed to the left of the pulpit and unveiled on 17 February 2008.

Present position: No minister; 110 members; Sunday Service and Sunday school morning or afternoon; annual Gymanfa Bwnc and occasional cultural meetings.
Further reading: Elsbeth Page, *Hanes Eglwys yr Annibynwyr Blaen-y-coed, 1801-2001* (2001).

75. CARMARTHEN, English Baptist (Be)

OS: SN 411 201

Early reports refer to a Baptist church in Carmarthen during the Commonwealth in the seventeenth century, and in the mid-eighteenth century Baptist services were held at Chapel Yard in Priory Street. A church was established in Dark Gate in 1782, and a substantial increase in membership during the pastorate of the Rev. Titus Lewis, the hymn writer, resulted in the opening of Tabernacl chapel in 1812. A further growth in church membership led to the rebuilding of Tabernacl in 1841-42. An English service was held in Tabernacl on a Sunday afternoon, but this practice came to an end following the opening of the English Baptist church in Lammas Street in 1870. 26 members, including several deacons, transferred from Tabernacl, and also Penuel, the Baptist church which had been founded in Priory Street in the late-eighteenth century.

The founding members of the English Baptist Church included George Morgan, the renowned chapel architect. Born in the parish of Laugharne but brought up at New Moat, Pembrokeshire, he had moved to Carmarthen c.1855 and had served as a Sunday school teacher at Tabernacl. He designed and built the new chapel on the site of the Black Horse tavern in Lammas Street, and subsequently became the secretary and life-deacon of the English Baptist Church. The site and the building costs amounted to £3,250, of which £1,250 had been paid by the opening service, and a further £900 had been contributed by 1877 at the time of the departure of the first minister, the Rev. Evan Thomas, whose ministry had commenced in 1873.

The new chapel, with its dramatic temple front and giant Bath stone Corinthian columns located at the end of a narrow courtyard, has a five-bayed façade. A detailed account of the new building and the opening service on 19 June 1870 appeared in the *Western Mail*. The chapel measured 67' by 37', and had a schoolroom and two classrooms in the rear. The columns measure 27' high, and whilst the front was of Bath stone, the sides and rear of the chapel were of local stone, hammer dressed, with freestone dressings. The interior, seating 450 persons, had a gallery, platform-pulpit and organ gallery under which a minister's vestry was separated from the chapel by a partition. The roof had a timber ceiling, with a handsome cornice, and all the woodwork was of pitch pine. The building was described as having "an eminently attractive appearance" and George Morgan, the 'architect and contractor' was praised "for the handsome building which he has designed". This is regarded as one of the finest examples of his work, and two other notable chapels designed by him are those of Mount Pleasant, Swansea (1874-76) and the Baptist Church, Newtown (1881) (entry 42).

A new organ, built by Messrs Wade & Meggitt, was installed in 1887, at a total cost of £571. The organist at this time was John Howard Morgan, son of George Morgan, and, in addition to the work undertaken at this chapel, he and his father

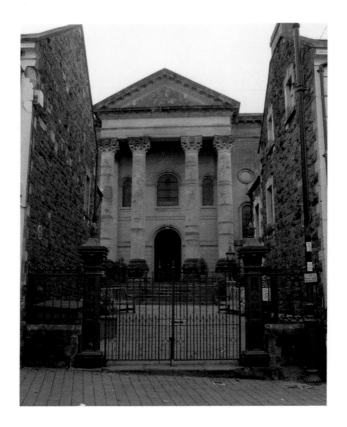

contributed significantly to the architecture of several chapels in Carmarthen, including the Tabernacl and Penuel Welsh Baptist chapels, Heol Dŵr and Bethania Welsh Presbyterian chapels, and Heol Awst and Priordy Welsh Independent chapels.

The ministers of the church have included the Rev. Dr. Gwilym Davies (1879-1955), the pioneer of social service in Wales, promoter of international peace whose writings are regarded as having influenced the constitution of UNESCO, and founder of the annual Goodwill Message annually broadcast from the Youth of Wales, who was the minister here from 1909 until 1915.

A considerable amount of work has been undertaken on the building in recent years, with a new minister's room/study behind the church, major refurbishment of interior walls affected by rain penetration, removal of the annexe which was detaching itself from the main building, addition of an atrium, refurbishment and modernisation of the downstairs centre, and the provision of a new kitchen area, lift and a disabled access, which is nearing completion. This work has been largely financed by substantial grants, including over £350,000 from the Heritage Lottery

Fund, and considerable sums also received from the European Union (1Fund), the Welsh Assembly Government (Cadw and Community Fund), Grantscape (Landfill Tax), National Churches Trust and Welsh Historic Churches.

Present position: No minister, 54 members, Sunday service at 11.00 a.m. followed by refreshments at the Lammas Street Centre; Junior Bible Club (in conjunction with Wesley Methodist Church – holiday schemes for children aged about 7-14); Messy Club (during school holidays in conjunction with Wesley Methodist Church); Christmas Lunch, usually attended by 40 to 50 people, mainly those who would normally be alone, organised by Church people with additional support from Salvation Army & funded by other chapels & professional people; Probation service, 'Away Days' – meeting place for those with mild mental health difficulties; Cellar café run by Church people, open for lunches & snacks 10 a.m. to 2 p.m. every Wednesday; Welsh and French classes; Art and ceramics exhibitions and pottery workshop.

Further reading: *English Baptist Church, Carmarthen, A Jubilee Retrospect 1868-1918* (1918); *Capel Information Leaflet* 31, Carmarthen (2007); Desmond Davies, *Pobl y Porth Tywyll* (2012).

Website: www.englishbaptistchurch.org.uk

76. CARMARTHEN, Heol Awst (I)

OS: SN 408 200

This church in Lammas Street (Heol Awst) was established in the period 1660-88, and the members were cared for by Stephen Hughes, 'the Apostle for Carmarthenshire' who had a close association with Carmarthen as his grandfather, father and brother had all been mayors of the town. It is therefore appropriate that one seat in the front of the present chapel is regarded as the mayor's seat.

The Rev. William Evans, the minister of Pencader, moved to the town in the early eighteenth century, and established an academy. One of the earliest students was Thomas Perrot, who came to Carmarthen as a minister and professor in either 1719 or 1720. He was responsible for moving the location of the church to Lammas Street (Heol Awst), and the first chapel on this site was built in 1726, following a gift of land by John Corrie, a silk merchant and member of the chapel which was enlarged in 1733. The academy was moved to Lammas Street during the long pastorate of the Rev. David Peter (1792-1837), and it developed into the Presbyterian College. A close connection was maintained between the College and the chapel over the years, and the door leading to the College may still be viewed near to the stairs leading to the gallery. The Rev. David Peter was the principal of the College for some forty years from 1795. He baptized 1,516 children and following a constant increase in the membership, a new chapel was built on the site in 1802 at a cost of £1,800.

The chapel was rebuilt in 1826-7 by William Owen, Haverfordwest, with seats for over 1,000, at a cost of £2,582. At the time, Heol Awst was regarded as one of the largest chapels in Wales, and today this is one of the finest chapels which has survived from this period and whose furnishings are largely intact. The chapel has a plain rendered, hipped front, with two pedimented Ionic doorcases, each of which has above an arched window. The chapel has been set back from the main road in a courtyard which also includes a very large schoolroom built in 1888-89 and designed by George Morgan. The Georgian square interior of the chapel has a panelled gallery on marble Ionic columns, plaster ceiling, box pews in two large centre ranks, and a rare, early- nineteenth century 'wine-glass' pulpit described as a 'witness-box' by the Rev. J. Dyfnallt Owen, (1873-1956), the Archdruid, crowned bard, writer and journalist, who was the minister here from 1910 until 1947.

In 1851 there were 200 free seats, 900 others and standing-room for 100 persons. On 30 March there were present 640 in the morning service, 170 in the afternoon and 802 in the evening service. The chapel was renovated in 1870, and a new ceiling, containing a large ceiling rose, was installed. A large pipe organ, built by James J. Binns, Bramley, was placed in the gallery. Two large stained-glass windows, made by Abbot & Co., Lancaster, were installed in 1922 behind the pulpit: one in memory of those killed in the 1914-18 war and the other to commemorate

Stephen Hughes. A third window, by the same firm, was added on the western side in 1946. A stained glass window in memory of the Rev. J. Dyfnallt Owen, the minister from 1910 until 1947, was placed in the chapel in 1960. His successor, the Rev. Emrys Jones, was the minister from 1949 until 1974, when the present minister commenced his pastorate.

The large schoolroom, which has a three-sided gallery, as if it were a chapel, supported by square, cast-iron pillars, has been adapted in recent years, and the large comfortable room is extensively used for a variety of services and meetings.

An extensive renovation programme was undertaken in 2010 and 2011, and grants of £150,000 were received from The Lottery Fund, Cadw and Carmarthenshire County Council. The chapel has been listed Grade 2* by Cadw.

Present position: Minister, Rev. J. Towyn Jones (since 1974), 199 members, 20 children, Sunday services, 10 a.m. including the children's Sunday School, 2.00 or 3.30 p.m.; Monthly cultural society, jointly with Smyrna and Elim churches, in winter; Plygain service Christmas morning, Illustrated newsletter *CWRDD* issued twice a year, with details of all activities, and with special emphasis on Easter and Christmas.

Further reading: J. Dyfnallt Owen, *Hanes Eglwys Heol Awst, Caerfyrddin* (1926); Noel Gibbard 'Heol Awst Congregational Church 1703-1837', *The Carmarthenshire Antiquary*, (2006), pp.5-17; *Capel Information Leaflet* 31, Carmarthen (2007).

77. CARMARTHEN, Heol Dŵr (Pw)

OS: SN 409 201

Calvinistic Methodists met in Carmarthen from *c*.1740, and a society is believed to have met in Goose Street (later Catherine Street) in 1748. The first chapel on this site in Water Street [Heol Dŵr] was located on a plot of land owned by Peter Williams (1723-96), the Calvinistic Methodist preacher, writer and Biblical commentator, who had been converted by the preaching of George Whitefield in 1743. The original chapel seems to have been built in his garden for his own use, but in 1771 was converted into a house and a second chapel built. This again was in many respects his private chapel, but after his death was sold by his widow in 1797 to the local Methodist society. Another chapel (*opposite*) was built on the site in 1813 and prominent members included David Charles the elder (1762-1834), the hymn-writer and one of the eleven preachers in Wales ordained as ministers in 1811, and his son David Charles the younger (1803-80), also a Calvinistic Methodist minister and hymn-writer.

The chapel was considerably modified in 1831, when the present gallery was installed. In 1851 there were 325 free seats and 685 others, and on 30 March 394 were present in the morning service with 43 scholars, and 470, with 42 scholars in the evening service.

The chapel has a long-wall front with pedimented porches on Tuscan columns, and a large arched window above each. Three slate monuments by Evan Harries were attached to the front and dated 1863. Inside, the gallery is supported by Corinthian columns, one of which is dated 1813. Box pews follow the line of the gallery, and the mahogany pulpit, of the 'wine-glass' type, stands between the entrance doors. The ceiling has a large plaster rose, added in 1892. An extension to house the organ was designed by J. Howard Morgan, and installed in 1922. Memorial tablets on the walls include those to the Rev. David Charles the elder, by Daniel Mainwaring in 1834, and to the Rev. John Wyndham Lewis, minister from 1870 until 1895, by W. Davies in 1895.

Heol Dŵr is the mother church of Y Babell, Pensarn (1834) and Bethania, Priory Street (1904), and also of Zion, Mansel Street (1850), which, established to cater for non-Welsh speakers, was designed by R.G. Thomas, the Newport architect, and has an elegant Classical façade.

Present position: No minister, 39 members, Sunday service, 10.00 a.m.
Further reading: *Zion 1850-2000, Celebrating 150 years of worship at Zion Presbyterian Church, Mansel Street, Carmarthen* (2000); *Capel Information Leaflet* 31, Carmarthen (2007).

78. DREFACH, LLANELLI, Capel Seion (I)

OS: SN 518 132

The first chapel is believed to have been built in 1712 on land granted by Philip Lloyd, Heol-ddu, Foelgastell, and within two years, nine members of the church at Pant-teg had been released to form a church at Capel Seion under the supervision of William Evans, principal of the Presbyterian College, Carmarthen. The chapel was extended c.1812, renovated in 1848 and in 1851 there were 300 seats and space for 400 persons to stand. On 30 March 250 were present in the morning service, 103 scholars in the afternoon and 168 in the evening service.

A lease of 1873 revealed that the land on which the chapel stood was owned by the Thomas family of Plas Cwmmawr, Drefach, and that, although a member of this family, the Rev. David Parry Thomas, rector of Llanmaes, Vale of Glamorgan had agreed to sign a new lease, he had died before the terms of a new lease were agreed. The trustees of the estate are believed to have attempted to turn the chapel into an Anglican church, but their efforts were foiled, and the lease recorded an agreement whereby the church would pay a sum of £100 and a rent of 10s a year for 1,000 years on certain conditions, including the reservation of mineral rights to the owner. In 1878 the present chapel was built, near to the existing chapel and services continued to be held in the original chapel whilst the new one was being built. This chapel, with its distinctive classical 'great arch' in pediment, was designed by the Rev. Thomas Thomas, Landore.

Following the Revival of 1904-05 it was considered that there was a need to improve the facilities, as the small vestry above the chapel house and the stable were too small. Additional land was therefore acquired facing the main road for the building of a vestry, kitchen and stable. The lease was extended for 99 years, and a rent of £2 was agreed. The owner by this time was Frances Ann Crosby, the grand-daughter of David Parry Thomas. Within a year the present vestry was built. The lands leased in 1873 and 1906 were bought in 1920, and thereby the chapel, chapel house, graveyard, vestry and land were acquired for £50.

The third minister, from 1720 until 1752, was the Rev. Samuel Jones, Pen-twyn, near Llwynteg in the parish of Llan-non, who held an academy at Pen-twyn. One of his students at the academy was Richard Price F.R.S. (1723-91), the celebrated philosopher whose writings influenced the Constitution of the United States of America. His successor as minister, from 1752 until 1802, was the Rev. Evan Griffiths, and during his ministry a theological debate resulted in the departure from the church in 1800 of a number of Calvinist members, who founded Bethania Independent Church in Upper Tumble. Other Independent churches in this locality which may be stated to have been directly or indirectly descended from Capel Seion include Nasareth, Pontiets (1803); Caersalem, Pontyberem (1816); Pen-y groes (1823); Crwbin (1829); Llwyn-teg (1845); Tabernacl, Cefneithin (1876); and

Bethesda, Tumble (1905).

Recent long-serving ministers include the Revs. Luther Moseley (1947-60) and Tudor Lloyd Jones (1968-95).

Present position: Arweinydd [Leader], Gwyn Elfyn, following the retirement in Decemebr 2012 of the Rev. Wilbur Lloyd Roberts, 204 members, 12 children, Sunday service, 10.30 a.m., Sunday school, 9.40 a.m.,monthly women's meeting, annual Singing Festival [Gymanfa Ganu] on Palm Sunday.

Further reading: Gwilym Evans, *Capel Seion, Drefach, Llanelli 1712-1980* (1981); Thomas Lloyd, 'Pre-1800 dated buildings in Carmarthenshire', *The Carmarthenshire Antiquary*, xxi (1985); Wilbur Lloyd Roberts (ed.) *Llusern Ffydd* (2012).

79. LLANELLI, Capel Als (I)

OS: SN 511 003

The history of the chapel may be traced to the year 1780 when a chapel was built to accommodate those members of the mother church, Llanedi, who resided in the parish of Llanelli. The original chapel, described as a 'tŷ bychan diaddurn' [a small unadorned house', was built on a plot of land where previously there had stood a cottage known as 'tŷ Alys'[Alys's house], and nearby was a well known as 'Ffynnon Alys' [Alys's well]. Llanelli soon grew rapidly as a result of significant developments in the metallurgical and coal-mining industries. Most of the members were colliers or copper workers, and the chapel, located between the Box and Bres collieries, was at the hub of the industrial activity, with much of the local traffic passing Capel Als, and coal wagons travelling on the railroad along the nearby Wern Road linking the town to the docks. After 1780 the building was extended and enlarged on several occasions, as in 1797, and a marble inscription on the wall of the outer vestibule at the entrance to the present chapel records outline various stages of rebuilding and extension, together with the names of the early ministers.

A marble memorial tablet to David Rees has been placed on the front wall of the chapel, to the left of the pulpit. David Rees, minister from 1829 to 1869, who was known as 'Y Cynhyrfwr' ['The Agitator'] on account of his admiration of Daniel O'Connell, was one of the notable leaders of nineteeth-century Wales, a redoubtable defender of Nonconformity who vigorously expressed his Radical views as editor of the Welsh journal, *Y Diwygiwr* (1835-1865). The 1851 Census recorded that the chapel contained 220 free seats and 630 others. On 30 March 800 were present in the morning service and 850 in the evening. No statistics were provided for the Sunday School, but the Rev. David Rees commented in a note that most of the Sunday School members attended services at the chapel, and that most of the congregation belonged to the Sunday School.

He had previously explained that many members had 'to work on the Sabbaths in copper and other works which required to be kept in order so that all the worshippers are never at the same time in any of the chapels at this place.' He added that there were "at least 1,300 who are in the habit of frequenting this chapel which is always crammed in the evening".

The statistics and comments emphasise the need for a new chapel, and in the following year the chapel was rebuilt and the architect was the Rev. Thomas Thomas, Landore. The minister's missionary zeal resulted in the building of the chapels of Siloa (1841), Y Bryn (1842), Dock Chapel (1876), and the English Park Street Church (1839).

During the ministry of his successor, the Rev. Thomas Johns, the first joint secretary of the Union of Welsh Independents, and editor of the children's magazine, *Tywysydd y Plant* for 44 years, Tabernacl Chapel, designed by John Humphrey,

Morriston, was opened in 1875 as Capel Als by that time was too small for its congregation. Even after the building of Tabernacl, there continued to be a problem of housing the congregation of Capel Als, and the chapel was extended in 1894 at a cost of £4,995. The four-wall framework was retained and the architect was Owen Morris Roberts, Porthmadog, a former ship's carpenter. Seating was provided for 1,100 persons with a gallery on four sides and a fully-integrated organ loft. Its frontage is in semi-Classical style, with a plain rendered finish, which contrasts with the warmth of the fine interior, with its decorated ceilings and stained glass windows. The renovated chapel evidently impressed the minister, the Rev. Thomas Johns who described the handsome and beautiful chapel as an 'addurn' ['adornment'] to the town, and the ceiling as "a real work of art".

Other previous ministers include the Revs. D.J. Davies, the chaired bard at the Aberafan National Eisteddfod in 1932 (1916-58); Iorwerth Jones (1959-1975) and Maurice Loader (1975-1994).

The new, large platform pulpit, which replaced the former 'witness –box tradition' one, provided a stage overlooked by a gallery which could be filled with a choir and orchestra. Capel Als is associated with the excellence of its musical traditions. The organ, made by Bishop & Son, has been maintained by Hill, Norman & Beard. The choirmaster for many years was Dr. Haydn Morris who conducted memorable performances by the chapel choir at the Market Hall. The string orchestra won first prize at the Llanelli National Eisteddfod in 1932. The first headmistress of Ysgol Gymraeg Dewi Sant, the first bilingual school established in Wales by a local authority, was Miss Olwen Williams, a deacon in the church, and the Sunday School evidently benefitted from this connection.

Considerable sums of money have been spent over the years in maintaining the chapel building. Major repairs included repairs to the roof timbers at the front of the chapel where extensive damage had been caused on account of the rotting of the main supporting roof-trusses.

Present position: No minister; 114 members, eight children, Sunday services at 10.30 a.m; monthly cultural society, 'Teulu Alys' in the winter, coffee morning to socialise and support Fair Trade first Saturday every month.

Further reading: Iorwerth Jones, *David Rees, y Cynhyrfwr* (1971); *Capel Als, 1780-1980*, ed Maurice Loader (1980); Huw Edwards, *Capeli Llanelli, Our Rich Heritage* (2009).

80. LLANELLI, Greenfield (Be)

OS: SN 506 001

This English-language Baptist church was established by the Welsh-language churches of Seion (see entry 81 Llanelli Seion) and Bethel, which were aware that David Rees, minister of Capel Als, had initiated an 'English cause' at the Park church in 1839. A plot of land known as 'the Greenfields' was bought, and a large chapel, measuring 60' by 41', was built at an estimated cost of £1,300. The chapel, opened in August 1858, was designed by Henry Rogers, and, with a handsome temple façade, was built in local grey-brown stone with Bath stone. Distinctive features include giant pilasters, columned Doric porch and long arched windows. A comparison may be drawn with the architect's Seion chapel which had been rebuilt in 1857. The new church had 23 members, including eight from Bethel and ten from Seion, of whom one, William Thomas, Cwmbach, a wealthy local resident, served as a deacon in Greenfield for many years, contributed substantial sums to the church and is commemorated by a memorial tablet in the chapel.

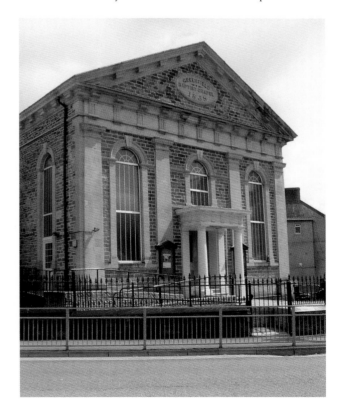

Galleries were added to the interior in 1861 and 1867 and the cast-iron gallery fronts probably date from the late-nineteenth century. A large new school-room, designed by George Morgan, Carmarthen, and comprising two large halls, two large classrooms in the rear and several smaller classrooms on the ground floor and on the galleries was opened in 1888, next to the chapel and cost £2,250. George Morgan also designed the renovations of 1902 and 1903 which included a new lobby, additional seating and a new organ by Harrison and Harrison, Durham, which was completely restored by the firm in 1969 and again in 1990.

Greenfield has been served by eleven ministers. The membership reached its highest number of 700 during the pastorate of the Rev. John M. Gwynne Owen, from 1909 until 1928, who came to Llanelli having previously served as minister in Devon, Manchester, Southampton and Birmingham. He baptized at Greenfield more than 400 persons, and queues are reported to have formed up to an hour before the commencement of the evening service.

The church experienced a difficult period in the 1970s when the proposal to demolish the 'New School-room' and build a complex of flats for the elderly resulted in a fierce debate among the members, was eventually approved by only a very small majority. By today the loss of the space which could provide improved facilities for the children attending on Sunday mornings, and the two youth groups meeting on Friday evenings, is greatly regretted.

Present position: Minister, Rev. David Jones (since 1989); 250 members, 50 children; Sunday services, 11.a.m (Family service with Junior Church and youth discussion groups) and 6.00 p.m. (with choir), Tuesday morning service, Prayer & Bible study meeting, Tuesday evening; Choir practice Thursday evening; Junior Youth Friday evening.

Further reading: Huw Edwards, *Capeli Llanelli, Our Rich Heritage* (2009).

Website: greenfieldchurch.net

81. LLANELLI, Seion [Zion] (Bw)

OS: SN 509 005

The words 'Jerusalem y Bedyddwyr yng Nghymru' [The Jerusalem of the Baptists in Wales] refer to the number and size of the Baptist chapels of Llanelli. The first of these chapels to be built was Seion, in 1822, as a branch of Adulam church, Felin-foel, which had been incorporated in 1735. In the seventeenth century Baptists of Llanelli had been among the early members of Ilston church, Gower, and they travelled to Ilston one Sunday every month, and to a house in the present-day village of Bynea on other Sundays. During the period 1766-1822 meetings were held in a small house in Spring Gardens opposite the location of the Town Hall today. Land was provided for a chapel on the present site and this was opened in 1823 with the minister of Adulam preaching here on Sunday evenings whilst the members were expected to attend the services at Adulam on Sunday mornings. An application to form a church in Seion was initially rejected but eventually approved in 1831 when 161 members of Adulam were released to form the church at Seion.

The 1851 Census recorded that the chapel contained 670 free seats and 130 others. On 30 March 1851, 400 were present in the morning service and 750 in the evening. The original chapel became too small for the growing congregation and a new chapel, designed by Henry Rogers and seating a congregation of 1,000 was built and this was opened in 1858. In the same year the Greenfield English chapel was opened and a number of the Seion members joined this church (see 80, Llanelli, Greenfield). The chapel was pedimented with giant pilasters, and was built of grey-brown local stone with brown sandstone dressings. The town of Llanelli continued to grow rapidly in the nineteenth century, and other Baptist chapels were opened. In 1872, 180 members were released to form the church at Moriah, and in 1881, 70 members left to form the church of Calfaria. Despite this, the membership increased from 281 in 1855 to 749 in 1900.

The minister during this period, from 1855 until 1900, was the Rev. John Rhys Morgan ('Lleurwg'), who was one of the most eminent Baptist preachers in Wales. He was renowned for his eloquence and mastery of the Welsh language, and other Seion ministers also regarded as 'giants of the Welsh pulpit' were the Rev E.T. Jones, the minister from 1900 until 1929, and Jubilee Young, the minister from 1931 until 1957. Oratorios were regularly performed by the chapel choir, conducted by R.C. Jenkins, who also conducted the 'United Llanelly Choir'. The choir's success in the main choral competition at the National Eisteddfod at Swansea in 1891 was acclaimed by a large and frenzied crowd which had assembled to greet the choir as it returned to the town. The Royal Commision Report of 1906 recorded that there were 996 members at Seion, the largest church in Llanelli, with congregations of 906, 967 and 812 on three Sunday evenings in late-September and early October. In the same year the highest number of members, 1,006, was recorded. In 1912-13 the

old schoolroom and two houses owned by the church were demolished, and next to the chapel was built the large schoolroom, designed by William Griffiths. This was built of local stone with Bath dressings, and comprising two storeys, has a pedimented centre and arched windows. The chapel and schoolroom were approximately the same size and both are listed Grade 2 by Cadw. The chapel was substantially modified in 1929 with the installation of a fourth gallery with an organ loft, housing a large three-manual organ built by W.C. Vowles, Bristol, and choir pews with dark wood panelling.

Concerts, lectures and political meetings have been held in the schoolroom, and speakers who have appeared here include Dr Martin Niemoller and David Lloyd George on several occasions. The first Welsh-medium school to be established by a local authority was opened in the schoolroom in 1947, and was housed here until it moved to a permanent home. The large room and the smaller one continue to be used for various meetings. Ambitious plans were announced in 2010 for a new cultural centre, Y Ffwrnes to be built next to Seion on the site of the Stepney Hotel. The intention is that the proposed retail, hotel and cinema development will include a main 500-seat auditorium, stage, and orchestra pit and flexible seating plan; offices to be provided for the University of Wales Trinity Saint David and as part of the proposal Seion chapel will be renovated. Several distinctive features of Seion, including the pulpit and *sêt fawr*, will be retained, and suitable premises provided for the church to hold its services. Services are held at the Glenalla Civic Hall and Community Centre until the anticipated completion of the building work in December 2012.

Present position: No minister, 55 members, Sunday service, 10.30 a.m. Tuesday morning prayer/Bible study meeting, monthly mission coffee morning and women's meeting

Further reading: E.T. Jones and T.R. Jones, *Hanes Eglwys Capel Seion, Llanelli* (1931); T.R. Jones, *Hanes Sion Llanelli* (1947); Huw Edwards, *Capeli Llanelli, Our Rich Heritage* (2009).

82. PEN-Y-GROES, Temple (A)

OS: SN 587 132

The Apostolic Temple is the fruit of the 1904-05 Revival and it became the centre of the world-wide Apostolic Church. It is therefore significant that the tablet on the outer wall proclaims 'in memory of the 1904-05 Revival'.

Daniel P. Williams (1882-1947), known locally as 'Pastor Dan', a coalminer and member of the Independent church at Pen-y-groes, experienced a conversion whilst listening to Evan Roberts preaching on Chrsitmas Day 1904. He later came into contact with a Pentecostal group when on holiday at Aberaeron in 1909. He joined an evangelical church which held services at the 'Hall gerrig' [Stone hall] in Pen-y-groes, and then, after leaving that church, the Babell meeting house was built in the village in 1913 for the local apostolic church. He was ordained an 'apostle' responsible for supervising the meeting houses of the 'Apostolic Faith Church' in Wales at a convention held the following year in London. The connection with the AFC was terminated in 1916 and a new body, the Apostolic Church in Wales was established. The first meetings of the Church were held at Skewen in January 1920 and all the minutes were in the Welsh language. A journal, *Riches of Grace*, was published and 'Pastor Dan' was its editor throughout its existence. A number of contributions, especially in the early years, were in Welsh, and the first issue referred to 19 churches in south Wales.

A convention was held in Pen-y-groes in August 1917, in a marquee with 1,000 seats. The convention developed into an international annual event, with missionaries sent to Africa, South America, India and a number of other countries. This was held at the Memorial Hall in Pen-y-groes after 1921, but despite establishing an appeal fund to build a temple to house the convention, it was resolved to spend the money collected to assist other congregations to build suitable buildings. An important development in 1922 was that several other Apostolic congregations joined with the Apostolic Church in Wales to form The Apostolic Church. The Church grew quickly and by 1930 there were 150 churches in Wales and 50 in other countries. A plot of land was purchased from a coalmine manager, and in 1933 the Apostolic Temple, with over 1,000 seats, was opened and all the costs had been paid. The Temple was built in the form of a cross, with a main assembly room, two transepts and a gallery above the entrance. By 1962 over 2,000 churches belonged to the Church, with 250 of these in the United Kingdom. By this time the Temple was too small for the convention, which was also an important event for the local community with several members from local churches attending services as well as members of the Apostolic Church, and many came from overseas countries. A large hall was built besides the Temple in 1967, and a considerable amount of the work was undertaken voluntarily by members of the Church. The hall was demolished in 2005 for safety reasons. Following an unbroken series of annual conventions held at

203

Pen-y-groes since 1917, the location was moved to Swansea in 2003, and to Cheltenham in 2012.

The education of the Church's prospective leaders and pastors has been provided at the Pen-y-groes Bible School established in 1933. A new hostel was opened in 1936, and although closed for a period in the 1970s and 1980s it was reopened in 1988. At present the Bible School is used by students from Korea.

Present position: Pastor: John Yeoman, 50 members, Sunday services: 10.30 a.m. and 6.00 p.m., Sunday school, 11.00 a.m.; monthly women's meeting, Tuesday; coffee morning, Wednesday; prayer meeting/Bible study Thursday evening; youth 'Crosswire' meeting, Friday evening; quarterly luncheon club with open invitation to villagers.

Further reading: T.N. Turnbull, *Brothers in Arms* (1963); James E. Worsfold, *The Origins of the Apostolic Church in Great Britain* (1991)

83. AMMANFORD, Bethany (Pw)

OS: SN 627 121

The present chapel was opened in 1929 after the old chapel and vestry were taken down in 1926. The first chapel on this site was opened in 1881 by the inhabitants of the village of Cross Inn, as Ammanford was known at that time. They were members of Seion church, in the nearby village of Betws, who were eager to build a chapel in a convenient location in the middle of a rapidly-growing coal-mining village. It is probable that the English form of the word 'Bethany', rather than 'Bethania' for a Welsh chapel may be explained by the intention to provide for the spiritual needs of the increasing number of English-speakers attracted to work in this area, and also possibly by a lack of optimism concerning the future of the Welsh language. One of those brought up in Bethany was the Rev. J.T. Job (1867-1938), the hymn-writer and chaired bard, who became a minister in Aberdare, Carneddi and Fishguard.

The third minister of Bethany was the Rev. W. Nantlais Williams (1874-1959), the hymn-writer, editor and poet, who was brought up in Gwyddgrug, near Pencader. He came to the attention of the members when he won the chair at the Ammanford eisteddfod in 1899. He was inducted as the minister in 1900 and his pastorate contin-ued for forty-four years. The 1904-05 Revival had a great influence on Bethany and on Nantlais who resolved to refrain from competing as a poet in eisteddfodau and to concentrate on proclaiming the Word. He composed a number of hymns, including several extremely-popular hymns for children, and he was the editor of *Trysorfa'r*

Plant, the denomination's children magazine, for thirteen years. An open Bible, music score and two pens, visual symbols of his achievements as a preacher, hymn writer and editor, appear above the words on his memorial tablet in the chapel.

An increase in the membership accounted for the intention to build a new chapel. After a decade of planning and collecting money, in a period of depression and poverty, and the damaging effects of the 1925 Strike, a new chapel was opened in October 1929. Nantlais was responsible for the selection of the wording on the foundation stone laid the previous year: 'I gofio 1904' ['To commemorate 1904' and 'I gofio y Maes Cenhadol' [To commemorate the Mission Field']. Whilst the new chapel was being built the pulpit, formerly in the old chapel and therefore the one used during the Revival, was safeguarded and continues to be used in the large vestry behind the chapel. The architect of the new chapel was J. Owen Parry, a member of the church, and the builder was William Evans, Ammanford, who was also responsible for building Gwynfryn, the Independent chapel in the town. A Classical façade was placed in front of the 1881 chapel, with a thin pediment, and the building was of stone with ashlar details. The interior is simple and dignified, with oak woodwork and a panelled three-sided gallery on iron columns. Seats were provide for 850 persons, and the cost was £12,000. An organ built by Conacher, Huddersfield was installed.

Nantlais was succeeded as minister by the Revs. J.D. Williams (1944-93), Gareth H. Davies (1982-93) and Meurig Dodd (1995-2001).

Present position: No minister, 53 members, Sunday services 10.15 a.m. and 5.30 p.m; weekly prayer meeting/Bible study, monthly sisterhood.
Further reading: J.D. Williams, *Bethany, Rhydaman, 1881-1981* (1981); Goronwy Prys Owen, 'Nantlais (1874-1959)' in *Nefol Dân, Agweddau ar Ddiwygiad 1904-05*, ed. Noel Gibbard (2004).

84. AMMANFORD, Gellimanwydd / Christian Temple (I)

OS: SN 633 123

There is a close connection between the history of Gellimanwydd / Christian Temple and the development of the town of Ammanford. The first chapel was built in 1782 near to the site of the present chapel, on a plot of land named Gellimanwydd. Although 'Capel Gellimanwydd' was the official name, the chapel was often described as 'Cross Inn Chapel', thereby referring to the original name of the village which developed into the town of Ammanford. Another chapel was built on the actual site of the present chapel in 1834, as a result of a substantial increase in the membership of the church following the Revival of 1829. A memorial stone near the door in the front of the chapel stated in English that this was the 'Cross Inn Chapel, built in 1782', followed by the Latin words 'Vox Populi' and that it was rebuilt in 1836 'Vox Dei'.

The 1851 Census recorded that on 30 March 280 were present in the morning service, 172 scholars in the afternoon and 226 in the evening service. The chapel was extended in 1865 with the Rev. Thomas Thomas, Landore, the renowned architect-minister, responsible for designing the improvements which cost £1,000. It is probable that his façade had two arched windows and arched doors. Another name, 'Christian Temple' was now adopted, and possibly reflects the contemporary negative view with regard to the future prospects of the Welsh language (see also 83,

Ammanford, Bethany). This is the name which appears on the tablet on the façade, and the full form, or an abbreviated version, 'Temple', was widely used by local residents. However, the minister and officials state that the official Welsh term 'Gellimanwydd' is generally used today.

A vestry was built in 1882, when the church celebrated its centenary, and for a period this was the location of the school of Watkyn Hezekiah Williams, 'Watcyn Wyn' (1844-1905), the schoolmaster, poet, and preacher. The missionary endeavours of Christian Temple resulted in the foundation of the Gwynfryn church in 1905 with 135 members enrolling in the new church, where Watcyn Wyn now established his academy to train prospective ministers. Gwynfryn, which has a stone gable front with Gothic tracery was designed by H. Herbert, who also possibly designed the interior of Gellimanwydd in 1910, when the chapel was renovated and the heavy pediment, Classical porch and large Gothic window probably introduced. The near-square interior had a strongly-panelled gallery, similar to the one at Gwynfryn, was supported on iron columns, with the gallery detail corresponding to that on the *sêt fawr* and pulpit.

In 1910 also a new organ built by Messrs. Norman & Beard was installed and formally opened by Caradog Roberts, Rhosllannerchrugog. Christian Temple is renowned for its musical tradition, with Gwilym R. Jones, its organist and choirmaster from 1914 until 1950, the conductor of the Ammanford Choir which achieved three successes at the National Eisteddfod. A new hall, Neuadd Gellimanwydd, was opened in 1970, and a number of functions are held here, including 'Drws agored' on a Thursday morning when a welcome is extended to socialise and join together in devotion.

Gellimanwydd has been served by nine ministers, including the Rev. Dr. Tegfan Davies (1915-1965) and the memorial tablet in the chapel refers to him as a friend to the people of Ammanford. He was described as a 'cyfaill mawr i'r glowyr' [a great friend to the coalminers] by the Rt. Hon James Griffiths (1890-1975), the Labour politician and cabinet minister. He and his brother, D.R. Griffiths, 'Amanwy' (1882-1953), the poet and writer, were members in Gellimanwydd throughout their lives and both are buried in the graveyard, together with Watcyn Wyn and also the Rev. J. Towyn Jones, another politician associated with the church.

Present position: Rev. Dyfrig Rees, 235 members, 25 children; Sunday services: 10.30 a.m with Sunday School, 5.30 p.m.; weekly prayer meeting, Bible study, preparatory meeting before Communion Sunday, i.e. the first Sunday of the month.
Further reading: Rachel L. Thomas, *Christian Temple, Eglwys Annibynnol Gellimanwydd, Rhydaman, 1892-1982* (1982).

85. LLANDOVERY, William Williams Memorial Chapel (Pe)

OS: SN 769 343

The Memorial Chapel (*over*) was built in High Street, Llandovery to commemorate William Williams (1717-91), the preacher and hymn-writer who lived in the neighbourhood of the town at the Pantycelyn farmhouse, and who was buried at the town's Llanfair-ar-y-bryn church. The need for an English church in the town was realised in view of the influx of many English-speakers to the town to build the mid-Wales railway. Previously English-language services had been held at the Tabernacl chapel, whose minister, the Rev. T. Thomas had organised the national appeal for subscriptions to finance the building of the chapel.

The chapel, costing £3,120, was designed by John Henry Phillips, Cardiff, with David Morgan the contractor. The foundation stones were laid by two Members of Parliament, David Davies, Llandinam and David Pugh, Llangadog. Measuring 43' long by 30' wide and 27' high, and holding 280 persons with a schoolroom for 80 scholars, the chapel was constructed during the period 1886-88. The chapel was built in a Decorated Gothic style, of grey Dunvant stone with Bridgend stone dressings and a slate roof with a coped gable. The interior is of an unusual ecclesiastical Gothic style, with a three-sided apse and a Gothic 'chancel arch'. To the left of the arch is located the Gothic pulpit in Caen stone, with stone steps and ornate panels on the five sides depicting Biblical scenes together with one of William Williams writing on an ancient sroll. An end-wall gallery over the entrance gallery is supported on two octagonal timber columns.

When the chapel opened, the *Carmarthen Journal* drew attention to this handsome building as one of, if not the very first, Calvinistic Methodist chapel to display artworks. A notable work of art is the stained glass window in four sections depicting Isaiah and St. Matthew in the centre, flanked by King David and Miriam, commemorating the Rev. John Roberts, 'Ieuan Gwyllt' (1822-27), the Rev. Thomas Phillips (1806-70) and the hymn-writer Ann Griffiths (1776-1805). The communion table in the centre of the chapel, together with four chairs, was donated by the Christian community of the Khasi Hills, north-east India, responding to the appeal before the chapel opened in view of their awareness that a number of William Williams's hymns had been translated into their language. Contributions were also received from the U.S.A. and Australia. The small harmonium was built by Dale, Forty & Co., Cheltenham.

A considerable amount of renovation work has been undertaken in recent years, and a substantial grant was received from the Heritage Lottery Fund. However, there is some uncertainty at present concerning the future of the church.

Present position: Rev. David H. Jenkins, 12 members, monthly Sunday service 6.00 p.m.

Further reading: *William Williams Memorial Chapel Centenary Souvenir, 1888-1988* (1988); Eifion Evans, *Bread of Heaven: The Life and Work of William Williams, Pantycelyn* (2010).

86. PONTARDDULAIS, Y Gopa (Pw)

OS: SN 602 034

A thatched roof chapel, Capel Iago, was built in 1773 following visits to the locality by Howel Harris in 1740, and the welcome he received at Llandremor Uchaf, the home of John Morgan, the old sailor, and where a society had been formed. This event has been recorded on the vestry wall behind the present chapel. Another name for the chapel was 'Gopa-fach'. The hymn-writer Dafydd Wiliam resided in a cottage near the chapel, and it is probable that he attended services at the chapel before he left the area in 1776-77. A description of this chapel has been provided by Hopcyn Bevan, who was the minister of Gopa in the period 1796-1809, and one of the first group of thirteen ministers ordained by the Calvinistic Methodists at Llandeilo in 1811. He referred to a small building accommodating about 100 persons, with its walls of local stones, a thatched roof and its earthen floor.

As a result of missionary activities by members of Gopa, a number of churches were established in this area. Capel Iago was rebuilt in 1837 and a schoolroom, 'Yr Hen Dŷ Ysgol' was opened in Pentre-bach in 1857. The considerable increase in the local population caused by the development of the coal industry and the establishment of two tinplate works led to the building of the present chapel in 1890, and Ebenezer in Pentre-bach in 1897 to replace the schoolroom. The chapel has a high ceiling, and the seats on the ground floor rise gradually. When he addressed the members in 1888, the minister, the Rev. W.E. Prydderch referred to the important work facing the church, that is, building a new temple [*teml newydd*]. The membership increased from approximately 156 to 327 during his pastorate (1874-1894). He was acclaimed as one of the most popular preachers in Wales, and Dr. Cynddylan Jones commented on the staunch Welshness of his style, and his masterly use of rural idioms.

The chapel was renovated in 1912 when a pipe organ built by Blackett & Howden, Newcastle-upon-Tyne, Glasgow and Cardiff was placed behind the pulpit, and the J.W. Walker firm continues to service and maintain it. The work of installing the organ was supervised by Dr. D. Vaughan Thomas, a member of a family prominent in the local musical and religious community. In 1942, at the end of the second period of the pastorate of the Rev. Thomas Francis Jones (1895-1908 and 1920-1942) there were 544 members in Gopa.

A centre for young persons, an educational room and new kitchen were provided in the space underneath the chapel during the pastorate of the Rev. J.E. Davies , 'Davies y Gopa', (1948-1968). Glyn Hopkin, the author of a history of the chapel, considered this period to be a golden age of the church in a cultural context. Extensive use of the chapel was made for concerts, and the high quality of the acoustics was highly praised. The Rev. J.E. Davies commented on the suitability of the chapel for preaching and public speaking, and also for choral as well as congre-

gational singing. The chapel was renovated in 2003, and is at present in a very favourable condition. The large vestry behind the chapel on a lower level and other rooms, together with a small one used for weeknight meetings, provide additional facilities.

The chapel has been listed Grade 2 by Cadw.

Present position: No minister, but valuable assistance provided by the Rev. D. Leslie Jones, the former minister, 60 members, 10-15 children attend Clwb y Bont held at the branch in Pentrebach on Monday evenings, Sunday services: 10.30 a.m. Bible study class every fortnight, and cultural society every month.

Further reading: Glyn Hopkin, *Hanes Eglwys y Gopa , Pontarddulais 1773-1973* (1973); *The History of Pontardulais*, ed. E. Lewis Evans, trans. Ivor Griffiths (1985); J.E. Davies, *O Graig i Graig* (1991).

87. PONTARDDULAIS, Hope-Siloh (I)

OS: SN 591 038

The early history may be traced to Hen Gapel Llanedi, the Independent chapel founded on the Carmarthenshire side of the county boundary in 1712. The small size of this building, together with the negative attitude of local landowners and the growth of the village of Pontarddulais as a result of industrial activities, with the Hendy, Tal-y-clun, Cambria and Ffos-yr-efail tinplate works opening in the period 1866-1875, led to the leasing, to 13 men for 99 years from 25 March 1869, of a plot of land, measuring slightly over half an acre, in the centre of the village beside the turnpike road to Swansea. The church was formally established on 22 August, 1869, and the trustees included Thomas Rees, Hendy, described as a Superintendent of Tinworks, and four tinplate makers, of whom one, John Edwards, was the first secretary of the church. The adoption of an English name 'Hope' for a Welsh chapel may possibly be explained, as was also the case at Ammanford (see entries 83 and 84), by a lack of optimism for the future prospects of the Welsh language, and the minute-book, significantly contained entries in English until 1924.

The first chapel was a plain, simple building, measuring 34 feet long and 24 feet wide, and was considered to be of a sufficient size for the 40 members. However it was soon realized that the chapel was too small, and the present chapel was opened in 1872, at a cost of £1,000. It was designed by the Rev. Thomas Thomas, Landore, and the builder was Thomas White, whose cousin, John White, was a deacon here from 1885 until his death in 1944, and secretary of the church for 42 years. The chapel is of a Gothic style in coursed brown rubble stone with Bath stone dressings and a slate roof. The long interior has a three-sided gallery with raked pews, and, with curved angles is supported on iron columns. The pulpit has curving steps on each side and the panelled front has rosettes. This chapel seated 450 persons, but had to be extended in 1880. The original chapel may well be the 'small vestry' or the 'old vestry' which continues to be used.

Two branches were opened in 1884, one in Waungron and the other one, Soar, at Hendy. Repairs to the chapel in 1893 cost £538. In this year there were 550 members but a number left to form another Independent church at Siloh. An organ built by John Davies & Son, Clydach, and with a Gothic pine case and painted pipes in five bays were installed in 1893 in the large rear organ arch. Concern was expressed with regard to the condition of the foundations of the building early in the twentieth century, but these were unfounded, and in 1909 a large vestry was built with a full-height interior and end gallery, and ceiling with a painted decoration in three pale-blue panels with ornate borders. This 'new vestry' seats 300 on the ground floor, and another 100 in the gallery. It cost £1,420, was designed by J. Davies & Son, Llanelli, and the builder was George Mercer from the same town.

The ministers of Hope have included the Revs. D. Lloyd Morgan (1891-1934),

E. Lewis Evans (1935-1967) and Caradog Evans (1978-2001).

In 2001 the Hope and Bethesda, Llangennech churches agreed to share a joint pastorate and in the following year the Hope and Siloh churches agreed to worship together for a period of six months. Further collaboration resulted in the decision in December 2006 to sell the Siloh buildings and renovate those of Hope. Services were held at Siloh whilst the renovation work was undertaken, and in June 2009 the two churches formally united to form the Hope-Siloh church. The provision for disabled persons has been improved and the panelled curved-ended *sêt fawr* has been removed with the result that the deacons now sit with the congregation. The adaptations resulted in improved facilities, and the buildings are extensively used, by the Welsh nursery school, and for practices by various local choirs: regularly by Lleisiau Lliw and Cantorion Pontarddulais, the pensioners'choir; and occasionally by the Glandulais and Pontarddulais Male Voice Choirs and also the Pontarddulais Town Band.

Present position: Minister, Rev. Llewelyn Picton Jones, 190 members, 54 youth and children, Sunday service with Sunday School, 10.30 a.m., Bible study group every fortnight, Cyfeillion cultural society every month, coffee morning on Fridays once a month; youth club every other Sunday evening, *Cwlwm* magazine.

Further reading: E. Lewis Evans, *Eglwys Hope Pontarddulais* (1969); *The History of Pontardulais*, ed. E. Lewis Evans, trans. Ivor Griffiths (1985).

88. LOUGHOR, Moriah (Pw/e)

OS: SS 577 981

Moriah stands on the main road (A 484) between Swansea and Llanelli. Following the visit of Howel Harris to the area in 1739, a small congregation met in the kitchen of the Tŷ-fry farmhouse, Loughor, as a branch of Gopa, Pontarddulais [see entry 86]. Increased numbers in the 1820s led to the need for a meeting house. The farm's barn was adapted for use as a chapel which was opened on 11 October, 1828, and was known as 'Capel to gwellt' [thatched roof chapel]. The first minister was the Rev. Hopkin Bevan, the first Calvinistic Methodist ordained minister from Glamorgan. A further increase in the congregation as a result of periodic revivals led to the building in 1842 on the same site of a new chapel, accompanied by a graveyard. A gallery was added in 1849, and in 1851 there were 12 free seats and 270 others, together with standing space in the middle of the chapel and on the gallery 'except the Front'. On 30 March 74 scholars were present in the morning, and there was a congregation of 200 in the afternoon and 261 in the evening service. A chapel house and stable were later provided on the eastern end. Other churches were established at Bethel, Gowerton, in 1873 and Libanus, Gorseinon in 1890. As the membership continued to grow, the present chapel, seating a congregation of 650, was built in 1898. William Griffiths, Llanelli was the architect and the work undertaken cost £1,700. In 1903 a sum of £500 was paid for restoring the old chapel and converting it into a schoolroom.

A memorial to Evan Roberts, the revivalist, (1878-1951), stands outside the chapel, and was erected after his death in 1951. His parents had been members at Moriah since 1873, and he, baptised here soon after his birth in 1878, became a member in the church. Following his conversion at Blaenannerch on 29 September, 1904 (see 63, Blaenannerch) he conducted his first week-long mission campaign in October and November 1904 at Moriah, and at the nearby branch chapel of Pisgah, Bwlch-y-mynydd, and at Libanus, Gorseinon. Moriah was filled to capacity every night of the week, and services continued until 4.00 or 5.00 the following morning. He was buried in the graveyard, where also was buried his brother-in-law and fellow revivalist, the missionary Sidney Evans.

Services were traditionally held in Welsh and the church belongs to the Welsh-language presbytery. In recent years there has been a tendency to hold the greater part of the services in English.

Present position: No minister, 15 members, Sunday service, 10.30 a.m. and 3.00 p.m., Sunday school at 2.00 p.m., prayer meeting Monday afternoon.

Further reading: A Short History of Moriah Chapel and the 1904 Revival; Eifion Evans, *The Welsh Revival of 1904* (1998).

89. BURRY GREEN, Bethesda (Pe)

OS: SS 462 914

Early developments in Gower included the establishment of circulating charity schools by the Rev. Griffith Jones in 1740, visits by Howel Harris in 1742 and 1743, and the formation of a group of six chapels in the early nineteenth century by Diana Middleton, later Lady Barham (1762-1823), the evangelical patron, whose father had been First Lord of the Admiralty in the period leading up to the battle of Trafalgar. The earliest of these churches was Bethesda, Burry Green, founded in 1814, and located a quarter of a mile from Lady Barham's home at Fairy Hill. When she discovered that a small number of local inhabitants intended to build a small meeting house, she persuaded them to allow her to pay for a larger building than originally proposed, and also a manse for the minister. William Griffiths, a native of Pembrokeshire who had been recognized as a preacher by the Calvinistic Methodists in 1816, was invited by Lady Barham to become minister in the following year. Ordained in 1824, he served here until his death in 1861 and was known as 'The Apostle of Gower'. At his request, the Gower churches built at Lady Barham's expense were donated by her son, Lord Barham, to the Calvinistic Methodist Connexion.

Water and electricity supplies were introduced in the early 1950s. The absence of street lights in the village was graphically described by the Rev. Tudor Lloyd when reminiscing about the early days of his pastorate which extended from 1956 until 1994. He also recalled the large marquee erected in the field behind the chapel when Dr. Martyn Lloyd-Jones came to preach in 1963 at the 150th anniversary of the church. The pastorate today also includes Trinity, Cheriton, another of the original group of Lady Barham's churches; as well as Ebenezer, Old Walls; Tabernacle, Pen-clawdd; Zion, Llangennith; and Zoar, Crofty.

Present position: Minister, Rev. Iain Hodgins, 12 members, Sunday Services 11 a.m. and 6.30 p.m., Sunday School at 9.45am and a children's meeting (King's Club) on Thursdays at 4.45 p.m.at Llanmadoc Village Hall where more space is available, Bible studies and prayer meetings held jointly with, and in the other churches in the pastorate.

Further reading: Eifion Evans (ed.), *Pleasant Places, A Tribute to the Gower Ministry of Rev. B. Tudor Lloyd* (2006).

90. MORRISTON, Tabernacl (I)

OS: SS 670 978

Tabernacl has an unique place in the history of Welsh chapels and this is reflected in the title of Trebor Lloyd Evans's history of the chapel: *Cathedral Anghydffurfiol Cymru* [the Cathedral of Welsh Nonconformity]. When the chapel was opened on 3 January 1873 the *Cambrian Daily Leader* referred to it as 'a large oasis in the desert' and as a 'Cathedral', and this term has been used locally over the years.

There was a substantial increase in the local population as a result of the growth of the copper works established by Robert Morris, and his son John Morris, and 'Morris-town' or 'Tre-forris' was designed by William Edwards, the bridge-builder who was the minister of Groes-wen, Caerphilly (see 104). He had also, at the request of a local Independent congregation, designed Libanus chapel, which had opened in 1782 as a branch of the renowned church of Mynydd-bach on Llangyfelach Common, and although the 1851 Census recorded seating for 602, the need for a larger building was also noted. It was therefore soon decided, under the guidance of the minister, the Rev. W. Emlyn Jones, to build a new chapel, and he was assisted by two local industrialists, namely the architect John Humphrey, a deacon at Mynydd-bach, and the builder Daniel Edwards. Humphrey had already designed chapels and schools in the area, including the new Mynydd-bach chapel (1866) and Morriston school (1868), and he was the architect of a number of important chapels, including Ffald-y-brenin chapel (1873); Tabernacl, Llanelli (1875); Carmel, Gwaun-cae-gurwen (1877); Siloh Pentre (1877) and Zion, Llanidloes (1879). Having carefully supervised the building of Tabernacl, Daniel Edwards built the Duffryn tinworks in 1873 which developed into one of the largest iron and tinworks in Wales.

The three are stated to have visited a number of buildings in England before agreeing on an ambitious chapel which was originally known as the 'new Libanus' chapel. The foundation stone was laid on 26 November by Miss Annie Hughes (Morfydd Glantawe), the daughter of Richard Hughes, Ynystawe, who had secured the plot of land in Woodfield Street, on which the chapel now stands: she later married Sir John Williams, physician to the royal family and principal founder of the National Library of Wales. The construction work was completed within two years, at a cost of £14,000. The new structure made a tremendous impression with its pedimented temple front with four pairs of Corinthian columns, round-headed windows and square tower with octagonal spire and clock. The magnificent interior, seating 1,450, has an elliptical ceiling, continuous gallery with balustrade supported on iron columns, stencilled decoration, stained glass windows and large convex pulpit. A distinctive feature is the arrangement of the seating to concentrate on the pulpit, and on the gallery, behind the pulpit, the seating of the choir rises on an individual basis. The Rev. W. Emlyn Jones was a conductor of hymn-singing festivals,

and his choice therefore of the Biblical verse behind the pulpit, facing the congregation, is therefore very appropriate: 'Addolwch yr Arglwydd mewn prydferthwch sancteiddrwydd' [Worship the Lord in the beauty of holiness].

The highest number of members in the history of the church, over 1,000, was recorded in 1911, and there were nearly 800 members in 1945.

The interior was re-arranged in 1922 at the time of the installation of the organ built by the Hill, Norman & Beard firm. A sum of £75,000 was spent in 1998 on restoration-work by Harrison & Harrison, Durham on the organ, which has 2,310 pipes of various lengths. A grant of £63,000 was received from the National Heritage Memorial Fund, and the remainder was raised by means of an enterprising pipe-sponsorship scheme. A sum exceeding £1,000,000 was spent on renovating the chapel, and floodlights were installed so that the chapel could be seen from a distance. In 2001 the restoration of the organ was celebrated by means of the production of a CD prepared by Huw Tregelles Williams, who has been the organist here since 1983, and is one of the foremost organists in Wales. A sum of £18,000 was raised for the Morriston Hospital Heart Fund in a concert held in November 2001 to express appreciation for the completion of the work undertaken at the chapel.

Work undertaken in 2011-12 to safeguard the chapel for the future included the renovation of the windows, overhauling of the organ, painting of the ceiling, restoration of the tower, and re-wiring. A grant of £100,000 was received from Cadw, and the total cost was approximately £360,000.

The prominent ministers who served as pastors of the Tabernacl, and who have been commemorated in memorial tablets on the chapel's walls include the Revs. W. Emlyn Jones (1872-1914); J.J. Williams (1915-44), the poet/preacher, chaired bard and archdruid; and Trebor Lloyd Evans (1945-64), who later became secretary of the Union of Welsh Independents. Memorial plaques to Daniel Edwards and W. Penfro Rowlands, the composer of the hymn-tune 'Blaenwern' have been placed in the porch.

Tabernacl is closely associated with a fine musical tradition, which has been established by precentors and choir-masters such as David Francis (1872-89), Eos Morlais (1889-92), W. Penfro Rowlands (1892-1919) and Edgar Hughson (1919-66). Choral singing continues to be an important feature of the life of the church, and the tradition of presenting works by significant composers has continued to the present day. Annual concerts are held in the chapel by a number of choirs, including the Tabernacl Choir, the Morriston Rugby Club Choir, the Morriston Orpheus Choir and the Morriston Ladies Choir: the four choirs participated at the service held on 1 July, 2012 to celebrate the re-opening of the chapel after the completion of the restoration work.

Present position: No minister, since the retirement of the Rev. Ieuan Davies; 135 members, 15 children, Sunday service at 10.30 a.m. with Sunday school, Services are held jointly with Bethania, Presbyterian Church of Wales, once a month, and the two churches join together for the Communion service on the first Sunday of the month. The Tabernacl choir practices on a Sunday evening, a prayer meeting is held in Bethania on a Monday evening, and a sisterhood is held every other Wednesday afternoon.

Further reading: Trebor Lloyd Evans, *'Y Cathedral Anghydffurfiol Cymreig'* (1972); David Farmer, *The Remarkable Life of John Humphrey, God's Own Architect* (1997).

91. GELLIONNEN (U)

OS: SS 701 042

A tablet on the wall of Gellionnen chapel, built in a remote location on Mynydd Gellionnen records that 'This place of worship for the use of Protestant Dissenters was first erected 1692, under the patronage of the Hon. Bussy Mansell, Esq. and rebuilt 1801 under the direction of the pastor for the time being, the Rev. Josiah Rees, in the 38th year of his ministry hereat'. Bussy Mansell had been a Member of Parliament and commander of the parliamentary forces in the seventeenth century Civil War, and was said to have "retained enough affection for his former beliefs to help provide Dissenters with land, stone and timber for their chapels". Chapels in west Glamorgan regarded as off-shoots of the church founded at Cadoxton-juxta-Neath included Cwmllynfell, which was in existence by 1715, and Gellionnen, sited at a crossroads where four roads converged leading from Swansea to Brecon, Ammanford to Neath. The first minister of Gellionnen was Robert Thomas, who died in 1692. Llewelyn Bevan was ordained at Gellionnen in 1697, and served as minister at Cwmllynfell and Gellionnen in the period 1701-1723. Roger Howell was his co-minister for a time, and he was assisted by Joseph Simonds, a Calvinist, in 1724. After the death of Roger Howell there was no regular minister for 16 years, and a theological divergence resulted in an increase in Calvinism at Cwmllynfell, and of Arminianism and Arianism at Gellionnen. Josiah Rees came to preach at Gellionnen on a monthly basis in 1764, and from 1767 Cwmllynfell and Gellionnen had separate ministers.

Josiah Rees (1744-1804) became the minister in 1763, and lived at Gelli-gron where he kept a school. By the end of the eighteenth century he was a staunch Unitarian, and the chapel was rebuilt in 1801 during his pastorate. He had published in 1770 on a fortnightly basis *Yr Eurgrawn*, claimed to be the first Welsh magazine, and the chapel was rebuilt in 1801 during his pastorate. He had preached at the first public assembly of the South Wales Unitarian Association held at Cefn-coed y-cymer on 26 June, 1803. He died the following year and was buried near the chapel. His son Thomas was the minister of various churches in England from 1802 until 1831, but also served as minister of Gellionnen in 1805-06. Other sons included Owen, who became a partner of the Longman publishing firm, and Josiah who served as British consul at Smyrna. Thomas Rees was succeeded as minister by the Rev. David Oliver (1806-14), and then the Rev. John James (1815-62), who was known as the 'quick silver' of his denomination. A friend of Iolo Morganwg, he kept a boarding school at Clydach. He was assisted in the final year of his pastorate by his co-minister, the Rev. John Evans, who became minister in 1863. He established a school at Trebanos, and in 1871 the congregation purchased for £160 the lease of the land on which the chapel and cemetery stood and also another acre for extension: previously a rent of £5 had been paid for the chapel. After renovation work had been completed the chapel re-opened in 1873.

A substantial increase in the local population as a result of industrial developments resulted in the opening in 1894 by the Unitarians of Capel y Graig in the rapidly-growing village of Trebanos, and in 1904 a large vestry was built beside the chapel. A new manse was built in 1932 to replace the previous one which was a conversion of John Evans's school, and a spacious new hall was opened in 1938.

On the wall of Gellionnen chapel a stone plaque records that the ancient Gellionnen Stone was moved from this site to Swansea Museum in June 1967.

The chapel was badly damaged in March 2008 by vandals who pushed out a 12 foot tall window, smashed the pulpit, and damaged the walls. Soon afterwards a fund was established to finance restoration-work, including the refurbishment of the windows, restoration of the pulpit and plaques, and removal of the blue paint thrown at the walls undertaken by the retired minister, the late Rev. Eiron Phillips, members and supporters of the church. Other significant recent developments include the installation of a wood burning stove and a land drain.

Present position: Minister: the Rev. Lewis Rees, Sunday service, 10.45 a.m.

Further reading: John Henry Davies, *History of Pontardawe and District* (1967); Glanmor Williams, 'The Dissenters in Glamorgan, 1660-c.1760', *Glamorgan County History*, Vol 4; *Early Modern Glamorgan: from the Act of Union to the Industrial Revolution*, ed Glanmor Williams (1974).

website: www.gellionnenchapel.org.uk

92. RESOLFEN, Tabernacl (Pw)

OS: SN 831 025

The small number of Methodists in this area in the late-eighteenth century were probably members of Capel y Gyfylchi, a chapel on the mountain above Pontrhydyfen, where they attended services on a Sunday morning, and received Communion, and they then held prayer meetings in the evening in various farmhouses. This was probably the background to the fellowship meetings held in the village, and the cause at Resolfen may probably be dated to the year 1799. A new chapel, 'Sion', was opened in 1821 on land acquired from John Edwards, Rheola, on a 99-year lease and for a rent of one shilling a year, and enough land was obtained to ensure the creation of a cemetery in front of the chapel, a chapel house across the road and a stable to house the horses of preachers and the congregation. There were 18 members in 1851 but in this year the Census recorded 24 free seats and 120 others, and that on 30 March 70 were present in the evening service. The membership had increased to 46 by 1866, and with probably a greater number of listeners again attending, Seion was demolished in 1867 and a new 'Seion' was opened in the following year at a cost of £550. Seating was provided for 400 persons, and the chapel was built by William Herbert and sons, and John Michael. There was a further increase in membership and attendance in the late nineteenth century, especially during the pastorate of the Rev. Moses Thomas (1877-95), who had first come to Resolfen to keep a shop and a post office. The chapel choir regularly performed cantatas at singing and catechism-testing festivals: the Gymanfa Ganu and the Gymanfa Bwnc: and after 25 years as precentor Daniel Herbert resigned in 1892 and was replaced by David Evans who later became Professor of Music at the University College, Cardiff. He was in great demand as a conductor of singing festivals throughout Wales, as also was his successor in 1899 as the organist of Seion, his cousin Tom Hopkin Evans.

The membership had increased to 143 by 1901, approximately 100 children were associated with the church, and the large number of listeners swelled the congregation to nearly 400 on Sunday evenings. This led to a demand for a new chapel, and a plot of land was obtained on a 99-year lease. The high rent of £5.17s 9d per annum may possibly be explained by a dispute between the local landowner, Vaughan of Rheola, with a prominent member of the church. The new chapel, named 'Tabernacl', was designed by W. Beddoe Rees, built by the Couzens firm from Cardiff, and opened in October 1904. This was a handsome chapel in a 'mock Gothic 'style and seated 650 persons. 100 seats behind the pulpit were removed in 1944 for the installation of a second-hand pipe organ purchased from Stockport. In 1910 the Salvation Army established itself in the village, and held their services in the old Seion chapel.

Tabernacl was renovated and re-roofed in 1953-54, but severe problems were

experienced in 1963 and all the seats on the ground floor in contact with an outside wall had to be removed. Despite valiant efforts to safeguard the building, a decision was taken in 1983 to abandon the building which was demolished in 1987. Some of the land was sold to a building firm, and a small new chapel was built by the Neath Borough Council Training Agency. The total cost was £41,000, the pulpit and communion table were made by Clive Morris, an elder and treasurer of the church, and the congregation occupied the new chapel in June 1995.

Present position: No minister, 12 members, Sunday services, 10.30 a.m. (with Sunday school for adults and children) and 5.00 p.m., weekly devotional service and monthly missionary prayer meeting.

Further reading: Phylip Jones, *History of the Methodist Cause in Resolfen* (1999).

93. MARGAM Beulah (Pw/e)

OS: SS784 874

Beulah has been listed Grade 2* by Cadw as the only surviving octagonal chapel in Wales, and as a special example of the round-arched style in chapel architecture. The vestry beside the chapel, together with the gates and railings, are listed Grade 2. The chapel is also known as Capel y Groes as it was originally located in the Groes village. In spite of the opposition of local residents in 1974, the village was demolished to make way for the construction of the M4 motorway, but the chapel was preserved and rebuilt at a cost of more than £80,000 on a new site at Tollgate Park. Margam. A dedication service was held at the chapel on 22 March 1976.

Methodists in the Margam area had held services in various homes, including the home of Thomas Jenkins, in the village of Groes. Following an increase in the number of those attending the services, the local landowner C.R.M. Talbot was requested to provide a site for the building of a chapel. At the time the village was being planned to replace Margam village as part of Mr. Talbot's development of Margam estate. He approved the request and probably influenced the design, ensuring that the chapel would be of an octagonal shape. It has been suggested that he had admired octagonal churches which he had seen on the continent, and that he wished to see a similar structure on his land. Also, that the chapel was based on the Margam chapter house. Another possible explanation was that Mr. Talbot was concerned at the increase in the number of local Methodists, and that he was aware of the advantages of building a place of worship which could not possibly be extended.

Beulah was built by Thomas Jenkins at a cost of £800, using coursed sandstone and with a slate roof. It was of a Lombardic style, with a bell cupola. The gallery is supported on two cast iron columns and the ceiling has high moulded coving and a plaster rose with foliate decoration. A wooden pulpit was provided and seating for a congregation of 200 persons. In 1851 there were 72 free seats, 198 others and standing space for another 60 persons. On 30 March 28 persons were present, together with 12 scholars in the morning, and 200, together with 35 scholars in the afternoon. The chapel was under the control of Mr. Talbot for a number of years, but the only occasion when he is reputed to have been directly involved was when he refused to allow the chapel to be lit for the evening service as he had been wrongly informed that two maidservants who often arrived back late at the castle had been attending services at Beulah. When he learned that they had been enjoying the 'night life' of Taibach on each occasion, he changed his mind and evening services were resumed at Beulah after a lapse of some weeks.

In 1872 the chapel was leased to the Calvinistic Methodists. In 1903 the chapel was renovated at a cost of £400. The architect was the Rev. William Jones, Tonpentre, who had been raised at Capel y Garn, Bow Street (see 50), and was responsible for designing many chapels in south Wales, and the builder was Thomas

Williams, Port Talbot. The roof has recently been repaired and maintenance work is regularly undertaken.

Present position: No minister, 13 members, Sunday service at 10.30 a.m, and most of the services are held in English, sisterhood every other Thursday, annual carol service.

Further reading: E.W. Pearce, *Beulah, Margam, 1838-1938*.

94. MAESTEG, Bethania (Bw)

OS: SS 858 909

Bethania was built in 1908 on a prominent elevated site behind a railed forecourt, and facing Ewenny Road. The chapel has been listed Grade 2* by Cadw as one of the finest examples of the work of a distinguished chapel architect in the Beaux Arts style.

Bethania was the mother church for local Baptists, and other chapels had been built on the same site, one in 1832 and the other in 1841. There were 372 free seats in 1851, 318 others and standing space for 60 persons. On 30 March 302 were present in the morning service, 236 scholars in the afternoon and 700 in the evening service. At approximately the same time a geography class studying the geography of Canaan was held on Saturday evenings. Another chapel was built on the site in 1858, and this was rebuilt in 1878.

The 1908 chapel was designed by W. Beddoe Rees, Cardiff who was a native of Maesteg. It was built of costly Portland stone with panels of Pennant sandstone in a mixture of Beaux Arts and Art Nouveau styles, with seating for a congregation of 1,000 persons. It has a slate roof and the front is divided into three sections, and the central bay has circular windows on either side of the entrance doors, Ionic columns and a large, 80-paned window. The impressive interior has a vaulted ceiling with a series of arches and is supported by cast iron columns made by W.A. Baker & Co., Newport. The recessed pointed arch in the back wall is occupied by a large pipe organ built by Binns and maintained by Rushworth and Dreaper. In front of it the pulpit is in the part-octagonal centre, with the *sêt fawr* below enclosed by a moulded timber rail and covering the immersion font, whose access is below the pulpit gallery. Behind the rear wall a two-storey wing contains a series of small rooms, and to the right of the wing a large schoolroom is divided into two parts by a three-arched partition, and contains a large stage. White marble tablets commemorate two former ministers: the Revs Richard Hughes, a poet and author (d. 1885), and Iorwerth Jones (Iorwerth Ddu), who was president of the Welsh Baptist Union in 1925. Another former minister, the Rev. Geraint Owen, was closely involved in establishing the Welsh school in Maesteg, with classes held in the schoolroom in its early days.

The problem of maintaining a large building by a small congregation prompted the closure of the chapel in 2004, and for the ownership to be transferred to the Welsh Religious Buildings Trust. An application is at present being submitted to the Heritage Lottery Fund to finance the conservation and repair of the chapel to the highest standards, with a sensitive conversion of some areas to enhance the public use of the building. This project, entitled A Story of Dissent, Bethania, 'A Palace of the Oral Arts', seeks to present the history, and influence upon Wales, of Dissent / Nonconformity. Preliminary work costing £48,000 involved repairs to the roof,

guttering, leadwork and front pediment, and measures have also been taken to tackle the infestation of Japanese knotweed in the large chapel burial ground.

The officials of Bethania had carefully compiled and safeguarded various documents, including minute books, correspondence and architectural drawings. These were catalogued to a high standard by students studying for a higher degree course in Archive Administration at Aberystwyth University in the 2010/11 session, and have been placed on deposit by the WRBT at the Glamorgan Archives.

Present position: Following the closure of Bethania, 14 former members of Bethania have joined the local Independent Church to form the Carmel-Bethania Church, Maesteg. No minister and Sunday service at 10.30 a.m.
Further reading: 'Bethania Maesteg', *Welsh Religious Buildings Trust Newsletter*, 2, (2007); 'Bethania funding bid' *WRBT Newsletter*. 5 (2012).

95. EFAIL ISAF, Tabernacl (I)

OS: ST 085 845

The first chapel was built in 1843 in the centre of the village of Efail Isaf, approximately eight miles north of Cardiff on the northern side of Mynydd y Garth. Previously members of the Groes-wen and Taihirion churches had been active in this area before meetings were held at the Carpenters Arms during the 1840s. On 30 March 1851, 62 were present in the morning service and 93 in the evening service, with 53 scholars in the afternoon. It was recorded that there were 200 free seats and also standing room for 200 persons, and the "whole of the building will contain about 300 persons." This information was provided by William Lewis, a deacon described as an 'iron miner'. The present chapel, designed by the Rev. Thomas Thomas, Landore, was built in 1870 and has a small gallery. The building cost £830, and the work of transporting the materials was provided voluntarily by the members and local farmers. There were 71 members at this time but the number had increased to 144 by 1878. The closure of local coal mines resulted in several members having to leave the locality, yet, in 1898 a vestry was built to house the Sunday school, with a stable underneath it for the benefit of those members who used horses to bring them to the services. A marble tablet, installed in 1906 at a cost of £30 above the pulpit commemorates the Rev. John Taihirion Davies who served as minister from 1851 until his death at the age of 70 in September 1904. He had a considerable influence on the locality, and was known as 'Esgob y Fro' [Area Bishop]. Electricity lighting was introduced in 1916 at a cost of under £24, and by 1926 the membership had increased to 176.

The past half century has been a very successful period in the history of the church. Towards the end of the 1960s the membership had fallen to approximately 40 and the usual congregation to 15 persons, with most of them pensioners who represented the last generation of native Welsh-speakers in the village. The English language was used in the Sunday school, and the possibility was discussed of changing the language of services to English. This suggestion was rejected, and the practice was commenced of holding a Welsh-language Sunday school on a Sunday morning following the movement of Welsh-speaking families into the village and surrounding area. The numbers at the local Welsh primary school increased, and so also did the attendance at the chapel following an invitation in 1973 to the Rev. Eirian Rees, who had become a member and deacon in 1970, to be the minister.

There were 143 members in 1980, and the church has developed over the years with various activities organised by a number of groups. This is the only place of worship in the village of Efail Isaf, and the chapel is used for separate English and Welsh services. A major decision was to form a charitable company. The adaptation of the vestry to form a multi-purpose community hall, designed by the Alwyn Jones firm, Taff's Well, and built by Neil Smith & Co., was completed in the summer of

2010. The total cost was £450,000 and sums of £300,000 were received from the Welsh Government, and £122,000 from the National Lottery. Changes to the chapel include the removal of the harmonium from the great pew to provide more space. Substantial sums of money have been raised for charities, and members of the youth club, Teulu Twm, have been actively involved in various fund-raising ventures. Nearly £4,000 was raised for Christian Aid in 2009, and a close link has been developed with Lesotho with three members visiting the country in 2010. Goods were collected for and distributed to victims of disasters, such as those who suffered from the effects of the Tsumani in Asia at the end of 2004. The church has become a centre for Welsh-language activities in the locality, and the Côr Godre'r Garth, Côr Merched y Garth and Parti'r Efail choirs practice here. The chapel is occasionally used for wedding and funeral services in the television programme *Pobol y Cwm*, so thousands of S4C viewers are familiar with the chapel's interior.

Present position: Minister, Rev Eirian Rees (since 1973), 185 members in the Welsh congregation and 15 members in the English congregation, 50 children in the Sunday school, Sunday services: English service at 9.30 a.m., Welsh service at 10.45 a.m., with Sunday school, Teulu Twm youth group and discussion group, 5.30 p.m. *Further reading*: *Gwres yr Efail*, ed. Allan James & Emlyn Davies (2010); *Capel y Tabernacl Efail Isaf, Bywyd a Bwrlwm* (2010).

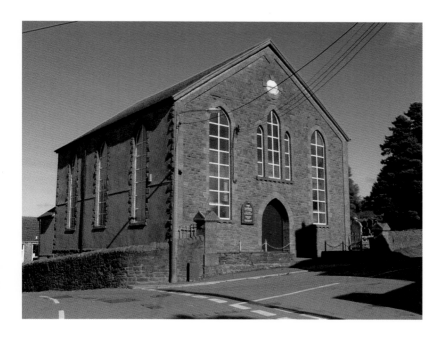

234

96. GWAELOD Y GARTH, Bethlehem (I)

OS: ST 117 836

The first chapel was built in 1832 as a branch of Taihirion church, and was sited on the edge of the village of Gwaelod y Garth, on the slopes of Mynydd y Garth, in the Taff valley to the north of Cardiff in the direction of Pontypridd. The present chapel, Bethlehem, was built in 1872. It is of a plain, Classical style with a small gallery.

The pulpit, like the chapel, is simple and unadorned, and this reflected the views of the Rev. R.G. Berry, the minister for 48 years, from 1896 until 1944, who strongly believed that nothing should interfere with the Gospel being preached. A native of Llanrwst, he was a prominent literary figure and a pioneer with regard to Welsh dramatic productions. When he was ordained as minister, Gwaelod-y-garth was a rural, completely Welsh village with many of the inhabitants working in local coal mines, such as the one at Nantgarw, or at the Pen-tyrch ironworks. During his long pastorate the distinctive Welsh character of the village was retained despite the increasing Anglicisation of the surrounding areas, and this was emphasised in the obituary written by his friend W.J. Gruffydd and published in the Welsh literary journal *Y Llenor* in 1944. Admiration for their minister was also expressed by other members at Bethlehem, including Professors T.J. Morgan and G.J. Williams. Other former ministers include the Revs. Gwilym Morris (1947-68), Rhys Tudur (1974-84) and Dr. T.J. Davies (1985-2000). The latter was a prolific author, and of special relevance for this volume are his recollections of rural chapels in north Ceredigion attended by him as a child and recorded in his autobiography, *Pridd o'r Pridd* (1988).

The chapel has recently been re-roofed with grants of money from Cadw and the Lottery Fund. In 2011 a Viscount (unico 400) electronic organ with three new keyboards was presented by one of the members to replace the old two keyboard (GEM) organ which had been used for 23 years and was nearing the end of its life.

The chapel has continued to the present day to be an important Welsh centre and an extremely active church, and indications of the liveliness are the universal and timely church announcements which have been published for several years in the Saturday edition of the *Western Mail*.

Present position: Minister, Rev. Dr. R. Alun Evans, 150 members, with 30 children, Sunday service with Sunday school at 10.30 a.m., monthly women's meeting on Tuesdays, monthly 'Drws Agored' discussion meeting during winter months.
Further reading: Huw Ethall, *R.G. Berry*, (1985).

97. PEN-TYRCH, Horeb (Pw/e)

OS: ST101 821

The first Association in Wales of the Calvinistic Methodists held at Watford Chapel, Caerphilly in January 1743 appointed the counsellor Thomas Lewis to care for the society at Pen-tyrch under the general supervision of Thomas William (1717-65), who was responsible for the societies of the Vale of Glamorgan and Monmouthshire. The small group of nine Calvinistic Methodists at Pen-tyrch originally held their services at local farmhouses or in the open air until an old barn, Brista Fach, was rented at £3.00 with a nearby stable housing horses for carrying the preacher and members of the congregation.

One of the early members was Evan Thomas, Pentwyn farm, who accommodated visiting preachers and provided stabling facilities for their horses. Services were normally held on Sunday mornings at 9 a.m., followed by a Sunday school, with another school in the afternoon, and a service in the evening. On his preaching tour of Glamorgan in 1806, the Rev. Thomas Richards preached at Brista Fach and recorded his impressions that at Pen-tyrch it was "… rather dry at the commencement but an improvement was made as we went on, and at the finish a fine climax was reached". Increasing numbers led to the construction of Horeb Chapel in 1839 on the site of the present building, and in 1851 the chapel contained 120 free seats and 170 others. There were present 120 persons together with 85 scholars on the morning of 30 March, 118 in the afternoon and 50 in the evening service. In 1884 there were 100 members, but the permanent closure of the Pentyrch Iron Works in 1885 resulted in the movement away from the village of several members. However, a new vestry was built in 1895 at a cost of £300. Services were held every evening during the revival of 1904-05, and it was estimated that approximately 60 converts were made. In 1930 there were 70 members, and 50-60 in the middle of the twentieth century. In 1959 it was decided to hold the evening service in English, and in 1971 the church joined the English-language West Glamorgan Presbytery. By 2003 the membership had fallen to 12 and the church closed in 2005.

Horeb was bought by Hywel Wigley and Catrin Finch in 2007 and has been extensively renovated with one area converted into the Acapela recording studio and the greater part of the chapel into the concert hall, with the traditional timber flooring and high ceiling providing excellent acoustics. The main change involved the removal of the *sêt fawr*, but the pulpit has been retained as also has most of the seating, and whilst there was seating at the chapel for a congregation of 250 persons, an audience of 180 may now attend the concerts regularly held in the concert hall.

Further reading: *The Garth Domain, no 22*, Miscellany (4), compiled by Don Llewelyn (November 2003).

Website: www.acapela.co.uk

98. ST ATHAN, Bethesda'r Fro (R)

OS: SS 992 691

This chapel is associated with the hymn-writer Thomas Wiliam who composed some of the most familiar hymns in the Welsh language, which were published in the collection of hymns, *Dyfroedd Bethesda*.

Part of the background to this chapel was the debate among the Calvinistic Methodists meeting at Aberthin chapel concerning the excommunication by the Calvinistic Methodists in 1791 of the Rev. Peter Williams (1723-1796) because of his unorthodox views. In 1798 several members who supported Peter Williams left Aberthin to establish a new church, and Thomas Wiliam (1761-1844) was ordained as the minister. The secretary was another notable hymn-writer, John Williams, St Athan. In 1806 a plot of land was acquired in the parish of Llantwit Major, near to Fisher's Bridge, and the chapel known as Bethesda'r Fro was built. The church was registered in 1807, and two ministers were named: Thomas Redwood, who had provided the land for building the chapel, and Thomas Wiliam. When the chapel was opened Thomas Wiliam preached in Welsh, and Thomas Redwood preached in English. The church was originally non-denominational but in time became an Independent chapel, and, with the services conducted in English for many years, today belongs to the United Reformed Church.

Few changes have been made to the whitewashed chapel since it was built. It has an unusual design as the pulpit has been placed half way on the right hand side, as one enters the chapel, with tapering windows behind it. There is no porch, and the door leads straight into the chapel. On the left hand side there is an entrance to the small vestry. A major development in 2012 was the installation of electricity.

Thomas Wiliam died in 1844 when he was 83 years of age, and he was buried near the chapel. He was described by Thomas Rees as a quick-witted, striking and exceptionally-effective preacher, by W. J. Gruffydd as a lamenting hymn-writer in the Vale of Glamorgan, and by Wyn James as a skilful, Biblical and confident melancholic hymn-writer. During his final years he was concerned at the spiritual deterioration in this locality, and in the elegy to his wife, he referred to 'Bethesda anniolchgar' [ungrateful Bethesda]. This greatly disturbed one who had been inspired by the Methodist Revival, and it was therefore appropriate that his hymn 'Y Gŵr wrth ffynnon Jacob' [the Man beside Jacob's well] should be extremely popular during the Revival of 1904-05.

On 30 March there were present 75 in the morning service, together with 30 scholars, and 30 in the evening service. There was standing room for 'about 200' persons. The chapel was renovated in 1853, when a new pulpit was installed, together with more comfortable seats following the removal of the benches. The chapel was re-opened on Wednesday and Thursday, 11 and 12 August, 1853, and on the Thursday ten sermons were preached, with the first one at 7.00 a.m.

Thereafter, the chapel became weaker, as also did the use of the Welsh language in the area, and disappointment at the deterioration was expressed by T. Rowland Hughes in his poem when he referred to a lack of fire on the small hearth of the old meeting-house, and an absence of anything to keep the Devil away. A significant development in this locality was the establishment of the Royal Air Force camp nearby at St Athan, and for some years after the Second World War the chapel was used by the camp with services organised by the chaplain. In 1969 the servicemen and workers based at the camp, under the direction of the chaplain, the Rev. J. Couch, voluntarily repaired and renovated the chapel. The vestry was re-roofed, and the chapel was painted. A financial appeal was organised, and the Union of Welsh Independents, a number of Welsh churches in Glamorgan and the wives of service-men at St Athan were among the contributors. W. Rhys Nicholas referred to the irony of the situation, with military planes flying above the chapel where the author of the Welsh hymn 'Adenydd colomen pe cawn' [O for the wings of the dove] had served as minister for many years.

Present position: No minister at present. 16 members (with Ebenezer, Llantwit Major), Sunday services, 9.30 a.m., 1st and 3rd Sunday of month, other Sundays presently at Ebenezer.

Further reading: W. Rhys Nicholas, *Thomas Wiliam, Bethesda'r Fro* (1994).

99. ST FAGANS, Pen-rhiw (U)

OS: ST 117 773

Pen-rhiw chapel now stands in The National History Museum, St Fagans, and is the chapel which attracts the greatest number of visitors in Wales every year. Soon after it was moved to St Fagans, Dr. Iorwerth C. Peate, the Curator, expressed the view that the chapel was a classical example of the simple and dignified architecture of Welsh meeting houses at its best. This must be set against the description in 1898 by the local historian, Daniel E. Jones, that the chapel was completely unadorned and old-fashioned, and uncomfortable for the congregation.

The history of the chapel commenced in 1777, in the village of Dre-fach Felindre, Carmarthenshire, when a plot of land was acquired on a 500-year lease for an annual rent, if requested, of 5s.6d. Another 500-year lease was obtained in 1798, but at a lower rent of 1s per annum, and again the words 'if requested' were added. The chapel was built and the graveyard enclosed that year. The chapel has an earth floor and plain wooden pews, whose size and design vary as they were built for different families, which each commissioned their own pew. The members had left Dre-fach church in 1756 because of their Unitarian beliefs: the Dre-fach church later developed into the Independent church of Saron. The first minister was the Rev. David Lloyd, from the beginning until his death in 1779, and in 1769 David Davies, Castell-hywel was ordained as his assistant. He also cared for other churches, and was in turn assisted at Pen-rhiw by other ministers. In 1786 Christmas Evans joined the church for a short period, but later turned to the Baptists and became one of the leading preachers in Wales. The Rev. David Davies retired from the ministry in 1820 having cared for his churches for over 50 years. Pen-rhiw was associated with Llwynrhydowen for a period, and Gwilym Marles was the minister from 1871 until 1873. Pen-rhiw was considered to be a thriving church for many years, with its members including several prosperous farmers.

When inspected after it was moved to St Fagans, it was suggested that a stone or tile roof had replaced the original thatched roof in the eighteenth century. The chapel was renovated in the period 1797-9, new windows were installed and a stable was added. In 1851 there were 164 free seats and 36 others. On 30 March 43 persons were present in the afternoon service, but it was also stated that the average attendance was 80. A gallery was added in the nineteenth century. The chapel was renovated in 1870 at a cost of £30, with thinner stones replacing thicker ones in the roof, and the chapel was painted.

At a further inspection following the removal to St Fagans old ink bottles and quills were found on the floor, and also a piece of wood used as a 'Welsh Not' in the period when the children were forbidden from speaking Welsh. These items belonged to the era when the chapel was also used as a school, with the Unitarian congregation seeking to provide for the education of the local community. A daily

school was held here initially, and then an Academy or Grammar School was opened in 1877. The pupils included Daniel E. Jones, author of the history of the parish of Llangeler and Pen-boyr, which contains the early history of Pen-rhiw, and whose views on the condition of the chapel are cited above.

Services continue to be held occasionally at the Pen-rhiw chapel at the National History Museum, and these include the annual Harvest and Christmas services.

Further reading: D. J. Goronwy Evans, *Penrhiw* (1977); Daniel E. Jones, *Hanes Plwyf Llangeler a Phenboyr* (1899); Iorwerth C. Peate, 'Symud capel Penrhiw', *Yr Ymofynnydd*, 56, (1956).

100. CARDIFF, City United Reformed Church (R)

OS: ST 189 768

Presbyterians from Scotland had been attracted to Cardiff in the wake of the advent of the Bute family with the third Marquess of Bute, reputed in the 1860s to be the richest man in the world. They were largely responsible for the establishment of the Presbyterian Church in Windsor Place in 1866. They had initially worshipped with members of the Charles Street Congregational Church, but having formed a separate church in 1864 they held services in an upstairs room in the Cardiff Arms Hotel. The Presbyterian Church of England contacted the local congregation, and in December 1864 Cardiff was accepted as a 'Preaching Station' of the Presbytery of Lancashire. A sum of £1,000 had been raised for a new chapel within three months, and in the period leading up to the opening of the church, 28 ministers conducted services in Cardiff, and of these 20 came from Scotland. The Rev. John Fordyce, a minister in Duns, Berwickshire, was inducted as minister at a service held at the Cardiff Arms Hotel on 1 August 1866, with the Moderator of the Presbytery of Lancashire presiding. The entire cost of the new church, amounting to £4,520, was raised in slightly over two years to pay for the church which opened on 9 October 1866 on land owned by Viscount Tredegar. The architect chosen for the work was Frederick Thomas Pilkington, the member of a family firm in Edinburgh who designed several chapels in Scotland, including the Barclay Memorial Chapel in Edinburgh. The chapel was designed in a spiky, ornate early Gothic style, of a square shape with curved sides, with buttresses extending to the spire which was a striking feature of the townscape before the building of tall office blocks. Inside, galleries cross the transepts and nave and create an amphitheatre effect. In 1873 a hall was built at the rear of the church, at a cost of £1,443 and in the following year the rear wall was extended to provide space for an organ.

In 1893 the west wall was moved outwards and reconstructed on the south side next to the tower. The architect was Col. Bruce Vaughan, and he also designed the rebuilding of the interior, costing £9,500, which involved the installation of a hammer-beam roof, highly-decorated pulpit and fine organ case following the fire which gutted the building in February 1910. The five stained-glass war memorial windows on the south side were unveiled and dedicated in 1921. Extensive renovation-work, which included the accommodation of the old north porch in the new entrance to the church was undertaken in 1980-81 and designed by Wyn Thomas & Partners. A further development in 1992, designed by John Partridge of the Chris Lodge Partnership, involved providing access from the main south porch to the new bookshop, and installing a new vestibule at the rear of the church, and a lift to ensure access for the disabled to the upper room which replaced the gallery.

The church today is part of the United Reformed Church, which was established in 1972 following the union of the Congregational Church in England and Wales, and the Presbyterian Church of England. It seeks to make use of its city centre site by enabling the buildings to be used for various activities which include the ecumenical Cardiff Adult Christian Education Centre. The Asylum Justice programme which provides legal advice to asylum seekers is supported by the church which is committed to providing a 'safe space' for marginalised people in the city. The Churches Together Bookshop and The Refectory Coffee Shop are located on the premises, which also host meetings of Gamblers Anonymous and Alcoholics Anonymous.

Present position: Minister, Adrian Butley, 90 members, Sunday services, 10.30 a.m with crèche, Junior Church and youth group; lunchtime prayers every Tuesday at 1.10 p.m.
Further reading: *City United Reformed Church, Windsor Place, Cardiff, The Story and Richness of the Building* (n.d.); *One HundredYears, Windsor Place Presbyterian Church, Cardiff* (n.d.); John B. Hilling & Mary Traynor, *Cardiff's Temples of Faith* (2000).
Website: www.CityUrc.org.uk

101. CARDIFF, Eglwys y Crwys (Pw)

OS: ST 186 773

Following the visit of Howel Harris to Cardiff in 1738 a society was established the following year. A meeting-house seems to have been built in 1810 in the centre of the town, near to the Glamorganshire Canal, probably on the site of the present-day British Home Stores in Queen Street. A larger chapel, Seion, with a gallery and a mahogany pulpit, was opened in 1827 in Trinity Street on the site presently occupied by the Old Library. In 1851, 'Zion' was recorded as having 140 free seats and 366 others, and on 30 March 340 persons together with 27 scholars were present in the morning service, and 392 with 60 scholars in the evening service. The growth in the town's population resulted in the establishment of new branch churches in 1856 in Canton, in the west (see 102, Cardiff, Salem, Canton), and in Loudon Square, in the dockland area to the south. Seion was closed in 1878 and the site sold to the town corporation for £6,500. A new chapel, designed by Henry C. Harris, a Penarth architect who had designed his first chapel, Bethania, St. Mellons, when he was only 18 years of age, was built in 1877-78 in Pembroke Terrace, the present-day Churchill Way. The plans were exhibited at the Royal Academy the following year, and attracted the derisive comment in *The Builder* that "at this rate of progress in ecclesiastical architecture, the Welsh Calvinists will hardly know themselves soon". The chapel had French-Gothic towers with octagonal turrets and semi-cylindrical stair-towers, and an interior with red-brick walls and the stairs and lobbies slotted into angles. Following its closure in 1975, when the church was united with Capel Heol y Crwys, the building was converted to office-premises in 1983 and is at present occupied by the Leo Abse & Cohen legal firm.

The Pembroke Terrace church served central and eastern areas of Cardiff, but the increase in the population of the Cathays area led to a Sunday school and prayer meeting being held in Munday Place, near Woodville Road, Cathays; and then to the building in 1884 of a schoolroom in May Street, on the junction with Fanny Street. The schoolroom developed into Horeb church, established in 1884. Its membership had increased to 163 by 1899, with another 150 'listeners', and there were 144 scholars and 17 teachers in the Sunday school. By that time permission had been granted to build a new chapel at the lower end of Crwys road in the middle of the catchment area roughly halfway between Cathays and Roath Park. This chapel, designed by J.H. Phillips, a member of the Pembroke Terrace church, who had also designed Horeb chapel, was opened on 19 May, 1900. The style has been described by J.H. Hilling as a "grotesque but lovable building" and as a "mixture of romantic medievalism and Dutch baroque, along with a hint of Art Nouveau" with features which "seem more reminiscent of a castellated railway terminus than a chapel".

The church has been described as being enthusiastic and active with a variety of members and talents, and in 1950 the membership reached nearly 500. Former ministers have included the Revs. William Davies (1903-35), Dr. T.J. Jones (1936-52), D. Lodwig Jones (1953-75) and W.I. Cynwil Williams (1976-2001). Improvements to the building were introduced regularly, and on several occasions concern was expressed with regard to the condition of the building and the need to safeguard the resources of the church in view of possible threats presented by plans to develop this area of the city.

A detailed report on the condition of the building drew attention to the immense costs involved in renovating it, with the problems accentuated by the heavy traffic passing along the road outside the chapel. In 1987 the vast majority of the members agreed to buy a chapel built in 1960 in Richmond Road and formerly used by Christian Scientists, providing that the price was satisfactory. Agreement was reached on a price of £225,000, including the seats and organ. An offer to sell the chapel to a brewery intending to turn it into a public house and prepared to pay the highest price, was rejected, and during the detailed discussions consideration was given to the legal requirement to sell the property to the highest bidder, and also the special covenant secured to prohibit the sale of alcoholic drinks. In 1988 the chapel was sold to a Muslim group which sought to convert the chapel into a religious education centre. By today it is the Shah Jalal Mosque, Islam Cultural Centre, and on the external wall may be seen the words 'None but Allah is worthy of worship. Muhammed is his messenger.'

A number of adaptations were made to the new chapel, designed by Gerald Latter, including a new roof, glass façade and a gallery. Classrooms, a handsome kitchen and toilets were installed, together with a new theatre located on an upper floor in the rear of the chapel. The church has received a number of gifts over the years, including a pulpit presented in memory of Mr. Lyn Howell, who had been a Moderator of the General Assembly of the Presbyterian Church of Wales. Also, two windows, one portraying William Williams, Pantycelyn, and the other Ann Griffiths, designed by Gareth Morgan and donated in memory of faithful members of the church.

Present position: Minister, the Rev Glyn Tudwal Jones, 330 members, 82 children and 14 adults in the Sunday school; Sunday services, 10.30 a.m. with Sunday school, and 6.00 p.m., weekday/evening activities include weekly devotional meeting, drama group, Bible study twice a month and monthly *Y Gorlan* society and women's group. *Further reading*: J. Gwynfor Jones, *Cofio yw Gobeithio: Cyfrol Dathlu Canmlwyddiant Achos Heol-y-Crwys, Caerdydd 1884-1984* (1984); John B. Hilling & Mary Traynor, *Cardiff's Temples of Faith* (2000). Website: www.eglwys-y-crwys.org.uk

102. CARDIFF, Salem, Canton (Pw)

OS: ST 168 765

This is one of the very few churches in Wales today where the membership is growing from year to year.

Early developments in Cardiff included the establishment of Salem, Canton in 1856 with 25 members, when the membership of Calvinistic Methodist residents in the rapidly-growing western suburbs of Cardiff were transferred to the new church from Seion, the mother church (see 101, Cardiff, Eglwys y Crwys). The original Salem chapel was built in Edward Street, Canton, later re-named Albert Street. The Rev. Edward Matthews supervised the church from 1864 until 1876, and other ministers of Salem have included the Revs. Cuthbert Thomas (1908-40), D.J. Williams (1942-67) and D. Haydn Thomas for two periods (1967-9) and (1977-98).

An important contribution to setting and maintaining the standard of congregational singing was made by the family of Jacob Davies, an elder from 1880 until 1921, and main precentor for a very long period. His daughter, Clara Novello Davies, was renowned as the conductor of the Royal Welsh Ladies Choir which won a prize at the Chicago Eisteddfod in 1893. She was an organist at Salem and the children associated with the church included her son Ivor, who later added 'Novello' to his name. He has been commemorated by a statue outside the Millennium Centre in Cardiff Bay and a plaque placed at their home in Cowbridge Road.

The present chapel in Market Road, opened in 1911, was designed by Edgar Fawckner, from Abershon & Fawckner, Newport, and the copies of the original plans are displayed today in the vestry. The builder was James Stephens, a member of the chapel and he was later responsible for building Tabernacl, the new Calvinistic Methodist chapel in St. David's. Sir William Goscombe John (1860-1952), born in Canton, was responsible for the war memorial (1923) in the chapel vestibule commemorating members of Salem killed in the First World War.

The members made strenuous efforts to pay for the new chapel but generous contributions were also received from Henry Radcliffe, the shipowner and a prominent figure in the international coal-exporting trade centred on Cardiff docks. In addition to his financial contributions, he also insisted on high standards of workmanship in the construction of Salem. He was responsible for the installation of an organ by Watkins & Watson, London, and extensive use was made of oak in the chapel, in the pulpit, *sêt fawr*, the front of the gallery, the communion table and the 'Calvin & Knox' pulpit chair. The oil portraits of Henry Radcliffe and Jacob Davies housed in the chapel testify to the influence of the two men on the early history of the church.

The Welsh language was used for services in Salem over the years. The continued use of the language was discussed in the 1930s in view of the decline in the numbers of Welsh-speakers who resided in the vicinity of the chapel, but a determined effort was made to maintain the use of Welsh in Sunday services. By today, as a result of the large number of Welsh-speakers settling in the area, especially in Canton and Pontcanna, many young families attend services and have become members of Salem. There has been a remarkable increase in the membership: the gallery now accommodates part of the Sunday morning congregation, and an extension, designed by Alwyn Jones Architects, was opened in 2005 to provide additional facilities for meetings and the Sunday School, and modern kitchen and toilets: one room in the extension has been named in memory of Edwin Lloyd Jones, the hymn-composer who conducted the congregation-singing at the chapel for many years.

Present position: Minister, the Rev. Evan Morgan, 242 members, 243 children in Sunday School and associated with the church. Sunday services, 10.30 a.m. with Sunday school, and 6.00 p.m.; weekday/evening services include the weekly singing club, breakfast club for young mothers and small children, Urdd adran for primary schoolchildren; and monthly prayer/Bible study group, *Y Gadwyn* society, young members society, youth club, book-reading club, coffee morning club, walking society; and a cricket club which has a full programme of matches in the summer months.

Further reading: Richard Hall Williams & D. Haydn Thomas, *Hanes Salem Canton, Caerdydd o 1856 hyd 2000* (2001); J. Geraint Jenkins, *Evan Thomas Radcliffe, a Cardiff Shipowning Company* (1982).

Website: www. capelsalem.org

103. CARDIFF, Y Tabernacl (Bw)

OS: ST 183 761

The history of Tabernacl may be traced to those Welsh-language services held by Baptists upstairs in the Star and Garter inn, Cardiff. The first chapel was opened in The Hayes on 27 March, 1821, and following the growth of Cardiff, it was extended in 1841, with space for a congregation of 900 persons. The 1851 Census recorded that 419 persons, with 124 scholars, were present in the morning service on 30 March, 218 scholars in the afternoon and 700 in the evening service, but it was also noted that the evening congregation was smaller by 150 than the average because the minister was away!

The present chapel was built in a six-month period in 1865 at a cost of £3,000 with 950 seats and an extensive schoolroom. The architect, J. Hartland, was responsible for designing a number of chapels in the Cardiff area, but Tabernacl is considered to be one of his finest and most original, and John Hilling has referred to its "agreeable Regency air". A distinctive feature of this chapel is the absence of pillars and pilasters which are normally found in larger Classical chapels, and the four central large windows correspond to the four round-headed doorways below. The interior has a ceiling with a large metal rose, and a gallery to four sides on iron columns with floral capitals. Below the organ recess there is a wooden pulpit and *sêt fawr* enclosure with wrought iron balustrade. A number of improvements have been made over the years, as in early 2004 with the renovation-work undertaken in response to the damage caused by fire in November 2003.

The church has had ten ministers since 1815, and a number are commemorated by stone tablets, including the one to Christmas Evans (1766-1833), the third minister from 1828 until 1832, the preacher and hymn-writer and one of the giants of the Welsh pulpit in its 'Golden Age'. The elegant stained glass windows, featuring Biblical scenes and presented in memory of the Rev. Charles Davies, the sixth minister from 1888 to 1927, have been renovated and these light up the Hayes throughout the year. A tablet commemorates Howell T. Evans, the medieval historian, whilst one of the memorials to those who lost their lives during the Second World War was skilfully created by a soldier in Singapore. It was first placed in the church in Changi prison, and when discovered after the church had been destroyed, was re-situated in Tabernacl.

Located in a prominent central position the church has made a significant contribution to the public and cultural life of Cardiff, and also the city's Welsh character. Church officials at the turn of the twentieth century who contributed immensely to the civic life of Cardiff were the two deacons, Edward Thomas, 'Cochfarf', mayor of Cardiff in 1902, and Alfred Thomas, mayor of Cardiff in 1881, and Member of Parliament for East Glamorgan from 1885 to 1910, who was created Lord Pontypridd in 1912. Special services have been periodically held at Tabernacl to

celebrate special occasions, such as the 400th anniversary in 1988 of the translation of the Bible into the Welsh language, the Millennium in 2000 and the 200th anniversary of the establishment of the Bible Society in 2005.

In spite of opposition an organ built by Griffin & Stroud was installed in 1907. This was renewed in 1972 by J.M. Walker & Sons, London and again in 2011, at a cost of £100,000 by Henry Willis & Sons, Ltd. The completion of the restoration-work was celebrated by a concert featuring an organ recital by Huw Tregelles Williams, and afterwards a series of organ recitals by a number of distinguished organists including Martin Neary. The church has had a succession of gifted organists, and Arwel Hughes and Owain Arwel Hughes made a significant contribution to its musical traditions. A number of concerts have been arranged over the years by the Tabernacl choir, and during the Second World War hymn-singing festivals were held every Sunday evening for soldiers stationed at Cardiff.

It is intended to publish a volume in 2015 to celebrate the 150th anniversary of the church.

Present position: Minister, the Rev. Denzil I. John, 198 members, 30 children, Sunday services, 10.30 a.m with Sunday school (adults and children) and 6.00 p.m., weekly prayer meeting and Bible class, and, during the winter cultural society and women's meeting, Coffee morning on Saturday with proceeds to charities, and tea and sandwiches for the homeless on Sunday afternoons.

Further reading: Undeb Bedyddwyr Cymru [Baptist Union of Wales] *Y Tabernacl, Caerdydd* (1993), *Y Tabernacl, Caerdydd* (1996), *Y Tabernacl Caerdydd a Thonyfelin, Caerffili* (2003); John B. Hilling & Mary Traynor, *Cardiff's Temples of Faith* (2000); J. Gwynfor Jones, 'Cyfraniad Bedyddwyr Caerdydd i Dwf Ymwybyddiaeth Ddinesig Gymreig yn y Cyfnod tua 1890-1914' *Trafodion Cymdeithas Hanes y Bedyddwyr* (2004). Website: www.tabernaclcaerdydd.org.uk

104. EGLWYSILAN, Groeswen (I)

OS: ST 128 870

Following a visit to the area by Howel Harris in 1738, and a society formed soon afterwards, he was present at the meeting held in January 1742 at Plas y Watford, the home of Thomas Price, the local squire who was a fervent supporter of the Calvinistic Methodists. It was resolved there to build a chapel on the site proposed by Thomas Evans, in Groes-wen, and the chapel was built under the guidance of William Edwards, the mason and builder who lived at Groes-wen and who became famous as the builder of Pontypridd bridge, and the designer of Morriston (see 90).

The chapel was completed by 1742 when a meeting was held at the 'New House': this name was used to avoid the word 'chapel' because of its ecclesiastical associations, and the term 'meeting house' used by Nonconformists. The services were led by counsellors including Thomas Price and William Edwards, but tensions soon developed between some of them and Howel Harris, who insisted that the Calvinistic Methodists should remain within the Anglican Church, receive communion in the parish church and be buried in the church graveyard. The Groes-wen church left the Calvinistic Methodist movement in 1751, and in 1752 it was announced that Groes-wen was an Independent church. William Edwards and Thomas Wiliam were appointed the co-ministers, the sacraments were administered and in time burial services were held in the plot of land acquired near the chapel and which became the graveyard.

The chapel was either enlarged or rebuilt in 1766 and a graveyard was provided in the period 1798-1801. The membership had increased significantly, especially during the ministry of the Rev. Griffith Hughes, in the period 1798 to 1839 when 1,164 infants were baptised. The chapel was extended in 1831, and there was space in it for a congregation of 600. A document from this period names the chapel as 'Whitecross' rather than 'Groes-wen' and the word 'society' refers to the early history of the chapel. There were 418 members in 1832. Also, the branch-chapels of Ebeneser, Rudry and Winllan, Nantgarw were opened, but the members were expected to attend Groes-wen on a Sunday morning. On 30 March 1851 200 persons were present in the morning service, 59 scholars in the afternoon and 150 in the evening service. The average attendance was said to be between 250 and 450 in the morning and between 150 and 250 in the evening, and the Rev. Moses Rees, the minister from 1841 until 1856, commented that the evening congregation was smaller than that of the morning as the church held services in four places at that time, and four Sunday schools in the afternoon. The chapel, described as 'Whitecross', contained 196 free seats and 350 others, together with standing-room for other persons.

The complete renovation of the chapel in 1873-74 was designed by the Rev. Thomas Thomas. The total cost of £1,300 was paid when the chapel was re-opened

in November 1874 at the completion of the building work when overflowing congregations attended the services conducted by six visiting preachers, and the debt incurred by the renovation of the chapel had been discharged. The chapel is of a Classical style with a three-bay gable end façade, built of coursed rubble stone, rendered to sides and rear, with ashlar dressings. The interior has a three-sided gallery supported by narrow, cast-iron columns. The minister during this period, from 1872 until 1876, was the Rev. William Nicholson, and other ministers included two poets who were prominent figures in eisteddfodic circles: the Revs. W. Caledfryn Williams, 'Caledfryn', the minister from 1856 until 1869, described by the *Cardiff Times* as "a name for many years which has been a household word among the Welsh nation" and "one of the most remarkable Welshmen of his age"; and Cadwaladr Tawelfryn Thomas, the minister from 1880 until 1926, of whom the *Western Mail* stated, following his death in 1939, that "a link with the Welsh Congregational past has been broken... Almost the last of his generation... he had a unique knowledge of Welsh poetry and the Welsh Bible". They were buried in the graveyard, together with several eminent Welshmen, including the Rev. Evan Jones, 'Ieuan Gwynedd,' and for this reason the church has been described as the 'Westminster Abbey of Wales'. In 1906 a bronze memorial tablet, made by Sir William Goscombe John, was placed in the chapel in memory of the Rev William Edwards. It included a portrait of the church's first minister, who is described as a "self taught engineer and builder of the world famed bridge over the River Taff at

Pontypridd" and one who served the church faithfully for 40 years.

The membership gradually decreased over the years, and the church was severely affected by economic and social developments, with the closure of local collieries and the Anglicisation of the area. The membership of Groes-wen and Nantgarw decreased from 240 in 1909 to 219 (165 in Groeswen) in 1915, 186 (139 in Groes-wen) in 1926, 61 in 1939, 54 in 1950, 23 in 1965 and 15 in 1992. The chapel had been repaired in 1947 when electricity was installed. In 1982 the windows of the vestry were repaired, and in the following year, at a cost of £5,600, so also were the roof and the interior ceiling. New windows have also been installed and the exterior walls repaired. An appeal for funds was launched to finance a substantial renovation programme, and a sum of nearly £400,000 was collected from various sources. Having initially concentrated on the exterior of the chapel, the interior walls were renovated in 2011, and Cadw contributed £10,000 towards the costs of £30,000.

The chapel has been graded 2* by Cadw on account of its national historical importance as this was the very first chapel to be built in Wales specifically for the Calvinistic Methodists. The chapel today attracts visits from historical societies, and is often the venue for christenings, weddings and funerals, and also civic services attended by local community councillors.

Present position: 20 members (of whom 10 were received during the last six years), one monthly Sunday service, special anniversary service on August Bank Holiday, Christmas carol service (attended by approximately 100 persons).
Further reading: J. Basil Phillips, *Groeswen, 1742-1992* (1992); *Capel Local Information Sheet*, 24, Caerphilly [2004].

105. PONTYPRIDD, Tabernacl (Bw) [Pontypridd Museum]

OS: ST 074 904

An important early development was the baptism in 1809, in the river Taff, of Kitty Rowlands by the Rev. Rees Jones, minister of Seion, Merthyr Tydfil. Two families from Merthyr were among the early adherents and preachers from Merthyr came here on a regular basis, with services held in houses and in the open air. Kitty's husband Adam who had previously been baptised at Bethany Baptist Church, Cardiff, had led a group which rented a loft which, forming part of the White Horse public house located adjacent to the old bridge, was described in a letter sent from the United States in 1860 as "a very shabby place". They then built Carmel chapel, the first Nonconformist chapel in Pontypridd, and the church here had been established by 1811, with the Rev. John Jenkins, Hengoed, the first minister. In 1833 there were 120 members when Robert Pritchard was the minister, and the membership had increased to 128 in 1838, 205 in 1848, and 311 in 1852, with branches at Llantrisant and Hopkinstown. The Rev. Edward Roberts moved from Rhyl to become the minister in 1859, when the revival of that year boosted the membership to 394 by 1860. He designed in a simple Classical style a new chapel, Tabernacl, which was opened in 1861, and located on the bank of the river Taff which provided baptism facilities, next to the Victoria Bridge completed in 1857 and also near to William Edwards's bridge of 1756. The new chapel had a symmetrical two-storey gable-end entrance with round-headed windows, and the exterior walls were built of local Pennant sandstone. The debt incurred by the construction of the new chapel, whose total cost amounted to £3,670, was cleared by the end of 1883.

A decrease in the membership of Tabernacl in the period following its opening may possibly be explained by the opposition of some members to the building of a new chapel. However, other, more significant factors were efforts to support new churches, with the departure of 100 members in 1861 to form the Rhondda branch of the church, and of 33 members in 1871 to join the English church at Carmel, formed in 1868 as a branch of Tabernacl. The local community also suffered from tensions in the coal-mining industry, such as those caused by the five-month strike at the Great Western Colliery in 1875. The membership of Tabernacl, recorded as 284 in December 1861, therefore fell to 260 in the following year, 202 in 1866, and 176 in 1876. The reversal of this trend, with Tabernacl containing 231 members in 1888, when the Rev. Edward Roberts retired, and 371 in 1895 reflected the considerable growth in the local population towards the end of the nineteenth century.

Major alterations were undertaken to the chapel in 1910, and the original handwritten specification documents are presently held by the Pontypridd Museum. The alterations included the provision of an assembly room and classrooms for the Sunday school; a new larger gallery and pipe organ, built by Conacher, Huddersfield; a new porch of Forest of Dean stone in neo-Baroque style; a new

elaborate ceiling with painted plaster panels; and new coloured glazing in the original cast-iron window frames: both the ceiling and glazing were in the Art Nouveau style: and the installation of electric lighting and a high-pressure hot water heating system. The changes were designed by the local architect firm, A.O. Evans, Williams and Evans; the builder was Richard Jones, Caerphilly, and the interior was painted by Edward Jones, Coedpenmaen.

A decreasing membership resulted in the closure in 1982 of the chapel, listed Grade 2 by Cadw, which was purchased by Pontypridd Town Council in the following year. It was reopened in 1986 as the Pontypridd Historical and Cultural Centre and is currently the Pontypridd Museum. Its conversion to a museum in 1985-86 involved the removal of the chimney and rooftop ventilation cowls, repair of the roof, eaves and cornice details, complete alteration of the basement to provide office space and ancillary services, the removal of the ground floor pews, construction of a platform across the raking balcony to provide a level first floor, and redecoration of the ceiling. A single-storey flat-roof extension in the late-twentieth century

257

provided additional storage space and a meeting room.

A conservation project, costing £152,000 designed by Alwyn Jones Architects and financed by the Heritage Lottery Fund and Pontypridd Town Council, was completed in 2011 and involved the renewal of the roof coverings, reinstatement of missing historic roof details and redecoration of ceilings and windows based on the original scheme.

Further reading: B. Davies, *Rise and Progress of Nonconformity in Pontypridd & District* (1897); *Pontypridd, Conservation Management Statement*, prepared by Alwyn Jones Architects (May 2010).

106. TRECYNON, Hen Dŷ Cwrdd (U)

OS: SN 995 035

The history of Hen Dŷ Cwrdd may be traced to the meeting of Dissenters held c.1650 on the mountain between Aberdare and Merthyr Tydfil. Divisions in the Cwm-y-glo church established in 1689 in a barn at Blaencanaid, after Independents in Aberdare and Merthyr Tydfil had left the church, had led to the establishment of the Hen Dŷ Cwrdd at Cefncoed y cymmer in 1747, Ynys-gau, Merthyr Tydfil in 1749, and Hen Dŷ Cwrdd, Trecynon in 1751. The theology of its early ministers fluctuated from Calvinism to Arminianism to Arianism and to Unitarianism in the period of Tomos Glyn Cothi.

The first chapel was a simple structure, built in the style of a barn with the entrance through a porch and with stone stairs outside. It is probable that the style was similar to that of Maesyronnen, with a rectangular form, and a long-wall façade and the pulpit in the middle of the long wall, facing the entrance. That chapel was demolished in 1861 and the present chapel was built in 1862 at a cost of £753 15s. 4d. The interior is of a square shape with a three-sided gallery supported by cast-iron columns. The entrance has a door with a rounded arch. The chapel was designed to be 'simple and solid' , and to reflect Unitarian principles of freedom and tolerance. The architect was Evan Griffiths, the son of Evan Griffiths, a staunch Calvinistic Methodist and owner of several large business concerns in Aberdare, and the architect who had designed in 1853 Bethania, the Welsh Calvinistic Methodist chapel; Trinity, the English chapel belonging to the same denomination, in 1867; and the Temperance Hall which is presently the Palladium Bingo Hall.

Hen Dŷ Cwrdd had several prominent ministers, including the Revs. Edward Evans, poet and friend of Iolo Morganwg, the poet and antiquary, from 1772 until 1796; Tomos Glyn Cothi, the fervent supporter of the French Revolution, from 1813 until 1833; John Jones, a prominent Chartist and one of the founders of the politically-radical, denominational journal, *YrYmofynnydd*, from 1833 until 1863; and his son Rees Jenkin Jones, minister for two periods, from 1863 until 1872, and from 1879 until 1909. The chapel was in the midst of the contemporary ferment arising from the interchange of political and religious ideas, and John Jones kept a school near the chapel which was known as Jones's School or the 'Trecynon Seminary'. He was succeeded by his son not only as minister but also as schoolmaster and editor. A significant contribution to the cultural life of the valley in the twentieth century was made by ministers, such as the Revs. E.R. Dennis (1916-49), the drama producer who founded the Little Theatre; D. Jacob Davies (1952-57) the poet, journalist and broadcaster, who wrote a history of the chapel; and J. Eric Jones, who has been one of the mainstays of the Welsh-language community in the valley in recent years, from 1962 until the closure of the chapel in 1994.

Prominent members included William Williams, '*Y Carw Coch*', the Chartist,

who was largely responsible for promoting local eisteddfodic enthusiasm; Rhys Hopkin Rhys who was closely-involved in the establishment of Aberdare Park which opened on 16 July, 1869 at a cost of £6,300; Griffith Rhys Jones, 'Caradog', who conducted his choir 'the United Choir of South Wales' or 'Y Cor Mawr' [the Large Choir] to victory at the Crystal Palace Challenge Cup in London in 1872-73; and the local historian William Watkin Price (1873-1967). A statue commemorating Griffith Rhys Jones by Sir W. Goscombe John was unveiled in Victoria Square, Aberdare in 1920.

Following its closure in 1988, the chapel was transferred to the care of the Welsh Religious Buildings Trust. The first phase of repair works, completed in April 2010, included fitting a new Welsh slate roof, completely overhauling all the windows and doors, and dealing with cracks in the exterior walls. Funding was received from Cadw, Rhondda Cynon Taff County Borough Council, the Listed Places of Worship Grant Scheme and private donations. The next phase of repairs will focus on the interior. In 2010 a blue plaque was installed by the Rhondda Cynon Taff County Borough Council which has designated thirty sites in the county to commemorate famous people, events and landmarks, with the sites eventually forming a heritage trail.

Further reading: D. Jacob Davies, *Cyfoeth Cwm* (1965); D. Ben Rees, *Chapels in the Valley* (1975); *Cwm Cynon*, ed. Hywel Teifi Edwards (1997), especially the chapters by Gareth Williams D. Ben Rees and D. Leslie Davies; Gareth Williams, *Valleys of Song* (1998); Alan Vernon Jones, *Chapels in the Cynon Valley* (2004); D. Leslie Davies, *'They love to be Dissenters', The Origins and History of Hen Dŷ Cwrdd, Aberdare, 1650-1862* (2012).

107. MERTHYR TYDFIL, Salvation Army Citadel (Sa)

OS: SO 049 062

The history of this church may be traced to the arrival in Merthyr Tydfil, in February 1878 of Kate Watts and Harriet Parkin, two young evangelists, for the purpose of establishing a branch of the religious organisation known as the Christian Mission. They were succeeded by a Mrs. Sayers and a Miss Smith, and whilst they were active in the town, the name of the organisation for which they were working changed its name to that of the Salvation Army. Meetings were held in a variety of locations, initially at the old White Lion near St. Tydfil parish church, and with Sunday meetings in the Drill Hall. By 1904 the local Corps owned a place of worship located at the foot of the old Merthyr Ironworks cinder tip where the Abermorlais New Calvinistic Methodist chapel had opened in 1882. A fierce storm in January 1925 resulted in the collapse of the structure and from this date until April 1937 meetings were held in local churches and other venues. In November 1936 exceptionally stormy weather threatened the continuation of the stone-laying ceremony of the new hall on the site of the previous one, but four stones were laid during a lull in the storm and one of the guests on this occasion was the 80-year old Mrs. Josiah Taylor, who as the 21-year old Kate Watts, had established the first Christian Mission hall here. This was also a period of severe unemployment in Merthyr, and when opening the new Citadel on 24 April 1937, Canon Richard Pugh, the rector of Merthyr stated that "Anyone who builds in Merthyr at the present time must have wonderful faith in God". The building, which cost £5,320, was described as "one of the most modern and well-equipped in the Wales and Western territory". The senior hall accommodated 400 persons, and on the same floor there were band, songster, commanding officers and accommodation rooms, and beneath this hall the Young People's Hall had a separate entrance.

The Citadel has been extensively renovated during the last twenty years. The roof and windows were renewed in 1993, a second stage was undertaken in 1997, and a further major programme of works, which included an extension at the rear of the building was completed between October 2003 and November 2004. Whilst the renovation work was undertaken, services were held in the Church Hall of St. David's Church. Collaboration between the Salvation Army and the local authority resulted in the provision of a purpose-built day-care centre for the elderly, operated by the Social Services department of the local authority in what had previously been the Lower Hall of the Citadel, whilst the activities of the Salvation Army are concentrated in the Upper Hall. A sum of £750,000 represented the total cost of the modernisation of the Citadel, which continues to serve the community for which it was founded.

Present position: Officers: Lts. Andrew & Lorraine Warriner, Neil & Elizabeth Duquemin, 33 soldiers, 11 adherents, Sunday services: 10.15 a.m. and 6.00 p.m.; Weekday/evening services, Songster & band practice, Over 60 Club, Parent & Toddlers, Disabled Group, Talking Hands, Active 8.

Further reading: *Merthyr Express*: 18 March 1882, 23 April, 1904, 10 & 24 January 1925,* November 1936, 24 April & 1 May 1937.

Website: www.merthyrtydfilsalvationarmy.org.uk

108. MERTHYR TYDFIL, Soar / Zoar (I)

OS: SO 050 065

The origins of the church lay in the decision by some of the members of the Ynysgau Independent church, established in 1749, to leave due to their concern with regard to the theological views of the minister. They met for some time in a room behind the Crown Inn, and in 1789 the first Quarterly Assembly for churches in south-east Wales was held at the Zoar church. A Mr. Powell, from Carmarthenshire, commenced his work as the minister in 1798. By this time, the expansion of industrial activities, in the ironworks of Cyfarthfa, Dowlais, Penydarren and Plymouth, was accompanied by a rapid growth in the local population. Aware of the need for a suitable building, Zoar chapel was opened in 1803, and was described as "one alley from the door through the building; seats on either side of it". The small chapel contained a fireplace, and the entrance to the gallery was from the inside. The claim for expenses submitted by the Rev. D. Lewis in relation to his efforts to raise funds to clear the debt incurred in building the chapel resulted in the departure of some members, and this dispute forms part of the background to the establishment of Bethesda church. Zoar was extended in 1810 with an entrance provided to the gallery from the outside. A further extension in 1825 cost £600 and two entrances were now installed for the gallery. The Rev. Samuel Evans, the minister since 1810, supervised the extension-work, and he was the president of the Four Counties Assembly held at Aberdare on 3 June 1831, the same day as the major confrontation in Merthyr which became renowned as the Merthyr Riots. Zoar had received 55 new members in 1829, and a decision was made to further extend the chapel, with the minister, by this time the Rev. Benjamin Owen, again supervising the project and the building-work. The new chapel cost £2,300, and when it was opened on 6 March 1842 a debt of £1,830 remained. Fund-raising events organised to clear the debt included various musical activities, and a tea-party on Christmas Day 1844 when over 4,000 persons attended, and a profit of £140 was made.

In 1849 the cholera epidemic afflicted Zoar, and the town of Merthyr Tydfil. The 1851 Religious Census recorded that there were in Zoar 457 free seats and 962 others. There were present 791 persons and 300 scholars in the morning of 30 March, 406 scholars in the afternoon, and 1,378 in the evening service. In 1854 two large schoolrooms were opened by Zoar, costing £300, in Penydarren and in Cae-draw. There were 410 members in 1869, and a thriving Sunday School of 388 scholars in 1897: in this year the chapel was closed for four months for the installation of new heating equipment. The increase in the membership to 471 in 1908 may probably be explained by the influence of the 1904-05 revival. In addition to the Sunday services, the numerous weeknight meetings held in the first decade of the twentieth century included those of the Fellowship and the cultural society, Band of Hope, and prayer and missionary prayer meetings. A similar pattern prevailed in

1926 when the membership had fallen to 417, and in this year the composer Haydn Morris was appointed to the post of organist and choirmaster. He was succeeded in 1928 by D.T. Davies, conductor of the Dowlais United Choir, and the two arranged several successful oratorios, concerts and organ recitals. Lectures were also delivered at the chapel. A dramatic society and gymnasium class were formed in the chapel, and a number of plays and gymnastic displays were performed at the Zoar Hall and also at the Miners' Hall. These activities provided opportunities to raise funds for the church, but there was also an awareness of the financial difficulties faced by many members at a time of economic depression. There were 232 members in 1945, and various activities, including lectures, musical and hymn-singing festivals were again held after the Second World War.

A further reduction in the number of members contributed to the closure of Zoar. A Welsh bookshop was opened in 1992 in a small side room off the main hall in the Zoar chapel vestry buildings. By supplying the growing demand for Welsh books across the Heads of the Valleys region its profits ensured an income to fund activities, events and social gatherings for Welsh speakers and learners at the newly-opened *Ganolfan Gymraeg* (Welsh Centre) in Merthyr Tydfil. A further development was the establishment on 1 May 2003 of *Menter Gymraeg Merthyr Tudful* (Merthyr Tydfil Welsh Venture) with the objective of broadening and strengthening services for the Welsh speakers and learners of Merthyr Tydfil County Borough. A determined effort to renovate the Zoar Chapel and the adjacent vestry, and transform the buildings into a community arts venue involved six years of planning, development and building largely financed by a £527,000 Heritage Lottery Fund Grant and Welsh Government grants. The result was the opening on 27 June 2011 of a 200-seat theatre, versatile studio space suitable for dance, arts and training workshops and two music/sound rooms. The adaptation was designed by Geoffrey Lapider, of Lapider, Penarth, and a significant feature of the present theatre is the covering of the seats in cloth by Cefyn Burgess. The chapel organ, built by Peter Conacher & Co. Huddersfield, is available for musical events. The first year's programme included theatrical and musical events and variety and children's shows performed by professional and community groups. Various courses are organised by the University of Glamorgan at Soar, and a number of voluntary groups make use of the facilities. The Welsh Language *Menter* / Venture is based at Soar, the bookshop continues to operate, the Cwtsh cafe is open from 9.00 a.m. until 4.00 p.m., and a licensed bar is also available.

Present position: Contacts, *Menter*: Lisbeth McLean, *Theatre*: Einir Sion.
Further reading: Angharad Lewis, *Zoar Chapel* (2008).
Websites: www.merthyrtudful.com and www. theatrsoar.com

109. LLANWENARTH (Be)

OS: SO 267 137

This is the oldest Baptist church in Wales which has met continuously since it was established. The Abergavenny church was established *c.* 1652 and there was a reference to Llanwenarth in 1655 as a branch of this church. Services were held in homes in the village of Govilon, in the parish of Llanwenarth, and in 1690 there were 110 members in Llanwenarth church, including 80 in Llanwenarth and 30 in the branch at Blaenau. In 1695 it was decided to invite Joshua James to assist William Pritchard who had been ordained as minister in 1653.

In the same year a plot of land was acquired in the village by Christopher Price, a wealthy apothecary who lived in the neighbouring village of Llanfoist. He was a prominent Baptist and a member of Abergavenny church. He represented a link with Baptists in England and was present at the meeting which framed the Confession of Faith, 1689. The plot of land was known as *Y Groes Newydd* [The New Cross] and a 199-year lease was secured for 2s 6d to build a meeting house. This was registered on 3 April by the Bishop of Llandaff. Missionaries were sent throughout Gwent and a number of branches were established which developed into churches, including those of Blaenau Gwent in 1660; Pen-y-garn, Pontypool in 1729; Abergavenny in 1769; Llangynidr in 1794; Blaenavon in 1823; Nantyglo in 1830 and Brynmawr in 1835. A 30-foot long banner illustrating the various churches founded by Llanwenarth was produced in 2002, when the 350th anniversary of the church was celebrated.

The broad chapel has a slate roof with round-headed sash windows. The largely-eighteenth century interior has a three-sided gallery supported on cast-iron columns, and box pews with panelled backs and doors. There are staircases on either side of the lobby, and a fireplace on the east wall.

The membership grew during the pastorate of the Rev. James Lewis, who accepted a call in 1792, from 119 in that year to 145 in 1793, and to 349 in 1811. The need to enlarge the chapel was appreciated and a sum of over £550 was collected between 1807 and 1809. The minister was assisted by Francis Hiley after 1810, and he was ordained here in the following year. A notable minister in this church until his death in 1860 and an inspiring preacher, he was known as '*Utgorn Arian Gwent*' [The Silver Trumpet of Gwent]. He was recorded as preaching to crowds of over a thousand at Nantyglo where 138 persons were baptised between June 1828 and May, 1829, and he and his predecessor baptised 1,471 individuals. On 30 March 1851 262 were present in the morning service, 164 scholars in the afternoon and 371 in the evening service. A note was added that many members and 'listeners 'resided in neighbouring parishes, and only attended services once a month. This explains the different numbers recorded as the average attendance, that is, 650 in the morning and again in the evening services. However, no explanation is provided for the limited space within the chapel, bearing in mind the statement that

the chapel contained 162 free seats and 90 others.

A considerable amount of renovation work was undertaken in 1869, with the construction of a vestry, a stage replacing the pulpit, and the installation of new seats and a baptistry in front of the stage. However, the outside pool, filled with water from the nearby Monmouthshire and Brecon Canal, continued to be used until 1943. Another important development related to the language issue. Services had initially been conducted entirely in the Welsh language, but whilst attempts were made in 1872 and 1873 to use both the Welsh and English languages, efforts to safeguard the use of the Welsh language were unsuccessful, and soon, with the rapid Anglicisation of the area, the English language became the sole language used in services.

The long association of the Hiley family has continued to the present day, with the current organists including two direct descendants of the Rev. Francis Hiley. A pipe organ was installed in 1973 instead of the old pedal organ, and an electronic organ was introduced in 1996. The musical tradition extends back for over a century, and for many years the Baptist Music Festival was held at Llanwenarth.

Present position: Minister, the Rev. Peter Baines, 80 members, Sunday services, 10.30 a.m. and 6.00 p.m., 52 children, 8-10 teenagers in the Sunday school; Weekday/evening activities include Bible class, coffee morning, luncheon club, youth club (travellers club), Mums & Toddlers group, women's meeting. Also occasional events include autumn fair, flower festival.

Further reading: Peter Baines & Govilon Village History Group, *Llanwenarth Baptist church, 1652-2002* (2002).

110. ABER-CARN, Welsh Church (Pw)

OS: ST 217 951

This church is distinctive in that whilst belonging to the Presbyterian Church of Wales, it had since its foundation adhered to the devotional practices of the Anglican Church.

The distinctive nature of the church stemmed from its early history and the association with members of the Llanover family who resided locally at Llanover House. Before his elevation as Lord Llanover, Sir Benjamin Hall was Chief Commissioner of Works in Lord Palmerstone's government during the period 1855-58, responsible for the improvement of London's parks and for the construction of Big Ben: a name which reminds us of him. His wife Augusta, known as 'Gwenynen Gwent', was a fervent supporter of the Welsh language and culture. The place of worship erected in Aber-carn was presented to the Church in Wales on condition that all the services should be in the Welsh language, with the original intention to provide for the lord's Welsh workers. The report on the opening of 'the new Welsh Church at Abercarn', published in the *Illustrated London News* on 16 December 1854, referred to the lord's opinion on the deterioration of the Church in Wales as a result of holding English-language or mixed-language services in parish churches established by "pious Welshmen for the benefit of the aboriginals of the soil."

The Book of Common Prayer was specifically adapted by Lady Llanover for use in the church which for nine years was in the care of a curate. Following a dispute with the vicar of Mynyddislwyn, who was supported by the Bishop of Llandaff, concerning the condition relating to the use of the Welsh language, the Llanover family invited a prominent minister with the Calvinistic Methodists, the Rev. David Charles, the Principal of the Trefeca Theological College and grandson of the Rev Thomas Charles, Bala, to be the minister. He left his post at Trefeca, and was the minister of the Welsh Church from 1862 until 1868. His successor was the Rev. David Saunders, another prominent leader with the Calvinistic Methodists and minister of Princes Road, Liverpool, one of the largest Calvinistic Methodist churches, and it was during his ministry that the church, together with its generous endowment, was transferred to the Calvinistic Methodist Connexion, and this explains its association with the Presbyterian Church of Wales up to the present day. The bilingual memorial tablet in the church to the Llanover family refers to Sir Benjamin Hall building the church in 1853 to enable the local residents of Aber-carn to worship God in their own language, and to his widow Augusta, for the support of the church, together with its minister, for the benefit of the Welsh people and the continuation of its language.

The chapel has been listed Grade 2 by Cadw as a chapel of special interest in the ecclesiastical history of Wales and one in which there has been little change since it was opened in 1854. It is of a revised Gothic style and has seating for a congregation of 300. The *Illustrated London News* report of its opening provided details of a building designed by the lord, and constructed of the best stones found on his estate. Reference was made to the simple style which was a feature of traditional Welsh ecclesiastical architecture, with a bell-tower.

The church was lit by four lanterns hanging from the ceiling, and was heated by hot water pipes running under the floor. The stone work, undertaken by local workers, was of the highest standard, and the stone corbels and window frames exhibited fine craftsmanship. The date of the building, 1853, was placed at the entrance, together with the Llanover coat of arms, and this coat of arms, together with the royal one also appears on the front of the gallery. The pulpit was made of pine, as also were the Communion rails, chair and frame surrounding the slates which present in black lettering the Ten Commandments, Credo and the Lord's Prayer.

Stained glass windows and Gothic altar rails previously in the Anglican St. Luke's until the closure of this place of worship in 1984 have been installed in the chapel. A sum of £40,000 was spent on repairing the exterior of the building, and financial support was received from Cadw towards the cost of the work.

Since 1984 the building had been shared with the local St. Luke's Anglican Church, following the closure of the Anglican place of worship, and was therefore a rare example of one building shared by the two churches. The closing Welsh-language service was held in January 2011 in a church which occupies an unique place in the history of the Welsh language in Gwent. The Welsh language had been used here from the very beginning, even though the language declined locally, but in recent years there had been a revival with the establishment of primary and secondary Welsh-language schools in the area. The continuation of the agreement whereby the building is used by St. Luke's Anglican church is at present under review.

111. PONTYPOOL, Crane Street (Be)

OS: SO 281 010

An early reference to Baptist activities in Pontypool is the record of a service held in Trosnant of a mixed congregation of Baptists and Independents. Pen-y-garn Baptist chapel was established by the Llanwenarth church in 1729 and doctrinal differences were probably responsible for the foundation of Trosnant Church in 1776. The future of the Baptist Academy at Abergavenny was discussed in 1836 at a meeting which resolved that the academy should be moved to Pontypool and that the President should hold the office jointly with that of minister of a new English church to be established in the town to cater for those who had moved to Pontypool and spoke no Welsh. The Rev. Thomas Thomas, a native of Cowbridge and minister of a church in London, accepted the invitation and Crane Street Church was established in the same year. The new church, whose services were held at the meeting-house of the Society of Friends at Trosnant, comprised 16 members, including the Rev. Dr. Thomas Thomas and his wife Mary, and he served as the minister until his retirement in December 1873. In 1871 he became the first Welsh-speaking president of the Baptist Union of Great Britain and Ireland, and is commemorated in the chapel by a tablet which contains profile busts of himself and his wife by J. Milo Griffith. Their son, the artist T.H. Thomas, 'Arlunydd Penygarn', was closely involved with the National Eisteddfod, Royal Cambrian Academy and the Cardiff Naturalists' Society.

A prominent figure in the church was the deacon William Williams Phillips, agent to Capel Hanbury Leigh, Pontypool Park, and descendant of the Rev. Miles Harry, the first minister of Pen-y-garn church. The growth in numbers led to the building of a new chapel in Crane Street which, costing approximately £2,200, was opened on the site in April 1847, when the church comprised 77 members. A sum of approximately £1,000 was collected before or during the opening services, and the debt of £1,200 had been cleared by 1868. The Classical building, designed by Aaron Crossfield with improvements by J.H. Langdon, was constructed of Bath stone ashlar with a central bay formed of a portico and two Greek Doric columns with a pediment. A distinctive feature of the interior includes the large glass panelled ceiling which was probably installed in the late-nineteenth century in the opening left when the chapel was built. This provides daylight throughout the building and the original intention was possibly based upon the contemporary view regarding the lighting of ancient Greek temples. The aisles now covered with carpet have glass tiles laid into the floor to allow light entering through the glass floor to filter through to the school room below the chapel. The baptistry for total immersion was placed below the floor of the platform pulpit which was appropriate for debate and teaching, rather than for eloquent preaching. In 1851 the chapel contained 100 free seats and 200 others. On 30 March there were present 110 and 30 scholars in the morning service, and 152 in the evening. The average attendance in the evening was 200, and Charles Davies, deacon, and ironmonger, commented that the smallness of the congregation could be explained by the absence on that day of the pastor. The membership increased to 197 in 1865, and in 1867 the Sunday school had 160 scholars and 16 teachers. The highest number of members, 220, was recorded in 1894 during the ministry of the Rev. John Williams (1878-1902). The chapel had been enlarged by A. O. Watkins in 1868-69. Most of the furnishings seem to date from this time, even though the pulpit may well be part of the original 1847 chapel. A pipe organ was installed in 1881, at a cost of approximately £300 and the galleries, surrounding the interior on four sides, were probably added at this time. A number of renovations and improvements were carried out between 1887 and 1897. A further extensive renovation, costing £820-850, was undertaken in 1908-09, and in 1910 two stained glass windows were placed in the chapel.

Significant decisions relating to church membership in 1946, 1950 and 1960 resulted in the acceptance into church membership of members of other denominations or those who could not accept the belief in 'believer's baptism'.

Major faults in the roof and portico were discovered whilst cleaning the stone work of the building in 1979-80, and the problems were compounded by the appearance of dry rot, the effects of flooding and further damage to the roof in a severe gale. Following an exceptionally positive response to an appeal for financial support, numerous fund-raising activities and grants from a number of organisations and local authorities, an extensive renovation-programme was undertaken in consultation with Cadw, which recognised the church in 1998 as a Grade 2* building. In 2009 the organ was rebuilt by the Midland Organ & Hele Co. Ltd. and the kitchen was upgraded and refurbished. An application has been submitted to Cadw for a grant of £79,000 to finance structural repairs to the roof.

In 2002 the Church united with the Mount Pleasant U.R.C. Church as a Local Ecumenical Partnership.. The twice-weekly coffee mornings attract members of the local community and a Yoga Group meets in the building on one evening.

Present position: Minister, Rev. Alvin S. Richards-Clarke, 16 members; Sunday service, 10.30 a.m; Wednesday 10.00 a.m ecumenical eucharist service led by Anglican church; twice-weekly coffee mornings for the local community.

Further reading: Crane Street Baptist Church 1836-1986, compiled by Dilys M Thorne, (1986); Arthur J. Edwards, *Thomas Thomas of Pontypool, Radical Puritan* (2009); *The correspondence of Thomas Henry Thomas, 'Arlunydd Penygarn'*, ed. Christabel Hutchings (2012).

112. NEWPORT, Havelock Street (Pe)

OS: ST 304 882

An awareness of the needs of the increasing number of English-speakers in the rapidly-growing town and port of Newport led to the establishment in July 1863 by Ebenezer, the Welsh Calvinistic Methodist Church, of a new English-language church. Early meetings were held in the Victoria buildings, later known as the Lyceum Theatre, attended by 12 members, and within three months the membership had grown to 26, and the Sunday School comprised 11 teachers and 51 scholars. Before the end of the year the Rev. John Davies, previously a minister in Bishop Auckland, co Durham, had been inducted as minister. Following the acquisition of a plot of land in Havelock Street and the preparation of plans by Messrs. W.G. Habershon and Pite, architects, a contract had been signed in April 1864 with L.B. Moore, a local builder, for the construction of a new permanent home at a cost of £1,170. In the same month the foundation stone had been laid by the Mayor of Newport for the new chapel which was formally opened on 19 October. The chapel, with its distinctive Italianate style, has been described as "one of the most remarkable buildings in Newport" with the building material a mixture of red and yellow bricks, and stones, including Bath Stone, Pennant Sandstone, Old Red Sandstone, granite and Devonian limestone: the latter probably derived from the Plymouth area: and many of the stones possibly derived as ship's ballast. A Lombardic-style entrance front had a wheel window over the porch. The interior comprises galleries on three sides with the organ above the pulpit under a large semi-circular arch.

In 1883 land next to the chapel was acquired and on it a Lecture Hall was built in the following year. A new pipe church organ costing £200, was installed in 1886, and paid for immediately. The organ was opened with a recital by George Rogers, the organist of St. Paul's Anglican church, and choruses from the Messiah were sung by the church choir. Fund-raising activities including two 'Grand Bazaars', in 1881 and 1891, and a Sale of Work in 1892 resulted in the clearing in that year of the total debt which had been incurred by the church, with a sum of £950 raised in these two years. A similar sum was spent in 1893 when the chapel, schoolroom and Lecture Hall were thoroughly renovated, following a fire in the chapel in April, and an organ chamber was erected at the rear of the chapel, thereby enlarging the interior. A further development in 1896 was the installation of electric light which, costing £78, was paid for at the same time. The significance of the church within the Calvinistic Methodist Connexion was recognised by the decision in 1898, following intense competition from Aberystwyth and Pembroke Dock, to be the venue of the 1898 General Assembly, thereby becoming the first English-language church to host the General Assembly.

The Havelock Street church actively supported the foundation of churches in other rapidly-growing areas of Newport. Developments in the eastern areas led to the establishment in 1893, initially of a Sunday school, and then of the branch mission church in Caerleon Road, whose original membership of 67 persons included 57 individuals transferred from the parent church of Havelock Street. This resulted in a reduction in the membership of Havelock Street to 173, but a consequence of the Revival of 1904-05 was an increase in the membership which in 1906 reached 248, the highest number in its history. In 1908 a church was established at Stow Park to cater for those attracted to live in the Stow Park, Caerau Park and West Park areas, and 27 members from the Havelock Street church joined the new church

A significant aspect of the history of the church was that the first Boys' Brigade company to be established in Wales was instituted here by George Philip Reynolds, an elder of the church and owner of a successful drapery business in the town. Having spent some time in Glasgow and admired the activities of the Boys Brigade he introduced the Brigade in Newport, by founding at the church in 1887 the 'first Newport (Mon) Company of the Boys' Brigade'. The constitution referred to him as the Captain, supported by three 'Lieutenants', a 'Band Master' and Gymnasium Club instructor, and the members were boys of between 12 and 17 years of age, on the roll of the Sunday school, and required to attend the Company Bible Class on Sunday afternoons. Activities included drilling and involvement in a gymnastic club and a pipe band, and a recreation room was open each weeknight, where books, papers and games were provided. A marble tablet was erected in the church in 1907 in memory of George Philip Reynolds, whose inscription contained the description of him as a 'Philanthropist, Social Worker and Christian Gentleman', and a reference to the 500 boys who passed under his care. A blue plaque on an outer wall of the chapel records that the site is the birthplace in Wales of the Boys' Brigade.

In the late-nineteenth century, and again in the twentieth century the church had been closely involved in the establishment and development of other Presbyterian churches in Newport, including the Caerleon Road and Stow Park churches and in 1962 the church amalgamated with the Great Central Hall. A sad event was the closure of the Sunday School in 2000 after the redevelopment of local streets in the 1980s and 1990s resulted in the movement away from the area of many families.

Present position: No minister but occasional duties undertaken by the Rev Dafydd H. Owen, 25 members, Sunday service 11.a.m., one devotional service every month on a Wednesday afternoon.

Further reading: *History of Havelock Street Presbyterian church, Newport, Mon, Jubilee Souvenir, 1864-1914*, compiled by A. Morris (1914); *Havelock Street Presbyterian Church, Portrait of a small Welsh church community*, Photographs by Ron McCormick (2009); Stephen Howe, 'The Building Stones of Newport' in *Welsh Stone Forum Newsletter*, no 4 (February 2007)

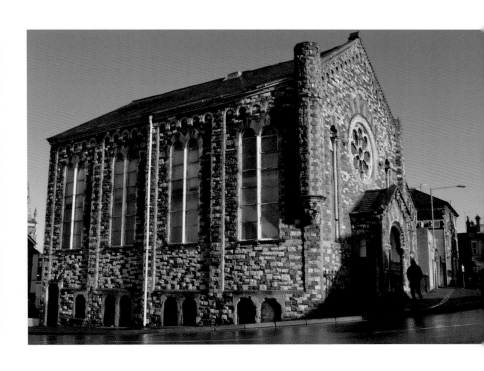

113. LLANVACHES Tabernacle (R)

OS: ST 437 912

The first Nonconformist church in Wales, and the oldest Independent church in Wales was formed here in November 1639. William Wroth had been the incumbent of Llanvaches since 1617, and since his conversion in 1620 he became renowned as an evangelical preacher. Large congregations were attracted here, with many travelling from neighbouring shires to hear him preach, and services had to be held in the graveyard as the church was too small. His co-workers included William Erbury, the rector of St. Mary's church, Cardiff, and his curate, Walter Cradock. The Bishop of Llandaff reported in 1635 that Wroth was "leading away many simple people". He was summoned before the Court of High Commision in 1635 and surrendered his incumbency in 1638. This forms the background to the establishment of the Llanvaches church in 1639. Wroth was assisted by Cradock and also Henry Jessey, who had been sent by All Hollows the Great church, London where John Penry had worshipped many years previously when he had visited the city. Following Wroth's death in 1642, he was succeeded by Cradock but soon afterwards, during the Civil Wars, he and his congregation were forced to flee because of threats delivered by royalist supporters in the shire. He was given succour in Bristol by the members of the Highmead church where William Wroth had preached on several occasions. After the surrender of Bristol to royalist forces they travelled under the leadership of Walter Cradock to London and joined All Hollows Church. After the Civil War the members of Llanvaches returned home, and it is probable that their enthusiasm had contributed to Walter Cradock's declaration in 1646, following his return after an absence of four years, that "The gospel has run over the mountains between Breconshire and Monmouthshire as the fire in the thatch".

Meetings were held for some time in members' homes and following the Restoration of 1660 the impression was given that the church was lively and successful. The 1689 Toleration Act granted the right to hold services in licensed meeting houses, and as a result members who had travelled to Llanvaches arranged services in their own localities, and henceforth only visited Llanvaches on an occasional basis. There was a failure to secure a plot of land to build a meeting house in Llanvaches parish, and the first Tabernacle was built in the village of Bryn Carw, in a neighbouring parish. In 1703 a joint pastorate was formed with the church of Mill Street, Newport, and a report prepared in the 1715-17 period referred to 236 members. By the end of the eighteenth century the church had weakened considerably and it was suggested that it should close. In the face of this threat, a plot of land was provided for the construction of a chapel in Llanvaches parish, and the new Tabernacl was opened in 1802.

There were periods of growth and of decline in the nineteenth century. In 1851 there were 150 free seats and on 30 March 45 were present in the morning service and 51 in the evening. In 1899 there were 20 members, 60 'listeners' and 50 scholars under 14 years of age in the Sunday school. By 1906 the influence of the Revival was reflected in an increase in the membership to 44, with a large number of listeners. Several improvements were made to the chapel, with seats replacing wooden benches on the ground floor, a new organ was bought and the chapel was painted. The need was expressed for a hall to be used for special occasions, and in 1924 the Wroth Memorial Hall, which had been presented to the church by Mrs. C.H. Bailey, was opened. A kitchen was built at the rear of the hall in the 1970s and the chapel was refurbished in 1982 in memory of the Rev. Charles Smith-Draper, who had been an energetic minister in the period 1974-82. The Rev. Shem Morgan served as part-time minister from 1982 until 2009.

Present position: Minister, Rev. Kevin Snyman, 37 members, 1st, 3rd and 5th Sunday afternoon at 3 p.m; 2nd and 4th Sunday 9.15 a.m.
Further reading: Shem H. Morgan, *A History of Tabernacle United Reformed Church Llanvaches, 1639-1989* (1989); Brian Ll. James, 'Llanfaches – The Background', *Capel Newsletter,* 10 (Spring, 1990).

114. LIVERPOOL, Bethel, Heathfield Road (Pw)

OS: SJ 394 885

The origins of Bethel extend back to the prayer meeting held at William Llwyd's home in 1782, the first religious service held by Calvinistic Methodists in Liverpool. 130 persons attended in 1860 the Sunday school established in 1859 by the Chatham Street Church and held in a rented room in Holden Street, a road located in the south of Liverpool extending from Crown Street towards Upper Parliament Street. The number had increased to 154 in the following year, and the growth in numbers led to the opening of a schoolroom in Smithdown Lane in 1864, when 170 attended. This had been built at a cost of £1,100 and in the following year the number had grown to 278, including 108 children. Most of the adults were members of either the Chatham Street or Bedford Street churches, but the increasing numbers and activities at the schoolroom resulted in the opening in 1889 of the Webster Road chapel, which seated a congregation of 300, and an associated small schoolroom. Sums of £805 were paid for the land, £1,766 to the builders and another £250 on various items. At the end of 1889 the Webster Road church had 203 members, 92 adults and 88 children under 15 in the Sunday school. The chapel was enlarged in this year with a small gallery built opposite the pulpit, the schoolroom was extended and a large schoolroom built on a plot of land behind the chapel.

The period extending from 1865 to 1935 has been described as the golden age of Welsh Calvinistic Methodism in Liverpool with large numbers of Welshmen settling in Liverpool, which was described by Lord Mostyn in 1885 as a city which had become "more than ever the metropolis of Wales". The elders of the church included two builders who had been born in Anglesey: John Jones, Mayfield, who had left school at 13 to work as a farm labourer; and John Hughes, Moneivion, They made a significant contribution to the development of the Liverpool area, building estates in Wavertree, Fazakerley, Walton, Bootle, Anfield and Birkenhead, and, in the case of John Hughes, in Newton-le-Willows, Birmingham and London. J.W. Jones, Hiraethog was responsible for building houses in Sefton Park, Allerton, Childwall, Wavertree and Mossley Hill; whilst yet another elder, John Jones, Salisbury Road, who had been born in 1831 in the chapel house of Penmount, Pwllheli, had come to Liverpool when he was 16 years of age as an apprentice builder with another Welsh builder. Having established his own business, he built several streets of houses in the Liverpool 8 area and also in Hoylake. These builders employed fellow-members who were stonemasons, craftsmen and labourers, who were also incomers, and thereby at the same time time both favouring them by providing employment but also punishing them by offering comparatively-low wages.

A rapid growth in the membership in the early twentieth century with 562 members recorded in 1906, and 606 members in 1922 led to repeated discussions on the need for a new chapel. A plot of land on the corner of Heathfield Road and

Smithdown Place was bought in 1923 and it is significant that the church's Buldings Committee was almost entirely composed of builders. The new chapel, designed by Richard Owen & Son, and built by John Williams, Collingwood Street, was opened on 26 March 1927. The total cost of the land and building-work was over £26,000. The chapel seated a congregation of 750, and an impression of extensive space was provided by the high ceiling and large windows. Associated with the chapel were two schoolrooms, one large and the other one small and compact. Also provided were a room for the minister and elders, two rooms for the Sunday school, kitchen, library and toilets. A chapel house for the caretaker was built beside the chapel. The highest number of members in the history of the church, 655, was recorded in 1930, with 424 members of the Sunday school and 798 listeners. However, a disturbing feature was the fall in the number of children from 162 to 93 in the period 1921-1930. Services continued to be held during the Second World War apart from Sunday, 11 May 1941 following a week when Liverpool was bombarded.

The decrease in the membership, partly caused by the increasing trend for families to return to Wales, and concern with regard to the need for extensive renovation of the chapel, resulted in discussions aimed at the construction of a new, smaller chapel. A report was prepared in 1997 but following protracted discussions eventually the chapel buildings were demolished and the new chapel on this site was opened in 2011.

Present position: Emeritus minister: Rev. Dr. D. Ben Rees, 138 members, 15 children and 5 adults in the Sunday school, Sunday service at 10.30 a.m., devotional service or cultural society on Monday evening, childrens' youth meeting on Friday evening. *Further reading*: John Hughes Morris, *Hanes Methodistiaeth Liverpool, 11* (1932); R. Merfyn Jones & D. Ben Rees, *Liverpool Welsh and their religion* (1984); D. Ben Rees, *Labour of Love in Liverpool, a history of Bethel Chapel, Heathfield Road, Liverpool* (2008).

115. LONDON, Castle Street (U/Bw)

OS: TQ 293 814

A group of approximately 70 Baptists, aware that Providence Chapel, at the rear of Tottenham Court Road, their former meeting-place, had become too small to accommodate them, had started to hold services in April 1865 at the Franklin Hall, located in a passage-way off the present-day Eastcastle Street. The Hall was rented for £35 per annum, but the 14 years of unexpired lease, which also included the two adjoining properties, was bought for £860 in 1880, and a further £500 was spent on improvements to the building. In 1888 the Duke of Portland, the landowner, was persuaded to grant a 60-year lease for a new meeting-house on the site, and building-work commenced in December 1888. The new chapel was designed by Owen Lewis, 'Owain Dyfed', a deacon at the church and the architect responsible for the chapel at Blaenwaun, Pembrokeshire where he had been brought up. The Castle Street chapel cost £ 4,800, seated 500-600 persons and contained a pipe organ, gallery, a large room underneath the chapel accommodating 500 persons and used for concerts and social gatherings, small rooms, library and tea-making facilities. Owen Lewis was highly praised for his work, and the *Baptist Times* described it as "an edifice worthy of a West end reputation" and "should it fail as a heavenly purpose, there will be no difficulty in selling the whole structure to a West end club, whose aristocratic members would be pleased to pay a subscription of so many guineas per annum for its social convenience." The church opened with a debt of around £2,000 but one of the major contributors to the building fund was D.H. Evans, the successful business man who established his store in Oxford Street, and who became a deacon during the opening services. A series of concerts and bazaars were also held to clear the debt. A further debt was incurred in 1909 as a result of the extension and modernisation of the chapel in preparation for the fiftieth anniversary of the church. The installation of a new organ, built by Hunter & Co. Clapham and costing £950, involved redesigning the ceiling coving, removal of seats from the front and side of the gallery, and extending the seating into the space created by the removal of two rooms behind the gallery. A large-scale fundraising sale of work was organised in 1910, with a profit of over £500 from stalls, concerts and plays, and two publications. Whilst Welsh was the language of the devotional services, and an eisteddfod was held by the Sunday school, English generally was the language of the social gatherings, and in 1910 the Rev. Herbert Morgan the minister from 1906 until 1912, was requested by the deacons to arrange the teaching of Welsh to children.

Twentieth-century ministers included the Revs. James Nicholas (1916-35, and 1936-7), Walter P. John (1938-67) and D. Hugh Matthews (1968-85). The membership had grown from 65 in 1866 to 508 in 1916, and to 700 in 1922. The 999-year lease had been purchased in 1921 for £1,500 with the landlord, Lord Howard de

Walden making a donation of £250 towards the costs. Extensive repairs were undertaken, costing over £1540 in 1924 and over £300 in 1925. In addition to raising funds to reduce the church's debt, collections were organised in 1926 in aid of strikers' families in south Wales, and for many years money and clothes were distributed to three specific churches in Glamorgan: Noddfa, Caerau; Seion, Maerdy, and Rhos, Mountain Ash. The numerous activities included the Sunday school, Saturday night Fellowship, choir practices, tennis and bowls clubs and the Whit Monday annual trip. In 1928 the Sunday school was invited to spend the day at Churt, David Lloyd George's country residence, where a marquee had been set up in the grounds. David Lloyd George, elected Member of Parliament for the Caernarvon Boroughs in 1900, attended services occasionally before becoming a member in 1906, but he also retained his membership of Berea church, Cricieth. On 26 October 1916, when he was the Secretary for War, he had chaired the induction meeting of the Rev. James Nicholas. A verse in Idris Davies's autobiographical poem, 'I was born in Rhymney' written in 1943 but referring to the inter-war period, reads: "To Castle Street Baptist Chapel / Like the prodigal son I went / To hear the hymns of childhood / And dream of a boy in Gwent".

The membership had increased to 1,012 by 1938 and, as the problem of overcrowding continued to present a problem, enquiries were made with a view to building an extension. However, the onset of the Second World War presented a different challenge, with 80 young members joining the forces and many moving away from London. Despite the bombing of the city, the doors of the chapel remained open throughout the war apart from two Sundays in September 1941 when services were abandoned because of an unexploded landmine. The membership had fallen to 788 by December 1945. Further renovation work was undertaken periodically during the second half of the twentieth century, as in 1950 and 1959, when sums of £2,000 were spent on each occasion; the 1960s when the sluggish pneumatic action of the organ was replaced by an electronic one; and in 1971 when the installation of a new electricity supply and fluorescent lighting, repairs and decorating the chapel cost over £5,000.

A number of distinguished organists have contributed to the renowned musical tradition of the church. They have included Dryhurst Roberts, Glyn Lang, who served as organist for nearly 70 years and is an honorary Life Deacon of the church; Carys Hughes and latterly Euron Walters and Gwenllian Joslin; and the numerous 'occasional' organists included Terry James and John Rogers.

The church has joined with the Tabernacle King's Cross and Radnor Walk Welsh Independent Churches to form Eglwys Gymraeg Canol Llundain (the United Welsh Church in Central London) and the opening service of the united church was held on 5 November 2007.

An interesting development is that a Korean church holds a service in the chapel on Sunday afternoon and on Wednesday evening.

Present position: Minister, Rev. Peter Dewi Richards, 110 members, Sunday services, 11.00 a.m. and 6.15 p.m., the Urdd Aelwyd meets on Sunday evenings at 7.30 p.m., Discussion group once every month.

Further reading: Walter P. John & Gwilym T. Hughes, *Hanes Castle Street a'r Bedyddwyr Cymraeg yn Llundain* (1959); D. Hugh Matthews, *Hanes Tŷ Cwrdd Castle Street Meeting House – A History* (1989).

Website: www.egcll.org

116. LONDON, Clapham Junction (Pw)

OS: TQ274 754

The history of this church may be traced to the concern expressed at successive annual meetings of the General Assembly of the Presbyterian Church of Wales in the last decade of the nineteenth century. The need to collect information on Welsh persons living outside Wales was emphasised in the meeting held at Morriston in 1891, and in 1893, at Bootle, reference was made to the spiritual requirements of the numerous Welsh persons living in the large cities of England, such as London, Liverpool and Manchester. In the following year, at Pontypridd, the London Presbytery was required to care for the Welsh persons residing in their midst, and the 1895 meeting in London resolved, on the basis of a report prepared by John Burrell, to appoint a missionary to work with some churches, and especially among the young Welsh women who had come to London. It was pointed out that it was not possible for Welsh persons living in areas such as Clapham, Lewisham and Wandsworth to attend Welsh-language services, and emphasis was placed on the importance of adding to the Welsh causes in London. A committee of the London Presbytery drew attention to the large numbers of Welsh persons living in Battersea, Clapham Common and Wandsworth, and the need for assistance to establish and maintain the Sunday school formed in 1893-94 in Wandsworth Road as a branch of the Sunday school of the Falmouth Road church. Despite its closure in the summer of 1894, the Sunday school was re-commenced in 1895, and was moved to a room in the Felix Institute, Lavender Hill which seated 80-100 persons.

The London Presbytery had agreed to establish a church in Clapham Junction, and the congregation meeting at the Felix Institute was incorporated as a church in January 1896 with 47 members. Later in the same year a room was rented in the New Hall, Battersea Rise which could accommodate 200-300 persons, and four elders were elected. The Rev. Llewelyn Edwards, one of the sons of Lewis Edwards, Principal of the Bala Theological College, accepted the 'call' to be the first minister, and a plot of land, measuring 80' on each side, was bought with the intention of building a chapel. A large house on the site could be adapted for a chapel seating 300 persons, and sufficient land was also available for the building of additional houses. After signing an 80-year lease, which stipulated a ground rent of £36, the building-work soon commenced. The report published at the end of 1896 referred to 91 members, and 87 members in the Sunday school, and an estimated cost of £5,833 which was higher than anticipated. Following fervent missionary activity in the area extending from Wimbledon to Vauxhall, and from the river Thames to Streatham and Brixton, and a determined effort to raise funds, the church had 204 members, 41 children, and a Sunday school with 145 members at the end of 1902, when the debt had been reduced to £4,400.

The minister retired at this time, and the six elders elected in 1903 included D.

Owen Evans (1876-1945), the barrister, industrialist and politician. The second minister, the Rev. D. Tyler Davies served from 1907 until 1916. On 27 June 1909 a stained glass window was unveiled in memory of Mair Eiluned Lloyd George who had died on 29 November 1907 at 17 years of age. Thomas Figgis Curtis was commissioned by her family to design this memorial which, created by T.F. Curtis, Ward and Hughes, Frith Street, Soho, shows Mair seated at a pipe organ, surrounded by angels and a number of panels including illustrations of Cricieth castle, the red dragon and the banner of the princes of Gwynedd. Mair and her brother Gwilym had been baptised and became members of the church, and their mother, Margaret Lloyd George, a very active member of the church, regularly distributed certificates to the children on Palm Sunday. By the end of 1912, the membership had increased to 289, and 91 children, and the Sunday School membership to 144. The chapel was repaired and cleaned in the summer of 1914, and electric light was introduced. The church rented and furnished a house in Lavender Hill to support refugees from Belgium during the 1914-18 war, and nine members were killed in the war. A tablet in their memory was unveiled by Margaret Lloyd George in 1921, and the tradition was established of placing flowers on the tablet on the Sunday nearest to Armistice Day. The debt had been cleared in this year and following the renovation of the chapel, its extension with the addition of additional seating and rooms, the purchase of an organ for £1,000 and the lease for £1,227.10s., another debt of £3,500 had accumulated by the end of 1926. The church had 409 members in 1927, and one of the three elders elected in this year was Sir David Hughes Parry, professor of English law and later vice-chancellor of the University of London who was regarded as one of the most influential Welsh jurists of the twentieth century. He and his wife Haf served as Sunday school teachers and founded a Welsh Sunday school at Kingston-upon-Thames. In 1928 some of the rooms in the chapel house were adapted to form an Institute providing recreational facilities for members, including the establishment of a bowls club and library, with Welsh and English books being available for loan, and the re-formation of a tennis club.

The 40-year celebration in 1936 was marked by the cleaning and repair of the chapel, rooms and houses, and in 1939 the membership has reached 457. The 1939-45 war had an immediate impact with the requisitioning of the room below the chapel by the Battersea Council and the strengthening of the walls with steel pillars, and as a result hundreds of Battersea families spent many hours here sheltering from the onslaught of bomb attacks. Considerable damage was caused in the vicinity of the chapel by the attacks launched during the war, with many persons killed and buildings destroyed. The arch above one of the chapel's windows was destroyed in September 1940 and the doors and windows damaged when extensive damage was caused to Lavender Hill, opposite Beauchamp Road in August 1944.

The organ was renovated and repaired in 1966, and the ceiling, chapel house and manse were renovated in 1972. In 1982 the chapel was decorated with the assistance of the Wandsworth Borough Youth Employment. Social activities arranged by the church included plays staged at the Battersea Town Hall, oratorios, eisteddfodau and classical concerts featuring masters and pupils at the Battersea Grammar School. For many years an annual English-language service was held on Armistice Sunday, and the preachers included the Rev. Dr. Martin Lloyd Jones, Lord Soper and George Thomas, M.P. Present-day services are predominantly in Welsh, with the inclusion of some English for the benefit of Welsh-language learners and those not fluent in the language. Long-serving ministers of the church have included the Revs. W.J Jones (1919-1955), O.J. Evans (1962-1981) and Geoffrey Davies (1982-1999). The pastorate was periodically extended to include Welsh churches in Croydon, Sutton, Walham Green, Lewisham and Charing Cross, and the Welsh churches of Lewisham and Falmouth Road have by now united with the church at Clapham Junction. The church presently forms part of the pastorate comprising the five Presbyterian Church of Wales churches in the London area.

Present position: Minister, Rev. Richard Brunt, 39 members, together with a number of 'listeners' who attend regularly or occasionally when in the area, Sunday service, 11 a.m. Services are predominantly in Welsh, with the inclusion of some English for the benefit of Welsh-language learners and those not fluent in the language.
Further reading: *Hanes Clapham Junction 1896-1996* (1996); R. Gwynedd Parry, *David Hughes Parry, A Jurist in Society* (2010).

117. LONDON, Jewin (Pw)

OS: TQ 322 820

The present chapel was built in Fann Street in 1961 after the original building on the site was bombed in 1940 during the Second World War.

In 1739 a society [seiat] was established in London following the visit of Howel Harris. Services were held in Cock Lane, Smithfield c.1774 and one of the preachers sent from Wales to minister there was Edward Parry, Bryn Bugad, Llansannan, the Denbighshire counsellor who has been commemorated at the chapels of Tan-y-fron and Capel Coffa Henry Rees, Llansannan. In 1785, Sion chapel Wilderness Row was built and it was extended in 1806. A 61-year lease, at a rent of £30 per annum, was signed in 1822 for a plot of land measuring approximately 421 square yards, in Jewin Crescent to build a chapel and house. The chapel, designed by Thomas Hughes, Liverpool, and measuring 60 feet long and 48 feet wide, opened the following year, and in the same year, 1823, James Hughes, 'Iago Trichrug', commenced upon his full-time pastorate. In 1865 a report in Y Drysorfa referred to Jewin Crescent chapel suffering from the effects of smoke and dampness, coldness and heat, and the chapel was renovated in that year.

The lease came to an end in 1876, and following determined efforts to increase the building fund, a new chapel was built in Fann Street in 1878-79. The connection with the old chapel was maintained by the use of the name 'Jewin Newydd' until 1917, and 'Jewin' afterwards. The designer was Charles Bell, who was also responsible for the restoration of Wesley's Chapel, City Road, which had been badly damaged by fire in 1879. The new Jewin chapel, built in the Early English style, whose style was designated as 'Old English', was constructed of Kentish rag and Portland stone. Having an oblong plan, with a tower and slated spire, it seated a congregation of 650. Henry Richard, M.P. presided at a public meeting which formally opened the chapel. A series of services was held the following week, and the preachers included Dr. Owen Thomas, Liverpool, who had been the minister from 1851 until 1865. Other former ministers included the Revs. David Charles Davies, from 1859 until 1882, and the crowned bard J.E. Davies 'Rhuddwawr' from 1886 until 1911. In 1898 the chapel was extended, and improvements were made to the chapel, designed by R.J. Lovell. These cost approximately £12,000, and this sum included a payment of £779 for the organ to Wadsworth & Bro. of Manchester. The debt was cleared by 1918, and in 1920 the chapel was renovated at a cost of £6,300 which was paid by the members. In this year there were 671 members, and this number increased by January 1939 to 1,148 and 245 children.

The outbreak of the Second World War in this year led to the evacuation of children and the return of many members to Wales, and in 1940 there were 1,082 members when the chapel was destroyed by fire bombs. Soon afterwards an Appeal Committee was formed, and following discussions concerning the possibility of

building a chapel on other sites, including one in Holborn Viaduct where land had been purchased by the church, the decision was made to build a new chapel, again in Fann Street. This was designed by Caroe & Partners and built by F. & M.F. Higgs, Ltd. in 1960-61. Whilst Philip Temple, the author of several volumes on London churches, was extremely critical of most of the churches built in London after the Second World War, referring to "eclecticism and experimentation", he expressed the view that Jewin was one of the few buildings "of real quality". It was of a rectangular plan, built of brick with a pitched copper-covered roof. The interior comprises a three-sided gallery with tiered seating, continuing as an organ gallery on the eastern end. The finish of the interior is of a very high quality, with the American oak representing a very attractive woodwork feature. The west window contains stained glass by Carl Edwards illustrating the spreading of God's Word and scenes of the London Blitz, and he also designed the window commemorating the Rev. D.S. Owen, the minister from 1915 until 1959 and the person who had organised the arrangements for building the new chapel. Associated with the church are the large hall with a stage, various rooms and a house for the caretaker.

The organ installed in the chapel was built by the John Compton Organ Co. Ltd, and the organ frame was made by I.A. Robinson who was also responsible for the pulpit and the *sêt fawr*. The building and its contents cost £84,666 and the organ £82,000. A number of donations were received, including two bardic chairs won at eisteddfodau, one presented by Dewi Emrys and the other by the former minister, the Rev. J.E. Davies, 'Rhuddwawr'.

The Rev. Elfed Williams served as minister from 1961 until 1990, and during the pastorate of the Rev. Dafydd Owen, from 2000 until 2003, Eglwys y Drindod, comprising Holloway, Wood Green and Leytonstone churches, joined with Jewin to form a new pastorate.

The church now forms part of the pastorate comprising the five Presbyterian Church of Wales churches in the London area.

Present position: Minister, Rev. Richard Brunt, 42 members, Sunday services, 10.45 a.m. and 3.30 p.m., weekday/evening meetings, devotional service, three times a month, cultural society, three times a month,

Further reading: Gomer M. Roberts, *Y Ddinas Gadarn, Hanes Eglwys Jewin Llundain* (1974); Philip Temple, *Islington Chapels* (1992).

118. MELBOURNE, AUSTRALIA, Welsh Church (Pw/e)

Welsh services have been held in Melbourne since 1852, when many Welshmen had been attracted to work in the gold mines in the state of Victoria. The discovery of gold in 1851 increased the Welsh population of Victoria from 337 in that year to 6,055 in 1861. There were at one time sixteen Welsh churches in Victoria, but at present only two remain, the Welsh Church Melbourne and Carmel, Sebastopol, near Ballarat, established by the Melbourne church in 1864. These two churches together form the Welsh Presbyterian Church Connexion in the state of Victoria.

In 1852 an advertisement in the daily *Melbourne Argus* announced that a Welsh service would be held at the Collins Street Baptist Church on Sunday afternoon, 12 December, conducted by two Baptist ministers who had recently arrived in Melbourne: the Revs. Abraham Parry Jones, from Merthyr Tydfil, and Zorobabel Davies, from Llanidloes. The meeting was publicised in English under the heading 'The World's Truth in the Welsh Language'. A congregation of 46 attended the service at which the Rev. Z. Davies preached. He soon left for the gold mines of Mount Pleasant, but the Rev. A.P. Jones continued to hold services in Melbourne every Sunday afternoon. The congregation moved to a schoolroom at the Scots Church on Collins Street in July, 1853 as these premises provided the opportunity to hold two services every Sunday. The members, comprising Baptists, Independents and Calvinistic and Wesleyan Methodists, decided to form a church, and as most were Calvinistic Methodists, the first service of the newly-formed Welsh Calvinistic Methodist Church, Melbourne was held on Sunday, 17 July. On the following Sunday morning, the first Sunday school was held before the service, and within three months, a Communion service was celebrated by the Rev. Z. Davies, who had returned to Melbourne for a short period.

Soon after the service on 17 July, an unsuccessful application, supported by the minister of the Collins Street Independent Church and 132 Welsh persons, was submitted to the authorities for a plot of land to build a chapel. A second application, signed by 380 persons, was submitted, and following discussions concerning two other sites, the church was notified in 1854 that a plot of land was available in La Trobe Street. By 1857 the first chapel, built of stone, quarried in the Footscray area, had been opened on the site. The chapel cost £300 and the builder was Dan Jones, a lay preacher. A chapel house was built in 1866, at a cost of £235, and in 1868 discussions commenced with regard to the construction of a larger and more modern chapel. However, financial difficulties were encountered, and these were largely surmounted through the efforts of the Rev. William Meirion Evans, who had been inducted as minister in 1871. A native of Caernarfonshire, he had preached in 1849 the first Welsh sermon in Australia at Burra, South Australia, where he was working in the earliest copper mine to attract Welsh settlers which had opened in 1845. Having subsequently returned to Wales and then settled with his family in the

Unites States, he had been the minister of the Welsh Calvinistic Methodist churches at Ballarat, Sebastopol Hill and Cambrian Hill since 1864. The new, and present-day chapel, designed by Crouch & Wilson with H. Ireland as the builder, was opened on 1 January 1871. The work of building a hall for social functions, soon regarded as the next requirement, was undertaken by two members, John Jones, from Corris, and Robert Jones, from Flintshire, and to a large extent, Welsh craftsmen were used. The cost was £815, and the new hall was used for the first time for the St. David's Day celebrations in 1893.

A pipe organ, costing £900 and built by J. Taylor, from the Hawthorn organ firm, was installed in 1923, and was formally inaugurated with a recital by Dr. Floyd, St. Paul's Cathedral Church, who had advised the church on its choice of organ. The organ, a rare example of a 'Taylor organ' which has not been significantly modified, has been considered by the National Trust to be an instrument of regional significance. The organ was moved in 1935 from the northern wall to the eastern wall, and a new pulpit, costing £100 was installed on the eastern wall. There was a theological significance to this change of location, and this is one of the few examples of a Presbyterian church with a pulpit which is not in the centre of the place of worship.

In 1988 the church organized the largest Gymanfa Ganu ever held in Australia, with approximately 1,300 persons present in St. Michael's Church, Collins Street. A gymanfa ganu is held regularly, with the special one on St. David's Day being one of the highlights of the cultural life of the Welsh in Australia.

The ministry of the Rev. Sion Gough Hughes, who has been the minister since 2000, represents the 21st period of ministry since 1857. The Rev. Dr. D. Egryn Jones was the minister for three of them: 1883-35, 1893-1906 and 1914-27, and with the exception of the Rev. Robert Caradoc Hughes (1936-62) most of the other ministers were here for relatively short periods.

Present position: Ministers: Revs. Sion Gough Hughes and J. Barr; 96 members; Sunday services: 11 a.m and 5.00 p.m; Bible Bash 2.00 p.m; afternoon Sunday service twice a month; Gymanfa Ganu at least twice a year.

Further reading: *Melbourne Welsh Church, 150th Year, 1853-2003* (2003); Gareth D. Evans, A *brief history of the Welsh 'Cause'* (Melbourne, 1971); Bill Jones, 'Y Parchedig William Meirion Evans', *Journal of the Historical Society of the Presbyterian Church of Wales*, 31 (2007).

Website: www.melbournewelshchurch.org

119. TORONTO, CANADA, Dewi Sant Welsh United Church (U)

The first major wave of Welsh migration to Canada occurred between 1901 and 1905. Many of the 16, 624 persons who came to Canada in this period probably settled in the growing city of Toronto, where a St. David's Society was established in 1906. The country they had left behind had witnessed the religious revival in 1904/05 and a group of Welsh immigrants soon established a Welsh Sunday school which met in a small room at Cook's Presbyterian Church, Simcoe Street between 2 p.m. and 4 p.m. every Sunday. 28 persons attended the Sunday school in July 1907 and meetings were also held in various homes. In the following year the growth in numbers led to the need to find larger premises, and, having reached an agreement to use the Temperance Hall, evening services were held here for the first time. Also a choir was soon formed which held concerts in the city. In 1909 a church, known as Capel Dewi Sant, was formally established and affiliated with the Welsh Presbyterian (Calvinistic Methodist) Church of America which provided valuable support to the new church. The first minister, the Rev. R.J. Jones was called and after his departure the Rev. J. Evans became the minister in 1912 when there were 124 members. New premises were secured in 1913, and again in 1915 when the Christian Workers' Church on Clinton Street was rented: the church was located here until 1960 with the exception of an interval between 1928 and 1933. Eight members of the church were killed in the First World War, and the names of the 56 members who served in this war are recorded on the Roll of Honour which hangs in the church today.

The Clinton Street site was purchased in 1917 for $6,000 and generous financial support was provided by the Welsh Presbyterian Church of America, which merged with the United States Presbyterian Church in 1920. By 1927 many members of the Dewi Sant Church were in favour of becoming affiliated to the United Church of Canada, an inter-denominational body which had been formed in 1925 as a result of the union of the Methodist Church, Canada, the Congregational Union of Canada, and 70 per cent of the Presbyterian Church in Canada. On the other hand, some members favoured retaining their links with the Welsh Presbyterian Church of America which had provided valuable support at times of great need, and left to join other churches. In view of the poor condition of the Clinton Street building, it was offered for sale in 1927, and sold in the following year. Considerable financial problems were again experienced during the Great Depression, and the minister voluntarily reduced his salary. The Dewi Sant church held services in a number of rented premises until 1933 when the Clinton Street premises were again bought following the failure of the new owners to meet their financial commitments. The lack of facilities to hold functions explains the decision to build a basement, and the result was that volunteers were responsible for physically raising the church building off the ground and digging the basement.

In 1946 the mortgage on the church building was discharged and the first manse was bought in this year. By the 1950s many members had moved to live in the suburbs, and as the building was in need of constant repair and maintenance, a decision was made to either buy an existing church or build a new church in a more central and convenient location. An attempt in 1956 to buy a Baptist church was unsuccessful, and in 1958 two houses in Melrose Avenue were bought, of which one became a manse and the other was demolished to provide a site for a new church. The Clinton Street building was sold in March 1960 to the St. Paul's Yugoslav Congregation for $35,000. The relocation was opposed by several United churches which feared that they might lose members to the Welsh church, but the move was eventually approved. The new church was designed by a leading firm of church architects, Bruce, Brown and Brisley, and built by the Carrol Construction Company, which was awarded the building contract for a sum of $113,944. An additional cost for furnishings amounted to $15,321 but most of the furnishings, including the pulpit, communion table, font, pews and chairs were donated in memory of various persons.

The first service in the new church was held on 16 October 1960, and despite the burden of a substantial mortgage the positive benefits of the new building were soon appreciated. The 1961 report stated that 'attendance at worship has improved, the church school has taken on new vigour'. There were 100 members in the Sunday school and the membership of the church had increased from 239 in 1959 to 293 in 1964. The small organ brought from Clifton Street was replaced in 1968 by a Conn organ purchased in 1968 for the sum of $4,664, and a new Allen organ, costing $33,000 was installed, dedicated and totally paid for in 1990. The centenary of the church was celebrated in 2007 by a number of events and activities, including the publication of Meriel V. Simpson's history of the church from 1907 to 2007, a commemorative booklet, 'Book of Memories' and a commemorative stamp.

The church has been served by a number of ministers, of whom some, such as the Revs. Elwyn Hughes and Deian Evans, came to Canada directly from Wales.

Present position: Interim minister: Rev. Eilert Frerichs [advertisement for minister has been extensively published in Welsh denominational newspapers in 2012], 225 registered members, some of whom are spread through Ontario and the rest of Canada. Church attendance is usually around 40 to 50 people, Sunday school of about ten children ranging in age from 4 to 13 years of age. English service every Sunday at 11.00 a.m., Welsh service at 7.00 p.m. (details on website).

Further reading: Meriel V. Simpson, *With a Song in our Heart: The First Hundred Years, A History of Dewi Sant Welsh United Church from 1907 to 2007* (2007).

Website: www.dewisant.com

120. DELTA. PHILADELPHIA (York County), U.S.A., Rehoboth (Pw/e)

Delta is located on the border of Pennsylvania and Maryland, near the Susquehanna river and the Mason-Dixon Line, the traditional boundary with the 'Old South'. Early settlers were of Scots/Irish origin, and the first Welsh association with the area was in the early eighteenth century when slate was discovered here. Welsh persons settled in a town they named West Bangor (the later Delta), and the first Peach Bottom quarry was opened in 1835: slate from this quarry was declared the 'finest slate in the world' at the London Crystal Palace exhibition of 1851. Welsh services were held in private homes in 1845 in the village of Stonetown, and a small narrow building, Capel Main [Narrow Chapel] was soon erected. A theological dispute with the Congregationalists led to the Calvinistic Methodists leaving Capel Main and, having first worshipped at the Slateville Presbyterian Church, formed in 1854 their own church, which comprising 84 members, they named Rehoboth. This new church was accepted as a member of the Southern Presbytery of the Calvinistic Methodist Church in the United States. A significant change occurred in 1935 when the Pennsylvania Gymanfa of the Calvinistic Methodists was dissolved, and the Southern and Northern Presbyteries were united in the Synod of Pennsylvania of the Presbyterian Church in the United States.

The members of Rehoboth built in 1854 a chapel and detailed instructions were recorded in the church minutes for the chapel. The façade was to face the highway with the pulpit on the opposite side if there was sufficient space, and the measurements were 54 feet by 30 feet, and the height to the ceiling 16 feet. There would be eight windows, each one of which would be seven feet high, and the chapel would be painted and built of bricks, provided that this would not cost more than 100 dollars if wood had been used. The floor should rise gradually towards the pulpit, and the comment was added that the work should be completed as economically as possible.

In 1890 a plot of land in Delta on the corner of Hill Road and Main Street was bought from Lieutenant Thomas S. Williamson. A larger and more modern chapel was built, based upon the design of the first chapel in west Bangor and retaining the best features. The foundations of the new chapel were laid on 18 August 1891, and a report of the impressive ceremony was published in the local newspaper. The membership peaked in 1913 at 193, and the children were taught in Welsh and in English at the Sunday school. Following the closure in 1916 of the Bethesda Congregational Church, which was sold with the site used for many years by the Delta Post Office, former members joined Rehoboth which then represented the only Welsh church in the town. The last slate quarry closed soon afterwards and the gradual decrease in the membership was accompanied by an increasing tendency to no longer use the Welsh language. In 1929, when the 75th anniversary of the church was celebrated, the chapel was renovated and refurnished, and the oil painting 'Christ in Gethsemane' was presented to the church. In 1993 a substantial sum of money was spent on renovating the interior of the chapel to rectify the damage caused by dust and soot as a result of a fault in the boiler, and in 1996 a Moeller pipe organ was installed.

In contrast to the trend in many overseas churches of Welsh origin, a conscious policy of introducing Welsh-language elements in the services was adopted during the pastorate of the Rev. Richard Price Baskwill, who was inducted as minister in 1982. Based upon a belief that the preservation of Welsh traditions in Delta involved the revived use of the language, the minister and members decided to learn Welsh from tapes and books. A bilingual service is held on Sunday evenings at 6 p.m., and before the service the congregation is invited to a Welsh-language class arranged voluntarily at 5 p.m. A Gymanfa Ganu is held twice a year, in May and in October, and attracts visitors from Canada and eastern areas of the United States. In 1995 Rehoboth sponsored the 64th Welsh National Gymanfa Ganu held in Harrisburg, Pennsylvania, and was one of the sponsors of the 2002 National Gymanfa Ganu. The growing interest in Welsh culture and traditions led to the formation of the Rehoboth Welsh Choir, whose members comprise not only church members but also individuals from the Baltimore-Washington metropolitan area and Delaware. The choir has a comprehensive schedule of public performances, and, singing in Welsh, was awarded fourth prize at the Royal Eisteddfod of Wales in 1992. Close links have been established with a number of Welsh choirs, including the Pendyrus and Brythoniaid male voice choirs, and the South Glamorgan Youth Choir. In addition to religious and musical activities, folk dancing classes and displays are organised by the church.

Delta, together with its sister community in Cardiff, Maryland, is very conscious of its historical background, and seeks to maintain the Welsh religious and cultural heritage in this part of the United States. In May 2010, the National Welsh-American Foundation (Sefydliad Cenedlaethol Cymru-America) designated Rehoboth Welsh Chapel (Capel Cymraeg Rehoboth) as 'A place of honor and significance in Welsh-American History'. An inscribed bronze plaque was donated to the chapel by the President of the Foundation on the occasion of its Gymanfa Ganu.

In May 2011, The Honorable Stanley E. Saylor, Pennsylvania State Representative of York County, PA, attended the Rehoboth Gymanfa Ganu and made a commemorative presentation to the chapel on behalf of the Pennsylvania House of Representatives. Part of the citation read "The House of Representatives of the Commonwealth of Pennsylvania heartily congratulates Capel Cymraeg Rehoboth upon the joyous celebration of its one hundred fifty-sixth anniversary, and offers best wishes for a continued tradition of devoted service to God and humanity".

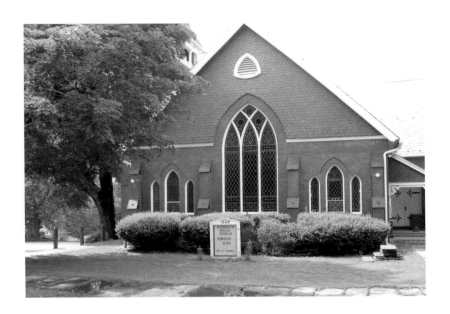

Present position: Minister, Rev. Richard Price Baskwill, 35 members, Sunday service: 6.00 p.m. according to Anglican Church in Wales, preceded by tea and cookies at 5.00 and an intensive Welsh-language class, occasional Singing Festivals (Gymanfa Ganu) featuring the Rehoboth Welsh Choir.

Further reading: Daniel Jenkins Williams, *One hundred years of Welsh Calvinistic Methodism in America* (1937); Jay Williams, *Songs of Praise, Welsh-rooted Churches Beyond Britain* (1996).

Website: http://homecast.net/~rbaskwil/chapel.html

121. BEAVERCREEK, OREGON, U.S.A. Bryn Seion Welsh Church (U)

Oregon, forming part of the region in the Pacific Northwest described as 'Farming's Last Frontier', was recognised in 1859 as a state of the United States of America. The fertile, affordable farmland of western Oregon attracted Welsh settlers who built in 1884 Bryn Seion (Mt. Zion), the oldest Welsh church on the west coast of the United States. A surviving letter from a certain David W. Thomas, Beaver Creek Farm, dated 12 June 1884, refers to his decision to leave Patagonia and settle in the United States. Having stayed in Nebraska for four months, he travelled to Oregon City, a journey of about 18,000 miles, via San Francisco, California and Portland, Oregon, where he saw ships from Liverpool, Cardiff and Swansea. He highly commended the local opportunities for settlers, and sought to persuade the recipients of his letter, a couple in Aberdare, to join him in Oregon. Land for the chapel in the small town of Beavercreek, a few miles south of Oregon City, was donated by a church member. The church was originally known as 'The Welsh Evangelical Church' but within a year became 'The Welsh Congregational Church'. Approximately ten years later a tea house was built behind the church and was used for meals after services and for conducting services. An eisteddfod chair, inscribed 'Eisteddfod, Talaeth Wash. 1890', is believed to have been won at a Washington State Eisteddfod by a person who gave it to a member of Bryn Seion, who then in turn donated it to the church. The chair today stands next to the podium above which hang the flags of Wales and the United States.

An important figure in the history of Bryn Seion was the Rev. John Rhys Griffith, who was the minister from 1908 until his death in 1946. He had resided in Wales when he accepted the call to be a minister here, and had not yet been ordained. In view of the small number of members, the church could not financially support a full-time minister, and the Rev. Griffith was employed as an executive with the Roberts Brothers Department Store in Portland.

Many members travel long distances to attend the bi-monthly services, and the church website states that 'What brings them together is the tranquil setting and a love of Welsh culture, language and singing.'

The church seats 160 persons, and occasionally, as at the time of the annual Gymanfa Ganu held since 1935 and attracting persons of Welsh origin from various areas in the northwest of the Unites States and also from western Canada, those attending have to sit outside on benches and chairs and rely on loudspeakers.

Bryn Seion formed a twinning link with Capel y Morfa, Aberystwyth in 2010 and reports on activities in Bryn Seion, such as the Easter Sunday service in 2011, have appeared in *Perthyn*, the monthly magazine of the Aberystwyth chapel.

Present position: Minister Pastor John Hasenjaeger, Sunday services, 11 a.m. 2nd and 4th Sundays of month except for August.

Further reading: *The Welsh in America, Letters from the Immigrants*, ed. Alan Conway (1961); Jay Williams, *Songs of Praise, Welsh-rooted Churches Beyond Britain* (1996).

Website: www.brynseionwelshchurch.org

122. GAIMAN, PATAGONIA, Bethel (U)

The close association of religious aspirations with the political and economic motivation for emigration was reflected by the frequent recruitment of potential emigrants by Nonconformist chapels in Wales, and also by the early actions of the Welsh settlers in the colony of Patagonia, with a chapel established in a central location in every settlement. Settlers who came to the Gaiman region in the Chubut valley in the period 1874-76 initially held services, and a Sunday school, in the homes of various members, and also at the home of the Rev. John Caerenig Evans. A native of Carmarthenshire, who had been the minister of a church in Cwmaman, Aberdare, he became the minister of the church which was established in August 1876. A chapel was built in 1878, known as Capel Cerrig [Rock Chapel] in the locality where the junior school is held today. This chapel became too small for them, and then collapsed during a storm. In 1880 they started to build a chapel on the other side of the river on land donated by the sister of the Rev. J. Caerenig Evans. They named the chapel 'Bethel' which is known today as 'Yr Hen Gapel' [the Old Chapel]. A vestry was opened by its side where the Sunday school was held. This was later extended and continues to be used for holding the Sunday School, young persons' services, Bible studies and prayer meetings, concerts and various cultural activities.

On the basis of the 1895 Census, Gaiman, with a population of 267 persons of whom 82.8% were Welsh, has been described as being "essentially a village which served as a dormitory for many employed in agriculture". Despite the extensive damage caused by the floods of 1899 and 1901, improved economic conditions in the early twentieth century led to the growth of the population of the lower Chubut valley, which attracted non-Welsh as well as Welsh settlers, and by 1915 the population of Gaiman had increased to 3,236. The membership of Bethel grew rapidly during the first decade of the twentieth century as a consequence of the 1905 Revival, and increased from 145 in 1903 to 242 at the end of 1905, with 56 persons received as members during that year. A letter dated 21 May 1905 and sent to Cwm Hyfryd in the Andes presented a graphic and detailed account of the intense spiritual experiences witnessed at services held in Gaiman on 17 and 20 May 1905. These specifically referred to the direct involvement of the Rev. J.C. Evans and Eluned Morgan, who had been brought up in the colony and was the daughter of Lewis Jones, one of the principal founders of the Colony. In 1906, she sent a letter from Wales to the Rev. J. Caerenig Evans expressing the hope that those Welsh people in the Camwy Valley who had experienced the force of the Revival would serve as missionaries in the Argentine Republic. The membership had fallen to 181 by 1913, but by that time the chapel was too small and work commenced on the construction of a new chapel next to the existing chapel. This was opened in 1914, even though the tablet above the entrance door refers to 1913. A brick building, measuring 12 metres long, 18 metres wide and 5.5 metres high, includes 12 windows, and with

space for 450-500 persons, this is the largest chapel in the Chubut Valley. The builder was Jack Jones, the wood work was undertaken by Egryn Evans and Llywelyn Griffiths, and the total cost was £1,500.

The Rev. J. Caerenig Evans died in 1913 before the new chapel was opened. His son Tudur served as minister for two periods, and together, the father and son ministered at Bethel for 64 years. Other ministers here have included the Revs. Alun Garner and D.J. Peregrine. Reminiscences of the chapel were recorded by Alwena Thomas, the Bethel organist, in her contribution to the volume *Agor y Ffenestri*. She described the chapel as being reasonably full during special preaching services or the Sunday school festival in the Welsh colony, and the chapel was full to capacity during the thanksgiving service held on the first Monday in April. She recalled Eluned Morgan responsible for planting trees around the chapel, and was present in the service held to bid farewell to the Rev. Nantlais Williams at the end of his visit to Patagonia.

A harmonium, made by Mason & Hamlin, Boston, U.S.A., is used in the chapel.

Welsh language services are held whenever possible. On the whole services, especially those in the Welsh language, are largely attended by elderly persons. Enthusiastic young persons are responsible for the Sunday school.

Present position: Minister; Rev. Carlos Ruiz (Union of Free Churches), 32 members;

35 children in Sunday school; Sunday services, 10.00 a.m, Sunday school, 11. 00 a.m., Evening service, 6.00 p.m. March to end of November, 7.00 p.m. January and February, (Welsh service once a month); Young persons' services, Bible studies and prayer meetings [latter also in private homes]; singing festivals [Cymanfa Ganu]in September and October; Mini-eisteddfod in the winter.

Further reading: Glyn Williams, *The Desert and the Dream, A Study of Welsh colonists in Chubut, 1865-1915* (1975); Robert Owen Jones, *Yr Efengyl yn y Wladfa* (1987); Glyn Williams, *The Welsh in Patagonia, The State and the Ethnic Community* (1991); 'Welsh Chapels in Patagonia', *Capel Newsletter*, 26 (Autumn 1995); Dorian Jones (ed.) *Capillas Galeses en Chubut* (1999); Alwena Thomas, 'Fy nghapel i', in *Agor y Ffenestri*, ed. Cathrin Williams (2001).

GLOSSARY

Definitions of selective architectural, buildings, ecclesiastical, Welsh-language terms used in volume. Sources: *The New Oxford Dictionary of English* (2001); *Oxford English Reference Dictionary* (2002); *The Oxford Dictionary of the Christian Church*, ed. F.L. Cross and E.A. Livingstone (1974); *Geiriadur Prifysgol Cymru* [A Dictionary of the Welsh Language] *The Welsh Academy Encyclopaedia of Wales*, eds. John Davies, Nigel Jenkins, Menna Baines, Peredur I Lynch (2008); L. Madden, Chapels, *A Guide to Denominations in Wales* (2010); relevant websites.

Anglican Church: The movement in Wales to disestablish the Church of England, formed during the Protestant Reformation in the sixteenth century, led to the creation of the Church in Wales in 1920.

aisle: passage between or alongside rows of seats.

altar: Communion table.

Apostolic Church: Christian Pentecostal denomination with origins in the 1904-1905 Revival, which emphasises baptism by the Holy Spirit, and whose church government is based upon the leadership of ' Apostles'.

apse: semicircular or polygonal recess.

arcade: series of arches supported by or attached to wall.

arch: structure, which is usually arched.

Arianism: popular belief among Nonconformists in the eighteenth century which developed into Unitarianism, and based upon views of Arius (*c*.250-*c*.336), who emphasised distinction between God the Father and Christ the Son of God, in opposition to the doctrine of the Trinity.

Arminianism: belief in Protestant theology, based upon the views of Dutch theologian, Jacobus Arminius (1560-1609) that individuals possess free will, and that the offer of salvation was open to all if they responded to God's invitation; strong influence on John Wesley and the Wesleyan Methodists.

Arts and Crafts: international design movement, flourished between 1860 and 1910, characterised by traditional craftsmanship using simple forms.

ashlar: squared, hewn stones.

Baptists: members of Christian Protestant denomination whose origins in Wales date from the seventeenth century, a distinctive feature is the emphasis on the baptism of believers by total immersion.

baptistry: part of chapel used for baptism.

Baroque: European architectural style, flourished from early seventeenth century to mid eighteenth century, whose characteristic features included an opulent use of colour and ornaments and a dramatic central projection of the external façade.

Boys' Brigade: Christian youth organisation, founded in Glasgow in 1883.

buttress: support built against wall.

Calvinism: belief in Protestant theology, based upon the teachings of John Calvin (1509-64), the influential French theologian, settled in Geneva, who emphasised predestination, that the elect who would be saved had been chosen by God from the beginning of time.

Calvinistic Methodists: members of Christian Protestant denomination formed in 1811 following separation from the Church of England, more commonly known today as the Presbyterian Church of Wales; strong influence, especially in early period, of Calvinism.

Chandelier: ornamental support for number of candles or series of lights.

Christian Scientists: adherents of a system of religious thought and practise influenced by writings of Mary Baker Eddy and the Bible; emphasis placed on healing and teaching by allegory.

Church of England: see Anglican Church

Church in Wales: see Anglican Church

Classical architecture: architecture partly influenced by Greek and Roman architecture of classical antiquity.

colonnade: row of columns.

column: upright structure, supporting pillar.

Congregationalists: members of Christian Protestant denomination with distinctive form of church governance based on the local congregation.

Congregational Federation: formed in 1972 by churches which declined to join the United Reformed Church, today an amalgamation of churches formerly belonging to the Congregational Church in England and Wales, Presbyterian Church of England, Churches of Christ and the Scottish Congregational church.

Corinthian [Order]: the most ornate of the three principal classical orders of ancient Greek and Roman architecture, whose features include slender columns with lavish ornaments carved to resemble leaves and flowers [see also Doric and Ionic].

cupola: small dome on a circular or polygonal base.

Dissenters: Protestants who dissented from the practices and structure of the Church of England, including sixteenth-century Presbyterians and Separatists, and seventeenth-century Baptists and Independents; allowed to worship in their own buildings by the Toleration Act, 1689.

Doric [Order]: one of the three principal Classical orders of ancient Greek and Roman architecture; characteristic columns stouter, and capitals simpler and plainer than those of the Corinthian and Ionic styles.

façade: main front of building.

font: receptable, usually of stone, for baptismal water.

gable: upper part of wall, generally triangular, between edges of sloping roof.

gable-end: end wall of building.

gallery: balcony overlooking main interior space of chapel.

Gymanfa Ganu: festival of sacred hymn-singing, with four-part harmony, by congregation.

Gymanfa Bwnc: festival for singing or reciting Scriptural catechism.

illuminated address: presentation of text, usually a tribute, in either scrolled form or as framed panels.

Independents: members of Christian Protestant denomination which emphasises the independence of the local congregation from any external authority.

Ionic [Order]: one of the three principal Classical orders of ancient Greek and Roman architecture, whose characteristic columns were more slender and ornate than earlier Doric style [see also Corinthian and Doric].

listener: person attending a Christian church service but not a member of the church.

lobby: foyer or waiting-room at or near entrance to building.

manse: home of minister.

Methodists: in Wales the term has been used for both the Calvinistic Methodists and the Wesleyan Methodists [see Calvinistic Methodists, and Wesleyan Methodists]

minister: person authorised to perform religious functions, usually in a Protestant church.

nave: body of church.

narthex: covered porch at main entrance of church.

Nonconformists: those who do not conform to an established church, especially the Church of England; or refuse to be bound by accepted beliefs, customs or practices.

organ loft: gallery in which organ housed.

parapet: low wall or barrier placed at edge of balcony, roof, structure,

pediment: triangular front part of building in Classical style of architecture, placed above doors, windows, portico.

Pentecostal: Christian renewal movement with emphasis on personal experience of God through baptism of Holy Spirit.

pew(s): enclosed seat(s).

pilaster: square or rectangular column or pillar.

portico: porch with roof and often a pediment supported by columns.

porch: covered approach to entrance of building.

precentor: person who leads the singing in Nonconformist service; occasionally conducting the congregation.

Presbyterians: members of Protestant Christian denomination influenced by Calvinist theology and with congregation governed or organised by assembly of elected elders.

Presbyterian Church of Wales: see Calvinistic Methodists

Protestants: members of major Christian grouping originating in early sixteenth-century Germany largely as a reaction against Roman Catholic practices and doctrines. Protestant doctrines include justification by faith alone, priesthood of all believers, and the supreme authority of the Bible.

pulpit: raised, enclosed platform used by minister for conducting service, including preaching of sermon.

Quakers: see Religious Society of Friends

Religious Society of Friends: also known as Quakers, founded in mid-seventeenth-century by George Fox (1624-1691); emphasis placed upon continuing revelation and the priesthood of all believers.

Revival: renewal in life of church congregation, successive examples in Wales and especially 1904-05 Revival.

Salvation Army: Christian, Protestant Church renowned for its charity work. Founded in 1865 by William Booth and his wife Catherine as the North London Christian Mission with a quasi- military structure. Name 'Salvation Army' adopted in 1878.

schoolroom: room used for Sunday school classes.

Scotch Baptist: Baptist denomination, with origins in Scotland, associated with Archibald Mclean, 1733-1812, and strongly influenced by Calvinistic theology.

sêt fawr: great pew in front of pulpit seating elders or deacons.

seiat: Calvinistic Methodist society, group.

spire: tall, tapering structure rising above tower.

stained glass window: coloured glass in windows of churches, often illustrating Biblical scenes; art form reached its height in the Middle Ages, but increased use in the nineteenth century was accompanied by a revival of the Gothic style in church buildings.

tablet: small slab with inscription.

transept: transverse part of church.

truss: supporting framework of roof.

turret: small or subordinate tower.

Unitarian: member of Christian church which defines God as one person, rejection of doctrine of the Trinity, that God, the Father, Son and the Holy Spirit are one and indivisible.

United Reformed Church: formed by union of Presbyterian Church of England and the Congregational Church in England and Wales in 1972.

vestry: a room in a building attached to a chapel, used for Sunday school, prayer meetings.

vestibule: lobby between entrance door and interior.

Wesleyan Methodists: members of Christian, Protestant denomination which originated as an eighteenth-century, revival movement within the Church of England, led by John Wesley (1703-91). Strongly influenced by Arminianism, successive secessions eventually resulted in the formation of the Methodist Church.

Word: the Bible or part of it.

SELECT INDEX

THE AUTHOR

Dr Huw Owen is a former Keeper of Pictures and Maps at the National Library of Wales. He is an active member of the Presbyterian Church of Wales, and of Capel – the Welsh Chapels Heritage Society, and is a trustee of the Welsh Religious Buildings Trust. *Capeli Cymru*, his survey of Welsh chapels, in the Welsh language, was published in 2005.